ALEX SALMOND is a Scottish p
First Minister of Scotland, serving for seven years. He was Leader of the Scottish National Party from 1990 to 2000 and again from 2004 to 2014, and was a Member of the Westminster Parliament from 1987 to 2010. He is currently the Member of the Scottish Parliament for Aberdeenshire East, and in 2015 he returned to the House of Commons for the Aberdeenshire constituency of Gordon.

THE DREAM SHALL NEVER DIE

ALEX SALMOND

William Collins
An imprint of HarperCollins Publishers
1 London Bridge Street
London SE1 9GF
www.WilliamCollinsBooks.com

First published in Great Britain by William Collins in 2015
This William Collins paperback edition first published in 2015

1 3 5 7 9 8 6 4 2

Picture section credits: all photographs by Allan Milligan, except: pages 6 and 7, Tom Farmer; page 11 (top), AFP/The Scottish Government; page 11 (bottom) courtesy of Fergus Mutch; page 12, Jeff J Mitchell/Getty Images; page 13 (top), Ian Rutherford/The Scotsman Publications Ltd; page 13 (bottom), Herald Scotland; pages 14 and 15, Dan Kitwood/Getty Images; page 16 (top), PA Images; page 16 (bottom), The Parliamentary Recording Unit. All rights reserved.

A catalogue record for this book is available from the British Library

ISBN 978-0-00-813978-0

Printed and bound in Great Britain by
Clays Ltd, St Ives plc

MIX
Paper from responsible sources
FSC C007454

FSC™ is a non-profit international organisation established to promote the responsible management of the world's forests. Products carrying the FSC label are independently certified to assure consumers that they come from forests that are managed to meet the social, economic and ecological needs of present and future generations, and other controlled sources.

Find out more about HarperCollins and the environment at
www.harpercollins.co.uk/green

Contents

To my dad, who believes in independence,
and my mum, who believed in me

PART I

Prologue

Day 100: Friday 19 September 2014

I phone David Cameron from a backroom in Edinburgh's Dynamic Earth exhibition centre, and congratulate him on victory. He congratulates me on an amazing campaign. He tells me that he has appointed Lord Smith of Kelvin to take forward the promises made to Scotland in the dying days of the referendum – the 'vow'. 'Excellent choice,' I say, and he pauses.

It suddenly occurs to me that he clearly doesn't realise how well I know Robert Smith. Why on earth does he think I appointed him to lead the Commonwealth Games? I press Cameron on whether he will have a Commons vote on the offer to Scotland before Easter, as Gordon Brown has promised. I know he won't.

With dawn approaching, the Prime Minister rings off to go and make his speech outside Number Ten, which I watch on TV. As he struts out to say that Scottish reform must take place 'in tandem with' and 'at the same pace as' changes in England, I immediately realise the significance. There was no mention of this last week when he was in a complete panic about the polls.

I think 'You silly arrogant man' and look around the room. The campaign team are totally exhausted, all passion spent, and no one realises the door that Cameron has just opened. I understand – no, I sense – what now must be done.

Just a few hours earlier, at 3.30 a.m., my wife, Moira, and I had left for Edinburgh from Aberdeen airport.

A snapper caught us at the gates. I had my head down, reading the referendum results on my iPad as they came in – far from the most flattering image of the campaign – and I saw the picture posted online before we had even reached Edinburgh. Anticipating the same thing happening at Turnhouse, I made sure I was sporting the bravest of smiles as we left the airport.

First we went to Bute House, where I phoned my Chief of Staff, Geoff Aberdein, to say that I would make the concession speech from Dynamic Earth as soon as the NO side had the official majority. The YES campaigners had been gathered there all night and would be gutted. They had to hear from me directly.

I delivered the speech that I had drafted very early in the morning when the first result from Clackmannan came through at 1.31 a.m. It was gracious in tone but resilient in defeat, celebrating the 1.6 million votes for YES and pointing to the future.

Following Cameron's appearance outside Number 10, and now back in Bute House, I sit down and write a brief resignation speech. I know exactly what needs to be said. It takes but one draft. I ask the press team to arrange for John Swinney and Nicola Sturgeon to come and see me at lunchtime, and to organise a press conference for the afternoon. Finally, Moira and I are able to catch up on an hour or so's sleep.

When getting dressed I reach for my favourite saltire tie, but Moira says that tartan would be better – softer – for this particular day. So a Lochcarron tartan tie it is.

Nicola and John arrive. We meet in the Cabinet Room. Nicola tries to talk me out of it, and at some length. She points out that there is no demand, no expectation, of a resignation.

'Yes,' I say. 'That is the time to do it.'

John, who was in this situation with me fourteen years ago, is emotional. Calmly, I explain that I am not resigning out of pique or even disappointment. I am heartbroken about the result, but that is not the issue now. Cameron has opened the door and we must drive through it quickly. This is about what best takes the country forward.

Peter Housden, my Permanent Secretary, arrives. Calm and authoritative as ever, he puts the arrangements into gear. He agrees that, despite the shortage of space, Bute House is the appropriate, indeed the only, place to deliver this speech. The drawing room is packed by 3 p.m. I thank people for coming at short notice and deliver the following address:

> I am immensely proud of the campaign which YES Scotland fought and particularly of the 1.6 million voters who rallied to that cause.
>
> I am also proud of the 85 per cent turnout in the referendum and the remarkable response of all of the people of Scotland who participated in this great democratic constitutional debate, and of course the manner in which they conducted themselves.
>
> We now have the opportunity to hold Westminster's feet to the fire on the 'vow' that they have made to

devolve further meaningful power to Scotland. This places Scotland in a very strong position.

I spoke to the Prime Minister today and, although he reiterated his intention to proceed as he has now outlined, he would not commit to a second reading vote by 27th March on a new Scotland Bill. That was a clear promise laid out by Gordon Brown during the campaign. The Prime Minister says such a vote would be meaningless. I suspect he can't guarantee the support of his party and, as we have already seen in the last hour, the common front between Labour and Tory, Tory and Labour is starting to break.

But the real point is this. The real guardians of progress are no longer politicians at Westminster, or even at Holyrood, but the energised activism of tens of thousands of people who I predict will refuse to meekly go back into the political shadows.

For me right now, therefore, there is a decision as to who is best placed to lead this process forward.

I believe that this is a new exciting situation that's redolent with possibility. But in that situation I think that party, parliament and country would benefit from new leadership.

Therefore I have told the national secretary of the Scottish National Party that I shall not accept nomination for leader at the annual conference in Perth on 13th–15th November.

After the membership ballot I will stand down as First Minister to allow the new leader to be elected by due parliamentary process.

Until then I will continue to serve as First Minister. After that I shall continue as member for the Scottish Parliament for Aberdeenshire East.

It has been the privilege of my life to serve as First Minister. But as I said often enough during this referendum campaign, this is a process which is not about me or the SNP or any political party. It's much, much more important than that.

The position is this. We lost the referendum vote but Scotland can still carry the political initiative. Scotland can still emerge as the real winner.

For me as leader my time is nearly over. But for Scotland the campaign continues and the dream shall never die.

Introduction

I have believed in Scottish independence all of my adult life.

The roots of this are not, as is often assumed, because of my background as an economist, although that undoubtedly helped. It runs much deeper than that.

In fact it was another Alex Salmond – my grandfather – who first sparked this Alex Salmond's belief in Scotland. This faith was instilled in me on my grandfather's knee when I was barely more than a toddler.

My wise granda – Sandy to everyone – had a town plumber's business in Linlithgow. He was in his late sixties and retired when I was young but kept his hand in by taking on odd plumbing jobs. I was his young apprentice, proudly carrying his tools.

As we trudged round the wynds and closes of the royal and ancient burgh my granda filled me with Lithgae folklore and Scottish history and how the two intertwined. He told me, for example, how King Robert Bruce's men captured Linlithgow castle by the simple expedient of blocking the portcullis with a hay cart.

More than that, he named the families involved: local folk in the town, families that I knew – the Binnies, the Davidsons, the Grants, the Bamberrys, the Salmonds and the Oliphants.

Oliphants were the local bakers. In my child's eye I imagined the boys in the bakehouse making the bread, dusting off the flour and then charging off to storm the palace.

I was taught no Scottish history at school, but years later at St Andrews University I finally learned the history of my own country and discovered that my granda's oral tradition wasn't too wide of the mark – if we forgive his artistic licence in the naming of names. Of course my grandfather wasn't really teaching me history but about life: how ordinary people could make a difference.

To my grandfather an honest man was the noblest work of God, Scotland was a special place on earth and Linlithgow was a very special place in Scotland. With this grounding it never even occurred to me that there was anything that could not be achieved with sufficient commitment and determination.

Robert Burns once wrote that a similar experience in boyhood gave him a Scottish view of the world which 'will boil alang there till the floodgates of life shut in eternal rest'.

So it shall be with me.

Everything else I have been taught or experienced, from the science of economics to the art of politics, is overlaid on these foundations: the belief that Scotland is a singular place and that the people of Scotland are capable of great things.

*

It was the best of times. It was the best of times.

For many people the Scottish referendum campaign was the best time of their lives, a far too brief period when suddenly everything seemed possible and the opportunity beckoned for the 'sma folk' to make a big impact.

We didn't win the vote but we did show the establishment circus – and its ringmasters Cameron, Miliband and Clegg – that major change is inevitable. The accepted order has been smashed – and it is the people who have achieved it.

There is a scene in the Ridley Scott film *Kingdom of Heaven* which sums up where we are now. Orlando Bloom, as the knight Balian, is left defending Jerusalem from the Sultan Saladin with no knights and only the dregs of the army. He has a brainwave: unite the remaining people by making them all knights, much to the disgust of the cowardly Jerusalem patriarch who wants to surrender.

'Do you think that merely by making people knights they will fight better?' asks the patriarch.

'Yes,' replies Balian.

And he was right. Trusting the common people with the future of their city, or their country, makes for better people and in our case for a better Scotland. Those metropolitan commentators puzzled by the surge in the SNP's fortunes since the referendum should understand this reality.

Once people have had a taste of power they are unlikely to give it up easily. The process of the referendum has changed the country. Many people felt politically significant for the first time in their lives. It has made them different people, better people.

This book seeks to explain that change, how we got here, why the people became enthused, what caused the big swing to YES, how success was just denied and, most crucially of all, what will happen now.

The events in Scotland underline the ability of grassroots movements to take on political establishments in modern democracies. A new and powerful force has been mustered – modern-day knights if you will. And the international community should sit up and pay attention.

*

But now to our referendum tale. Ours is but a new chapter – albeit a crucial one – in a much older story. Scotland is one of Europe's oldest nations.

In the late twelfth century, when Balian was busy defending the Holy City, Scotland had already been united as a kingdom for 300 years, with Picts and Scots forced together under the threat of Viking incursions. Richard Coeur de Lion never did manage to win back Jerusalem, but his crusade gave William the Lion of Scotland an excellent opportunity to be released from the feudal impositions Henry II had enforced upon him and therefore Scotland. He was able to fly his Royal Standard (the Lion Rampant) with additional pride.

The next affirmation of Scottish independence was somewhat bloodier but the outcome was the same. Robert de Brus did not seal Scottish independence by the storming of Linlithgow castle in 1313, or on the field of Bannockburn in the following year on midsummer's day, or even in the Arbroath Declaration of six years later, but at the Treaty of Northampton with England in 1328. However, Bannockburn was still one of history's decisive battles. It both preserved and shaped the nation.

The recognition of Scottish independence at Northampton did not finish the matter, and an uneasy relationship between Scotland and England was the norm for the next 300 years – border warfare tempered by the occasional dynastic nuptial.

From a Scottish perspective, for many years, union with the auld ally of France looked more likely than union with the auld enemy of England.

And when crown unity did come in 1603 it was through a Scottish king, James VI, becoming King of England. But Scotland remained an independent nation and it would be another century before the Union of the Parliaments.

When that happened, in 1707, Scotland had a collective history of statehood, stretching back for the best part of a millennium: three times the period that has elapsed since.

Scottish dissatisfaction with the government in London has ebbed and flowed since the Treaty of Union. There have been periods when support for the union was in the ascendancy. However, it is also true that every movement for radical change in Scotland, from Jacobite to Jacobin, from crofting Liberals to the early Labour movement, was overlaid with Scottish nationalism.

Even those famous Scots who are often regarded as pillars of the established order have displayed a sneaking sympathy for the nationalist cause. On the Canongate Wall of the Scottish Parliament are inscribed the words that Walter Scott put into the mouth of Mrs Howden in *Heart of Midlothian*:

'When we had a king, and a chancellor, and parliament-men o' our ain, we could aye peeble them wi' stanes when they werena gude bairns – But naebody's nails can reach the length o' Lunnon.'

The immediate aftermath of the Second World War was a high point of Britishness, which had a bearing on my own upbringing. My late mother, Mary, patriotic Scot though she was, would probably never have countenanced Scottish independence if her son had not become inveigled into the national movement. She was from a middle-class background and her views had been bolstered by the war: the Churchill pride.

My father, Robert, however, thinks rather differently. When I was a young MP, and didn't know better, I got into a spot of family bother. I made public the contrast between my mother's and father's views, revealing the capital punishment remedy my dad said was appropriate for Churchill's treatment of the miners.

'Salmond's father wanted to hang Churchill' screamed the newspaper headline. I phoned Dad to apologise.

'Did I teach you naethin?' said Faither reprovingly. 'Hingin was owr guid for thon man!'

The skilled working class like my father – from Robert Burns to the 1820 martyrs, and from Keir Hardie to the early trade union movement – have always been open to the great call of home rule.

James Maxton, the Clydesider MP, speaking in Glasgow in the 1920s in support of a Home Rule Bill (and for a Scottish socialist commonwealth), declared that 'with Scottish brains and courage … we could do more in five years in a Scottish Parliament than would be produced by twenty-five or thirty years' heart-breaking working in the British House of Commons.'

So it wasn't a great leap of faith for my dad to move politically from Labour to SNP in the 1960s. Nor was it for the many others who followed suit in the 1970s, forcing the issue of devolution onto the UK agenda.

The failed referendum of 1979 and the election of Margaret Thatcher seemed at first to have reversed the trend, but in reality it accelerated the underlying shift towards home rule.

A great deal of Scottish identity has been preserved for 300 years through the strength of institutions – Scottish churches, Scots law, Scottish education – and now the myriad of third-sector pressure groups that interact with that institutional identity.

Ironically, Margaret Thatcher's brand of Conservatism set about dismantling many of the key symbols of Britishness. So British Airways became BA, British Petroleum became BP, and British Rail became lots of things.

But Thatcher inadvertently managed rather more than that. A quarter of a century ago she swept into the General Assembly of the Church of Scotland and, in an infamous address, exposed the crass materialism of her creed. This was too much for the elders and brethren – and far too much for a Churchill Tory like my mother, who never voted Conservative again.

Margaret Thatcher had combined her visit to the General Assembly with an equally ill-fated visit to the Scottish Cup final, where she managed to unite Dundee United and Celtic fans in an ingenious and very effective joint red card protest.

Shortly thereafter, on 16 June 1988, Hansard records a brash young SNP member from Aberdeenshire, fresh from being restored to the House after expulsion for intervening in the Budget in protest against the poll tax, taunting the Prime Minister about what he described as her 'epistle to the Caledonians':

> Will the Prime Minister demonstrate her extensive knowledge of Scottish affairs by reminding the House of the names of the Moderator of the General Assembly, which she addressed, and the captain of Celtic, to whom she presented the cup?

Margaret Thatcher had given Scottish nationalism a new political dynamic and accelerated the long-term decline of the Conservative Party in Scotland, where it now commands a mere one-third of its popular support of the 1950s.

Other factors were undercutting support for the union. The Scottish economy had been underperforming the UK average for much of the twentieth century. The reasons were deep and complex but one key factor was the export of human capital. Often it was the best people, the people with get up and go, who got up and went.

When I was a lad, thanks to my grandfather's grounding, I knew that Scots had invented lots of things. He proudly showed me the plaque to David Waldie, born in Linlithgow and pioneer of chloroform, on the wall of the Four Marys pub. He told me that he had worked on the discovery with James Simpson of nearby Bathgate.

I soon discovered that, even beyond Linlithgow and Bathgate, Scotland seemed to have invented just about everything worth inventing – television, telephone, tarmacadam, teleprompter, etc. – and they are just a few examples beginning with the letter 't'!

It took me some time further to realise that Scotland's creative grandeur is not just down to natural ingenuity but springs from our most important invention of all: long before the Treaty of Union, Scotland legislated for compulsory universal elementary education at parish level. Indeed if we look at the list of great Scottish inventors of the eighteenth and nineteenth centuries almost all of them were people of humble origins, because almost all people had received an education. Few flowers in Scotland were born to blush unseen.

In no other society on earth, with the possible exception of Prussia, which embarked on this mission two centuries after Scotland, would such 'lads of pairts' have had the educational grounding to advance in business, science and medicine.

From the most developed education system in the world sprang the Scottish Enlightenment and out of the Enlightenment came the scientists, innovators and entrepreneurs who established Scotland as the pre-eminent industrial economy of the world by the end of the nineteenth century.

For most of the last hundred years Scotland was still producing the scientists and innovators but, by and large, they weren't staying in the country. Scotland started to export its human capital to a ruinous degree.

However, towards the end of the twentieth century things started to change.

In the 1980s, when I was working as an economist, I used to do a party trick during lectures by asking the class to write down the six top industrialists or business people in the country. The names provided were invariably a familiar litany of minor aristocrats, most of whom were running their companies less well than their fathers or grandfathers.

But by the end of the century there had been a significant shift. The most highly regarded business people in the country were no longer those who turned silver spoons into base metal but working-class Scots who had either built their own businesses or run companies on their own merits.

Thus the likes of Brian Souter, Jim McColl, Tom Hunter, Tom Farmer, Martin Gilbert, Roy McGregor and David Murray became the best-known entrepreneurs in the land. What's more, these people were popular and were often deeply influenced by the philosophy and philanthropy of another great Scot, Andrew Carnegie.

They were also generally sympathetic to either independence or at least home rule, and none of them rated the traditional unionist business organisations like the CBI. This directly affected Scottish politics.

In the 1979 referendum people in Scotland still listened to the CBI. By 1997 they were ignoring them. By 2014 they were laughing at them.

At the same time Scotland's economic performance improved. The country now has lower unemployment and, even more crucially, higher employment than the UK average. Indeed outside the south-east of England, Scotland now has the best-performing economy in the country.

Furthermore the second half of the century brought a revival in the arts in Scotland, which gathered pace through the millennium. From crime novels to Turner prizes to chart-topping groups, Scottish art forms flourished as the country moved through the self-government gear box. The balance of opinion in this burgeoning artistic community also favoured radical change or independence.

Against that background the movement towards home rule was irresistible. I committed the SNP to campaign with Labour to secure a double YES vote in the referendum of September 1997. The political price that the late Donald Dewar agreed to pay for securing a united campaign was his explicit agreement that Scotland could progress to independence if the people so willed. Labour, it should be said, made that offer confident that the introduction of proportional representation for the Scottish Parliament would be an insurance policy against any such eventuality.

After a successful referendum campaign, the Scottish Parliament was, in the words from the chair of its most experienced member, Winnie Ewing, 'hereby reconvened' in 1999. The 'recess' had lasted a mere 292 years!

In the elections of that year the SNP gained more parliamentarians in a single day than in the previous seventy-year history of the party, became the official opposition, and shifted the centre of gravity of Scottish politics irreversibly from Westminster to Scotland.

After a setback in 2003, the SNP, under its new and combined leadership team of Nicola Sturgeon and me, narrowly won the election of 2007, and in the process inflicted on the Labour Party its first defeat in a major Scottish election since 1955.

There followed four years of minority government with a plurality of one seat. This government was to face the challenge of the greatest squeeze on public spending since the Second World War.

However, thanks to the parliamentary skill of the business convener Bruce Crawford and the magician-type qualities of the Finance Secretary John Swinney, the minority government survived to prosper. In 2011 the SNP achieved what had, until then, been thought impossible: an absolute majority in a proportional system specifically designed to prevent that from happening.

This made a referendum on independence, a key manifesto pledge of the SNP, inevitable. In the first term of office the three unionist parties had held the line against the referendum apart from a brief period in 2008 when Wendy Alexander, as Labour leader in the Scottish Parliament, had unexpectedly proposed a referendum herself.

Unfortunately for Wendy, among those most surprised by this development was Prime Minister Gordon Brown, and the drama thus ended with her resignation. This was ostensibly for a minor infraction of donation declarations but in reality it was because of a complete removal of her political credibility by a London leadership team, which included her own brother Douglas, who gave her no support whatsoever.

This episode was a classic example of Labour in Scotland being treated as a London 'branch office', in the phrase of Johann Lamont (two Labour leaders after Wendy) in her spectacular resignation eruption of October 2014.

If the election result made a referendum certain, it did not define how exactly such a referendum should be structured. That was to be the subject of delicate negotiation between Downing Street and the Scottish government.

I had previously proposed to David Cameron, after his own election in 2010, that he should spring a political surprise and implement radical devolution for Scotland, often described in the shorthand title of 'devo max'. This initiative got short shrift from the Prime Minister.

Why this was the case I cannot be certain. It would have been popular with his Liberal allies and allowed Cameron to propose a statesmanlike solution to the West Lothian question,* and one effectively on his own terms.

---

* The political shorthand for the question of parity between Scottish MPs voting on English matters but English MPs not being able to vote on Scottish domestic issues. It was so called because it was most frequently raised by the indefatigable Tam Dalyell, MP for West Lothian in the 1970s, who used the examples of Blackburn in his constituency and Blackburn, Lancashire, to illustrate the point. Dalyell

The best explanation for Tory intransigence lies in the bowels of Westminster history and deep in the entrails of the Conservative interest. From Dublin to Delhi, Westminster governments have a dreadful record of conceding much too little and much too late to restless nations. In the case of Scotland the Tory attitude is further complicated by a proprietorial instinct. Regardless of their near total wipeout in Scottish democratic politics they regard our country as part of their demesne.

David Cameron stands in a long line of Tory prime ministers close to landed interests in Scotland. The Prime Minister's holiday retreat, the Tarbert Estate on the island of Jura, is popularly believed to be owned by Mr Cameron's stepfather-in-law, William Astor. In fact, it is owned by Ginge Manor Estates Ltd, a company registered in the Bahamas. The name tells the family story – Ginge Manor is William Astor's stately home in Oxfordshire.

This interest extends to the very top of the civil service. Many people were perplexed by the apparent willingness of the Head of the Treasury, Sir Nicholas Macpherson, to abandon any vestige of civil service impartiality during the referendum campaign. Some people assume that he was forced into it by a scheming and highly political Chancellor. I doubt that.

---

was well aware that the original concept was first mooted by Gladstone in the Irish home rule debates of the 1880s. The name 'West Lothian question' was then coined by the Ulster Unionist MP Enoch Powell in a response to a Dalyell speech, when he said: 'We have finally grasped what the Honourable Member for West Lothian is getting at. Let us call it the West Lothian question.'

Just after the election of 2011, I had a meeting with George Osborne and Sir Nicholas in the Treasury. Normally at these sorts of meetings there is an element of political sparring between the politicians while the civil servants stay suitably inscrutable. This meeting was different. Osborne was full of bonhomie while Macpherson radiated hostility.

I have no means of looking into the soul of the Permanent Secretary to the Treasury but my guess is that a background reason for his intense level of politicisation may well lie in his family's extensive land interests in Scotland.

Whether that is his motivation or not, there is now no doubting his politicisation. In an unwise series of admissions to the inaugural meeting of the Strand Group* on 19 January 2015 Macpherson wallowed in his new-found role as a politician. He defended his decision publicly to oppose independence for Scotland. He said that in such an 'extreme' case as the referendum, in which 'people are seeking to destroy the fabric of the state' and to 'impugn its territorial integrity', the normal rules of civil service impartiality did not apply.

---

* The Strand Group is a forum and seminar series of the Policy Institute at King's College London. It aims to explore how power operates at the very centre of government. The Group's events bring together senior figures from the worlds of governance, civil service, business, journalism and academia past and present to discuss the most pertinent government and political issues of the day. The group's establishment within the Policy Institute has been complemented by the appointment of new Visiting Professors including Sir Nicholas Macpherson. In his lecture Macpherson defended the Treasury's role in the referendum, stating that 'Her Majesty's Treasury is by its nature a unionist institution. The clue is in the name.' Given that the present monarchy is not itself a 'unionist institution', having been established more than a century before the Treaty of Union, we can safely assume that Professor Macpherson is not Visiting in History!

It is interesting to speculate how far Macpherson's rant could change the relationship between civil servants and politicians if others succumb to this pernicious nonsense. In the past his logic could have led officials to take action against any politician or indeed government 'destroying the fabric of the state' by, say, accession to the European Union, or 'impugning' its financial integrity by, say, attempting to join the Euro. In the future being 'extreme' in Macpherson's judgement could be, say, advocating the non-renewal of the Trident submarine fleet.

The solution to Macpherson's dilemma is obvious. He shouldn't wait for his inevitable seat in the House of Lords. He clearly needs to take his own manifesto to the people directly, by standing for election in the west coast of Scotland, perhaps in Plockton, Wester Ross, near his family estate. His father (a splendid chap by every local account) can give him bed and board while he campaigns to his heart's content, explaining to the natives what is good for us. At any rate Sir Nicholas should give up now the pretence of being a civil servant.

Macpherson was allowed to get away with it by a subservient House of Commons, united across the parties in their mutual loathing of Scottish independence. Only the independent-minded veteran Labour MP Paul Flynn saw and challenged this behaviour, recognising, for example, the dangerous precedent created by the extraordinary publishing of Macpherson's 'advice' to the Chancellor on sterling. Unfortunately, real Members of Parliament like Flynn are in short supply now in the Palace of Westminster.

In any case, and for whatever reason, Cameron rejected out of hand the idea of a démarche on devo max in 2010.

After the SNP landslide in the Scottish elections of 2011, I made another attempt to revive the devo max argument by means of a third question on the ballot paper, creating a choice between independence, radical devolution and the status quo. Three-way constitutional referendums are not unknown. Indeed the Cabinet Office itself organised one in Newfoundland in 1948.

This has been interpreted by some commentators and many opponents as indicating a lack of enthusiasm for independence on my part. How little do these people know me or my background.

I believe in Scottish independence. My mandate was to hold a referendum with independence on the ballot paper. I have always thought that it is possible to win such a vote. However, as I remarked to the Welsh politician Dafydd Wigley during the referendum campaign, a punter who places an each-way bet still wants his horse to win the race.

Cameron was having none of the three-way referendum. Buoyed by private polling and political advice which indicated a potential YES vote at around a maximum of 30 per cent, he was intent on a shoot-out between YES and NO with no intervening option. Given what was to transpire in the campaign with the last-minute 'vow' to Scotland of 'home rule', 'devo to the max' or 'near federalism', there is a certain irony in recalling his hard line of 2011/12.

Cameron's position was entirely consistent with the traditional Tory attitude in conceding the absolute minimum to Scotland. At the same time, the new Scottish Tory leader, Ruth Davidson, fought an internal leadership election arguing that there should be a 'line in the sand' against any further devolution proposals.

An agreement with Westminster was necessary to put the referendum beyond legal challenge and, more than that, to have the aftermath of the ballot navigated in a positive manner. The central difficulty that Scottish nationalism has faced throughout its democratic history has not been persuading people that it *should* happen, but that it *could* happen.

Therefore, Cameron made his red line in negotiations the requirement for a single question in the belief that NO would score a comfortable victory. My key objective was to secure an agreement which established independence as a consented process after which it could not – and never again – be argued that there is no means by which Scotland can achieve independence.

In contrast to that absolute strategic objective the tactical consideration of having devo max on the ballot paper was very much of secondary importance. There has been some debate as to whether this was a real position of mine or merely a negotiating posture. The truth is it was both.

Initially, in the aftermath of the 2011 election, I had hoped that we could gain substantial traction across the range of civic organisations who favoured devo max. Many of these were grouped around the Devo Plus campaign led by the economically liberal financier Ben Thomson, but there were others active in much of the third sector and the Scottish Trade Union Congress. It was clearly not credible for the SNP government to simultaneously bring forward into a referendum campaign two propositions: independence *and* devo max. The latter would have had to be the result of genuine work by a substantial body of opinion outside of government and also be radically different from the insipid offering of the unionist parties at the time.

However, a fully fledged proposition for devo max proved not to be possible, and in 2012 I had to come to terms with that reality. I led a Scottish Cabinet discussion on the issue.

On the whole, at least in my second period as SNP leader, since 2004, I have had little difficulty in securing consensus behind my strategy for progress towards independence. It was not always like that. In the days when the SNP were far distant from the independence objective, occasional outbreaks of ideological purity were often a comfortable substitute for progress.

In the 1990s acres of newsprint and many SNP Conference motions were devoted to attempting to interpret every single nuance of my attitude to supporting devolution as a staging post on the way to independence. Eventually I put the matter to the decision of the SNP National Council and successfully committed the party to campaigning YES/YES in the two-question referendum of 1997.

As the Party became increasingly capable of winning, then confidence grew in the likely success of my gradualist strategy. Despite this, by early 2012 I was perplexing some of my colleagues with my continuing support for a third question on the ballot paper. Even Michael Russell, the Education Secretary, who was the joint architect of my step-by-step approach towards independence, contributed powerfully to the discussion, suggesting that it was time to embrace a YES/NO referendum. After I heard them out around the Cabinet table I sprang a surprise by saying: 'Fine, let's do that. YES/NO it is then.'

I then confided to my colleagues that we should maintain our public pursuit of the third option, since it would put us in a strong position to negotiate the timing, the framing of the referendum question and votes for sixteen- to seventeen-year-olds – all crucial matters under the control of the Scottish Parliament. I knew that the UK government would concede much else in their anxiety to record a 'victory' in their red line.

In other words, my support for devo max on the ballot paper was not initially a negotiating posture, but when it eventually became one it was highly successful.

The Edinburgh Agreement between the Scottish and United Kingdom governments was duly negotiated. The most important clause, and the one that received the most entrenched opposition from the UK negotiators, was the very last one, clause thirty:

> *Co-operation*
> 30. The United Kingdom and Scottish Governments are committed, through the Memorandum of Understanding between them and others, to working together on matters of mutual interest and to the principles of good communication and mutual respect. The two governments have reached this agreement in that spirit. They look forward to a referendum that is legal and fair producing a decisive and respected outcome. The two governments are committed to continue to work together constructively in the light of the outcome, whatever it is, in the best interests of the people of Scotland and of the rest of the United Kingdom.

And so when David Cameron came to St Andrew's House on 15 October 2012 with his Secretary of State Michael Moore to conclude the Edinburgh Agreement with Nicola and me, he signed a deal which both sides believed had fulfilled their key objectives. That is, of course, the best sort of deal. They had the YES/NO choice which they believed they would win comfortably. We had a referendum legislated for by the Scottish Parliament and consented by Westminster, establishing for all time a process by which Scotland could become independent.

My remarks at the press conference were designed to move the YES campaign into ultra-positive mode:

> Today's historic signing of the Edinburgh Agreement marks the start of the campaign to fulfil that ambition [of independence]. It will be a campaign during which we will present our positive, ambitious vision for a flourishing, fairer, progressive, independent Scotland – a vision I am confident will win the argument and deliver a YES vote in autumn 2014.

The Edinburgh Agreement allowed for the referendum to be held up to the end of 2014. The proper parliamentary process meant that a year to eighteen months was the necessary preparation time, but basically this left a choice available for the referendum to take place at any point in 2014.

My decision was to go later rather than sooner. It was what I had committed myself to in the election campaign. In addition we were behind in the polls – perhaps not by as much as the Tories believed, but still well behind.

We needed the time to gear up a campaign to take us from the low 30s to over 50 per cent, a seemingly daunting task. However, we also knew from our private polling that the total potential YES support was up to 60 per cent ('potential' means the number of people who said they were prepared to vote for independence under certain circumstances).

But away from all the pomp and poignancy of the historic day, there were a couple of moments when I believe the Cameron mask slipped a little. Signs that suggested his absolute confidence of late 2011 was faltering and that his vaunted attachment to Scotland was based on precious little of substance.

I had asked for some private time with Cameron immediately before and after the signing of the Agreement.

Beforehand this was no more than making sure that the television shots of our entrance into my office looked natural. I confess to having arranged the room so that the all-yellow map of the 2011 Scottish election results was immediately behind my seat. I even moved in the Permanent Secretary's table for us to sit around. In the way these things work in the civil service, it is a rather more impressive piece of furniture than the First Minister's table! Cameron and I went in together to join our teams and I showed him my John Bellany painting which adorned the First Ministerial room in St Andrew's House. I mentioned to him that the painting was of Macduff Harbour and pointed out that it was pretty close to where his grandfather had founded a school in Huntly.

'Ah!' breezed the Prime Minister. 'I've never actually been there.'

Given the important business to hand, I suppressed my surprise that someone should be so rootless as to never have thought of visiting a place presumably of importance to their family origins. However, of more political significance was the conversation that took place after the Agreement had been signed and the others had left.

The Prime Minister asked me when we were intending to hold the poll. I said the autumn of 2014.

He replied: 'But that won't allow enough time before the …' and then stopped himself.

I took the half-finished sentence to mean that it wouldn't allow time to negotiate independence before the UK election of May 2015. In other words, he wasn't so absolutely confident that he hadn't considered the political implications of a YES vote on Westminster parliamentary arithmetic.

Westminster underrated the importance of the timing of the referendum. Everyone likes to be noticed and 2014 was set to be a huge year for Scotland when we could bask in the international spotlight.

Cameron had a blind spot on this. He believed the centenary of the Great War in 2014 would be of more significance in reminding Scots of the glory of the union.

This attitude betrayed a huge misunderstanding of the Scottish psyche. As a martial nation Scots tend to revere soldiers but oppose conflict. We have no time for politicians who believe, like Cameron, that the anniversary of the bloody carnage of the First World War should be celebrated 'like the Diamond Jubilee'.

There were more spilled guts than shared glory in the Great War.

Cameron thus overrated the impact of war and underrated the impact of peaceful endeavour. In 2014 Scotland would host the Commonwealth Games, the Ryder Cup, even the MTV awards. It was also the Year of Homecoming.* Into this heady mix there would come a referendum on self-determination.

Once the date was set the challenge was how to create a campaign that would increase support by the 20 percentage points required to win.

One thing was certain. If we fought a conventional campaign then we would conventionally lose. It was Churchill who said of Austen Chamberlain: 'He always played the game and he always lost.' We had to ensure that we did not just play the game.

The forces lined up against us were formidable.

Although we had drawn up spending rules to attempt to equalise the playing field, we would be heavily outspent during the campaign. The financial imbalance was partially corrected by the serendipity of Chris and Colin Weir winning the Euromillions lottery jackpot in 2011. The Weirs, longstanding and principled nationalists and also among the nicest people in the country, could be relied upon to help redress the imbalance.

The role of Chris and Colin in facing down the unpleasant media attacks on them is worthy of the highest praise. In the looking-glass world of the old written media it is fair game to

---

* Scotland's Homecoming years in 2009 and 2014 were a series of special events designed to generate interest from around the world in Scotland, particularly, but not exclusively, from those of Scottish ancestry. The first of these celebrated the 250th anniversary of the birth of Robert Burns, which provided a theme for many of the events, while the second coincided with the Commonwealth Games and the Ryder Cup. Both years are judged to have been highly successful in attracting additional visitors.

attack two ordinary Scots who invest part of their fortune in the future of their country while turning a 'Nelson's eye' to those London-based big business and financial interests who bankrolled the NO campaign. If campaign donations had been restricted, as they should have been, to those on the electoral roll of Scotland, the NO side would have been struggling to finance their own taxi fares.

This old press were almost entirely lined up on the NO side. In 2007 the SNP famously won an election with both of the main tabloids vying with each other to denounce the party. But we won that election with 33 per cent of the vote. To win the referendum we required 50 per cent plus one.

The ability of the press to determine elections has declined even since 2007, but there is a difficulty when it runs against you as a solid phalanx. It determines the media agenda, which has a follow-on impact on broadcasting, a medium that does still influence votes.

The full machinery of the British state was lined up against us. The three main Westminster parties would unite to see off the challenge with their own separate agendas. Luckily, each was vying with the other in a race to be the most unpopular, and the prestige of the Westminster system was at an all-time low. The very unity of the NO campaign was a disadvantage: the image of London Labour high-fiving the London Tory Party was a massive turn-off to Labour voters in Scotland. It still is.

This left social media and grassroots campaigning as areas where we had to excel. We needed to encourage the growth of a myriad of individuals and campaign groups who would be diverse, and therefore unregimented, but would also contribute to the overall campaign. We had to let a thousand flowers bloom.

In addition, many influential and progressive organisations in Scottish society were favourable to the YES campaign and were looking increasingly to Holyrood and not Westminster for their political objectives. The third sector in Scotland was either neutral or, by majority, supportive, given the experience of seven years of SNP government, and the trade union movement was fundamentally unhappy with the NO's Better Together campaign and was becoming increasingly sympathetic to our cause.

And so the picture, after the signing of the Edinburgh Agreement in the latter part of 2012, was not as bleak as it might have at first appeared. The key to progress was always to be on the positive side of the argument. The referendum question – Should Scotland be an independent country? – gave us that firm platform. It is simply not possible to enthuse people on a negative.

Our first key moment in the campaign was the launch of the White Paper on 26 November 2013. This 670-page document was intended to present independence as a positive but workable vision for the people of Scotland. The launch stood up pretty well to critical examination by the press, and on social media there were hopeful signs that our message was cutting through the usual fog of politics.

That night, in looking at the BBC online reaction, I was struck by an entry from Stevie Kennedy of Mow Cop, a village in Staffordshire: 'As a Scot living in England with an English wife and kids, I feel British first. Today, though, I see a politician talking and I feel hope kindle in my heart that the UK's future isn't all about Westminster and the corrupt industrial–political machinery that controls it regardless of what we vote for. It's been a long time since I felt hope or any other positive emotion when watching a politician speaking, yet I know the next 10 months will see relentless waves of cynical negativity from the No campaign.'

I have never met Mr Kennedy, but he sums up really well the position facing us going into 2014. On the plus side we were inspiring the people with a new vision. The difficulty would be sustaining it against the avalanche of 'cynical negativity' which he so rightly expected.

The most consistent and regular polling was carried out by YouGov, asking the same question as the one that would appear on the ballot paper.

In August 2013, according to the first YouGov poll, the NO side were 30 points ahead: 59–29. By the end of the year, after the launch of the White Paper, their lead had shrunk to 20 per cent: 52–33.

Through the spring and into the summer of 2014 the YouGov polls still recorded NO leads of between 14 and 20 per cent. However, the previous 'don't knows' were generally moving to YES at around 2–1. That group of undecided voters was around 15 per cent at the end of 2013, 10 per cent in the first half of 2014 and then a mere 5 per cent by August 2014.

At first sight, the effective stability in the polls in the first half of 2014 did not look like good news for the YES campaign. However, a deeper examination tells us otherwise.

In quick succession in mid-February the unionist forces fired their biggest guns. First George Osborne, hand in glove with Danny Alexander and Ed Balls, ruled out a currency union, while José Manuel Barroso, the President of the European Commission, popped up on BBC's *Andrew Marr Show* to say that it would be 'difficult, if not impossible' to secure the approval of member states for an independent Scotland's accession to the European Union.

This heavy artillery, which was meant to finish the argument, misfired. The first bombardment, on the currency, looked high-handed, with former First Minister Henry McLeish and even Gordon Brown expressing open or private doubts about the tactic.

The second barrage was regarded with even more incredulity. Sir David Edward, a former judge at the European Court of Justice and a unionist to his fingertips (albeit one who is increasingly despairing of the europhobic politics of Westminster), was moved to directly counter Barroso's bureaucratic bombast, arguing that the latter's comparison of Scotland and Kosovo was little short of preposterous.

Neither Osborne's 'sermon on the pound' nor Barroso's lecture on Europe cut the mustard. They were meant to close out the game but did not have the desired impact. Indeed in the case of the currency the effect was, on balance, counterproductive. And when big guns are fired too early it is sometimes difficult to reload in time.

The launch of the White Paper caused the first big shift to YES. After that, for the first six months of 2014, there was effectively a standoff between the fear-mongering of the NO side and the aspiration of the YES side. As we moved into the last 100 days, the grassroots campaign took off and momentum shifted towards YES.

And so battle was joined and the referendum decided. Of course it is possible to win a battle and lose a war, just as it is possible to lose a referendum and still win the end game. In the aftermath of the ballot the losing YES side have emerged looking like winners while the winning NO side are looking like losers. The full consequences of the Scottish referendum are only just beginning to be understood.

*

Politicians can so often sound mechanical, robotic even: pre-programmed with policies and beliefs. Possessing none of the necessary emotion that makes life worth living.

I believe that the referendum was Scotland's democratic hour, the moment of fundamental reassessment. A time when many people realised that, collectively, they could be more significant than they had ever previously believed. The moment to change, to influence. Rather than just listening to the weather forecast, the people got to decide what the weather should be.

I didn't have to see the world differently. My upbringing had grounded me with that same belief all of my life. I have always been fortunate to have had that at my core. There are now many more people in Scotland in that position.

The great impenetrable edifices, the blocks to progress – Westminster, the Labour establishment – are still there, but they have started to crumble and the people sense it.

I have my family history to thank for my convictions. Both of my parents eventually reached the same conclusion on Scottish independence in their own separate ways. As my father tells it, his moment of conversion happened during an exchange with a Labour canvasser on the front doorstep. Faither was asked how he would be voting.

'Labour,' he replied without hesitation. 'Always have.'

'That's great,' said the canvasser before inquiring about my mum's voting intention.

'No hope for her,' said Faither. 'She's a Tory.'

'Not a problem,' said the Labour man. 'Just as long as she doesn't vote for those Scottish Nose Pickers!'

'Wait a minute,' said Faither. 'My best pal's in the SNP.'

'They're all nose pickers,' said the canvasser.

Dad: 'No, they're no'!'

Canvasser: 'Aye, they are.'

Half an hour later and they're still at it – but, by this time, it wasn't just my dad's friend the canvasser was insulting. He was running down the whole of Scotland.

Finally Faither – ever thrawn – finished the fraught conversation.

'Look, when you arrived I told you I'd vote Labour as I have done in every election. I will now vote SNP in every election. I want you to remember that this is what you have achieved tonight.'

This exchange – which probably took place during the West Lothian by-election in 1962 – bears a striking similarity to Labour's attitude in the referendum.

It's not just that they campaigned side by side with the Tories, it's the fact that they were running down Scotland alongside them too, shoulder to shoulder, hand in glove.

And you don't have to be a member of the SNP to be angry when someone is belittling your country.

My dad has voted SNP for the past fifty years on the back of that conversation. Fifty years! And the Labour Party think they'll be able to wash their hands and, over the next few months, move on from what they've done.

As for my late mum, her route was rather different and more recent – and it was more about a mother's love than a political conversion, despite her distaste for high Thatcherism.

In the 1990s, during my first term as SNP leader, I was conducting a press conference in London when it became clear that the Labour-supporting *Daily Record* wanted to have a pop at me by 'exposing' Mum as a Tory. If he can't convince his own mother, why should people listen to him? That kind of thing.

I knew they were going to doorstep her and phoned with a warning. 'Leave it to me,' she said.

The *Record* duly turned up to quiz her on her Conservative leanings. 'That's true,' she said, 'but all in the past. I'm actually very disappointed in Mr Major and can tell you – and this is exclusive – that I will now be voting in the same direction as my husband – and my son.' Then *The Times* arrived, to whom she said she was papering the bathroom and didn't have the time to talk. Finally the *Scotsman* was rebuffed on the basis that she had already turned down the London *Times*!

Meanwhile, down in London, cut off from the turmoil and worried sick about the press persecution of my poor mother, I phoned home repeatedly for updates. Eventually my dad answered. 'Listen, will you stop phoning, your mum hasn't had as much fun since the Blitz!'

There you have it. That is the well from which I flowed.

*

This is my story of the last 100 days of the referendum.

By definition it is a story told from my vantage point. I know a great deal more about the YES campaign than I do about the NO campaign. It also tells the story from the point of view of the leader of the campaign.

Quite deliberately, the YES campaign was diverse and grass-roots-based. I didn't try to control all aspects of our campaign activity. To have attempted to do so would have been to nullify our greatest advantage: our ability to mobilise vast numbers of people. Rather, we tried to get our message and themes across and, by relaying them through a cast of many thousands, see them impact on the wider community.

None of that removes the responsibility that comes with leading a movement. The mistakes (and there were a few) were my responsibility and mine alone.

Would I do a few things differently with the benefit of 20:20 hindsight? Of course I would. However, my grandfather taught me not to dwell on the past but to learn from it.

Thus on the whole, and that is the only way you can judge these things, the Scottish summer of 2014 saw the most exhilarating, positive and empowering campaign ever to impact on democratic politics. It achieved a greater amount with fewer resources than any election campaign, not only that I have ever been part of, but have ever heard of. I am proud to have been a part of that experience.

It was, for me, the best of times and the best of campaigns. I hope my granda would have been proud.

The Run-Up

As the 100-day campaign approached, the scene was set and the political temperature was rising.

Thursday 5 June 2014

A game of Top Trumps with the US President. Think I may have won.

I've just announced the judge-led inquiry into the Edinburgh trams project. I fully expect this probe into the controversial project to lead the Scottish news.

My Chief of Staff, Geoff Aberdein, threatens to put my gas at a peep. He comes bounding into my office in the Scottish Parliament.

'Obama's come out for NO,' he says.

'What did he actually say?' I ask.

'He said NO,' says Geoff.

'Geoff, what did he say and where did he say it?'

'Well, he was standing with Cameron at a press conference and he said that the UK was a strong ally which should be unified but it was up to the folks up in Scotland.'

'Good,' I reply.

'How can it possibly be good?' asks Geoff.

'Three reasons – one he was standing beside Cameron. Two: Scotland likes to be talked about and three: these "folks" up here are nothing if not thrawn.'

I add: 'So we say, one: Cameron begged for the support. Two: America had to fight for their freedom whereas we have a democratic opportunity. And three: it is indeed up to the "folks up in Scotland".'

'Anything else?' says Geoff. 'Add Yes We Can,' I smile.

Staying in the Sofitel at Heathrow so that I can get to Normandy for the D-Day commemorations, at some unearthly hour tomorrow morning.

Dinner with John Buchanan, my security officer, and Joe Griffin, my principal private secretary. Also there is the really excellent Lorraine Kay, from my private office, who has just flown in from the USA. An English by-election sees the Tories hold from UKIP with the Lib-Dems losing their deposit. Much being made of the continuing tribulations of Nick Clegg.

Friday 6 June

Find myself on an RAF flight back from the D-Day commemorations in Normandy with Nick Clegg and Ed Miliband. Brings to mind a version of the balloon game and who should be pushed out of the plane first. Probably neither of them. They both have their uses.

Appropriately enough this has been, if not quite the Longest Day, then a pretty long one. I'd caught an early plane from RAF Northolt with Clegg (remarkably cheerful) and Miliband (remarkably pleasant).

It is, of course, undoubtedly the case that Nick is putting on an act for Ed's benefit – to show how unruffled he is by the slings and arrows of outrageous by-elections. Meanwhile Ed is on his best behaviour, as there is little or nothing in his current performance to suggest that Labour will be able to govern alone.

There is no purpose in politics in offending someone, at least unnecessarily.

In turn, I am really cheerful (at least for 7 a.m.). I want to give the impression that, despite the 20-point-plus leads for NO in the referendum polling, I might just possibly have something up my sleeve.

Also there are the Welsh First Minister, Carwyn Jones, and Peter Robinson of Northern Ireland, for once and for obvious reasons, without Martin McGuinness.

We are taken across the Channel in a very comfortable BAe jet from the Royal Flight, which I would strongly recommend to all air passengers. Laughingly make a note to self: if things go well perhaps we could get one of these – Scotforce One!

I'm offered a very nice breakfast, but it's too early for me. Anyway, I think: the food'll be much better in France. Our flight was certainly easier than the one which the parachutists put up with on D-Day.

In virtually no time at all we are at Caen airport heading towards the prefecture where the delegates are assembled for the first of several church services.

The highlight of the first service is the consecration of a massive bell in the middle of the Bayeux cathedral. I meet my first veteran of the day, from Southport, who asks me if I am the one who is 'causing all the trouble'. At least he says it with a twinkle in his eye.

On the walk from the cathedral to the cemetery for the second service the townspeople clap the D-Day veterans as they march forward in the sun. It is the first of a number of moving moments.

Foolishly having turned down some factor 50, and even more foolishly with no hat on, I am baked in a warm sun at the cemetery. However, the day is enlivened by some chats with the old soldiers from around the Commonwealth who are in robust form. And all of whom have brought their headgear.

I meet John Millin, son of Piper Bill, who featured in the film *The Longest Day*, and whose statue adorns Sword Beach. John tells me a couple of things.

First, despite sporting a set of bagpipes he is actually no piper but had promised his dad on his deathbed that a Millin would play at the unveiling of the Sword Beach statue. So he is able to play 'Highland Laddie', one of his father's tunes from D-Day, and pretty well nothing else.

He also discloses the real sequence of events on D-Day. Millin did not actually volunteer for a suicidal piping recital, but when ordered by Lord Lovat to play a tune demurred, pointing to the King's regulations aimed at stopping the demise of pipers in active combat.

'Ah,' breezed Lovat, 'that's English war office and doesn't apply to us Scots – so just play.' Bravely, Piper Bill followed this direct order and, with comrades falling like flies all around him, he miraculously escaped without a scratch.

The next day they asked some captured German snipers: 'Why didn't you shoot the piper?'

'He was obviously a madman,' they replied, 'and the Wehrmacht is not in the business of shooting lunatics.'

So, not quite as represented in the film but a cracking story. Come to think of it, rather better than in the film.

Piper Bill's role is duly celebrated in a pretty good pageant which is the centrepiece of the French commemoration at Sword Beach. Trouble is, they start an hour and a half late and have a dozen veterans lined up to meet the various heads of state, who all insist on arriving one by one.

The prospect of our heroes surviving D-Day only to be struck down by sunstroke at the commemorative pageant is too awful to contemplate. Fortunately someone has the presence of mind to get some umbrellas for shelter, although a French TV producer keeps pinching the veterans' water bottles because she thinks they are ruining her best shots.

While we wait I take the opportunity to have a quick word with US Secretary of State John Kerry, who is sitting just opposite me.

I start by suggesting that, given the President's pronouncements, I might expel John from the Scottish caucus – the group in Congress that Senator Jim Webb has brought together to promote the Scottish interest.

He seems to think this suitably funny and tells me that we have a 'big day' coming up and that 'it' (presumably Obama's statement) is 'the least we could say'.

Things are just starting to get really interesting when Carwyn Jones comes up to get a photo and all revealing chat stops. Kerry's last words to me are 'Good luck'.

After Sword Beach we are back to Caen, where all heads of state take off in strict protocol order, Airforce One first. This means that the very pleasant Prince Albert of Monaco takes off before the Deputy Prime Minister, the Chief of the General Staff and me.

We board a Hercules transport plane. The trip back is rather like the closing scene of *Where Eagles Dare*, with the top brass, Ed, Nick, Carwyn and me, sitting with our backs to the fuselage – and me wondering who should be jettisoned first.

Back to Northolt in double quick time before Joe and I fly on to Aberdeen. The crew are good sorts and for the final leg I am in the jump seat in the cockpit. They tell me that they did most of their flying time in Afghanistan, where the Hercules was the ideal aircraft: it has near-vertical take-off with a light load. This stops bandits being able to shoot at you – which seems like a pretty unanswerable argument.

Despite the best efforts of the crew and a very rapid flight straight up the North Sea to Aberdeen, the taxiing around the airport takes time and a dash to Inverurie mart has me arriving at 10.30 p.m. – quick enough for people to see me making the effort but not in time to address the Taste of Grampian dinner.

This is a great pity, since I had intended to open my speech with the line: 'I apologise for my late arrival but Airforce One delayed my Hercules taking off from the D-Day landings at Caen airport!'

Saturday 7 June

A day at home preparing for the 100-day sprint to the line.

I have some time to think about Cameron's pleas to everyone and their auntie for help against independence and about some people being daft enough to respond.

After the Obama 'intervention' we had been wondering who else Cameron and his crew would be successful in persuading to speak against us. We'd heard reports of the

Foreign Office briefing against us and we expected that all significant leaders had been asked for their view. Galling, since we pay those people's salaries.

But my hunch is still that it is good for YES and that is what I shall certainly suggest to Andrew Marr tomorrow.

Apparently Andrew Neil is tweeting that because I am on Marr then Nicola cannot be on the *Politics Show* – an illustration of the double-think that is now par for the course for the BBC. Clearly if one SNP politician is on one network programme, then we have exhausted our quota for the day.

Sunday 8 June

Use the interview on Marr to launch a further challenge to the Prime Minister to debate with me directly – First Minister to Prime Minister. He won't, of course, but that is no reason for not issuing the challenge.

Interviewed down the line from the Marcliffe Hotel, my favourite hotel in Aberdeen. Indeed it is everyone's favourite hotel in Aberdeen.

As it happens I helped Andrew with one of his first big stories in journalism.

Wind the clock back to 1982 and I was at the heart of the SNP 79 Goup's* industrial campaign, and British Leyland at

* The SNP 79 Group was a ginger group set up after the rout in the 1979 election which argued for a declared left-of-centre programme from the SNP. One of its campaigns in 1981–82 was in support of workforce occupations of factories in the face of industrial closures. Although the 79 Group was defeated internally, many of its ideas strongly influenced the development of the SNP and many key members, including the author, went on to achieve high office.

Bathgate was in terminal trouble. I had accumulated a great deal of material on how truck models were being systematically withdrawn from Bathgate to prepare for rundown and closure.

However, from the less than dizzy heights as assistant economist of the Royal Bank of Scotland, I was hardly in a position to release it myself. My solution was to give the story to a young *Scotsman* journalist – Andrew – who ran a very good three-part series based on the information.

As part of the job, Andrew came into 36 St Andrew's Square to interview me. Behind my desk I had a framed copy of the first-day cover of a magazine called *Radical Scotland*, which featured a cartoon illustrating a quote from historian Tom Nairn: 'Scotland will be free when the last Church of Scotland minister is strangled by the last copy of the *Sunday Post*!'

The depiction of a slightly panicky and very baldy meenister was not meant to be taken seriously.

Some six years later, when I was in Westminster, one of Andrew's great friends, the *Guardian*'s Ewen MacAskill, interviewed me and started his profile by suggesting that I was a very unusual Royal Bank economist, since behind my desk there was a copy of a Church of Scotland minister being strangled by a newspaper!

This led the local Conservative Association in Banff and Buchan to release a press statement saying that I wished to assassinate ministers of religion. The *Press and Journal*, delivered in those days to just about every home in my constituency, then put this nonsense on their front page.

As a newly elected member I was perhaps oversensitive about reputational issues, and a defamation action followed to bring the local Tories to heel, masterminded by my great friend and lawyer, Peter Chiene.

All of which is a reminder that stuff and nonsense in politics did not start with social media – it just makes it more immediate and more widespread.

Monday 9 June

Today is the day that the media has designated as the official launch of the 100-day campaign and so it is redolent with political opportunity. For my part I end up doing some personal polling in a golf club bar – and come away thinking we *really* can do this, despite the gap.

Nicola kicked it all off this morning with an all-women Cabinet and public question-and-answer session in Edinburgh. I take over in the afternoon and go back to Aberdeen to cover Sky and the BBC network.

I do the Sky piece from Nigg Bay Golf Club in Aberdeen, a municipal course with great views over Aberdeen harbour. Cheekily, someone – one of the green keepers I'm told – has hung a union flag on a fence in a vain attempt to get it into camera shot.

However, the guys in the clubhouse are very keen to see me, and after a few drinks I end up as an honorary member. It should be said that the folk in the bar are bang on a key YES demographic – mainly middle-aged, working-class men – but, even so, this crowd is a pretty easy and enthusiastic conversion to the cause.

I tell Geoff Aberdein in a phone call afterwards that, regardless of a general lack of encouragement in polls, I am confident that we have a real shot at this. The 100-day coverage also reinforces my view that as we move into the campaign period proper then the inevitable quickening of the pace will be of great benefit to YES.

Tuesday 10 June

I phone in to the YES campaign meeting tonight and find them a bit downbeat. Turns out that they've had access to a TNS opinion poll, which shows little or no movement to YES.

It is always a wonder to me that people in politics allow their morale to be affected by the latest opinion poll, instead of trusting their own political antennae.

It's hard to give a pep talk down the phone, but I'm open and direct with my feelings: that we might not be there or even close, but everything is possible at this point. We're not close to winning but we CAN win and the campaign has to believe that. Part of this confidence comes from my informal canvass in Nigg Bay Golf Club. My gut tells me that things are going pretty well.

Wednesday 11 June

Could be said that we held a Gunn to our own heads today.

Stayed in Strichen to cover the Oil and Gas UK conference in the Aberdeen Exhibition Centre. The speech goes well and I'm ready to face the cameras when I get a pretty panicky call from Geoff Aberdein to brief me on a self-inflicted wound.

For reasons (not altogether clear), my highly experienced special adviser [SPAD] Campbell Gunn decided to email the

Daily Telegraph to inform them that Clare Lally, the 'ordinary mother' who featured in their coverage of the 100-day Better Together launch, was actually a member of Labour's shadow cabinet and former Labour Provost of Glasgow Pat Lally's daughter.

The first suggestion is correct, the second total nonsense. I know Clare personally. She is the mother of a quadriplegic daughter and a carers' champion.

All of which wouldn't have caused much of a stir in normal times, but what on earth Campbell thought he was doing emailing the *Daily Telegraph* is beyond my ken.

The paper is the self-appointed ringleader of a madcap old-fashioned media preoccupied in their conspiracy to discredit the YES campaign and all our works. There is therefore no point whatsoever in engaging with them or wasting time on them or explaining ourselves to them. Still less in sticking out our chin and letting them hit it.

The *Telegraph*, true to form, conflates Campbell's foolish email with a story of the online abuse of Clare to concoct an attack. This is yet another episode in the claims of systematic online abuse from the YES side by so-called 'cybernats'. In fact it is not 'nats', it is nuts. I deal with the TV interviews easily enough. I'm also asked about J. K. Rowling, who has given a million pounds to Better Together and has also been attacked online.

It is pretty obvious that the Clare and J. K. stories will now centre on the online abuse and there is next to nothing we can do about it. This story now has all the ingredients to take it beyond the *Telegraph* obsessions and into the tabloids and TV.

The connection with politics is coincidental. Internet trolls get their kicks by attacking anyone in the news about anything.

In addition, the only research on the politics of this is by a Strathclyde University academic, Dr Mark Shephard, who has concluded in his interim report that the YES campaign is more of a target than a source of internet abuse.

However, the truth is that there is no high ground in this matter: any society and any subject is fair game for the pathetic clowns who get their kicks by abusing other people online behind the shield of anonymity. Most claims of the NO campaign don't touch us: they are too exaggerated or just plain silly. This might.

I instruct Campbell to apologise at once and to make it clear that he distances himself from the online abuse of anyone at any time. Of course the ability to stop internet trolls is non-existent.

Let there be no doubt about the reasoning behind the *Daily Telegraph* attack. They would like nothing better than to force us off social media where we are dominating and back to a conventional campaign which we would inevitably lose.

Ironically the latest Survation poll from the Labour-supporting *Daily Record* confirms my hunch about the way the wind has been blowing, with 46 per cent YES and a big lead for the SNP in the party ratings for Holyrood. In my opinion it overstates YES support but does give an indication of the direction of travel.

The 100 Days

Day One: Thursday 12 June

'Campbellgate' duly dominates First Minister's questions and I repel boarders as best as I can. Even for the rough old trade of politics there is something pretty unsavoury about today's line of questioning. All of the opposition leaders know Campbell and indeed have known him for many years. They all said wonderful things about him when he collected his well-merited lifetime achievement award for journalism earlier this year. They all know that his email has been taken out of context by the *Telegraph* and that he had nothing whatsoever to do with online abuse. Yet here they all are lining up to present him as the devil incarnate and baying to end his career in an ignominious sacking!

Ruth Davidson even compared him to Donald Dewar's SPAD John Rafferty, who was sacked in 1999 for allegedly making up death threats against then Labour Health Minister Susan Deacon. I have no intention whatsoever of sacking Campbell. My administration has been grounded on loyalty to colleagues. Even when they make silly mistakes. Leaders who fling people overboard can't lead.

I call Campbell in at 5 p.m. and administer a formal written warning, only the second one for a SPAD in seven years. The first was for an unfortunate who managed to leave Cabinet papers in a pub. The rules drawn up in the aftermath of the fall of Gordon Brown's spinner Damian McBride (resigned when caught trying to peddle made-up rumours about the private lives of Tory politicians) are poorly and loosely drafted. This seems the proportionate and fair action to take.

Day Two: Friday 13 June

Today is dominated by the highest YES poll so far – and meeting the real Inspector Rebus.

Launching the reindustrialisation strategy in Dunfermline at Greenfield Systems Ltd, a company which is a main supplier to the Falkirk bus company Alexander Dennis. It's a pretty good document drawn up by our economics team and the SPAD Ewan Crawford, who has done an excellent job.

Ewan is the son of the late Douglas Crawford, a brilliant and mercurial SNP MP from the 1970s, and Joan Burnie, the doyenne of Scottish agony aunts. This family background may explain Ewan's permanent hangdog demeanour. He gives the impression of being a melancholy chap in a constant state of anguish about something or other. It may be that he acts like a political sin eater – his worried looks serve to ease the anxiety of everyone else in the team.

At any rate it will be interesting to see how much this substantial document receives in terms of publicity compared with the contrived candy-floss of cyber abuse.

On the way back to Bute House I get the results of our own

latest Panelbase poll which has YES up to 48 per cent – the highest in the series. I suggest to Kevin Pringle that the *Sunday Herald* and the *Scottish Sun* might be the best release points for a neck-and-neck poll. Rather like the Survation figures, I don't think we are anything like as close as this poll suggests, but we are certainly in this game.

The artist Gerard Burns comes in with a choice of two portraits of me. I like the one he has set in Bute House, which will be auctioned for charity during the Commonwealth Games. The idea is called 14 for 14 – with 14 prominent Scots as his subjects and all proceeds going to 14 different charities. I choose CLIC Sargent, the children's cancer charity, which arranges family support and respite and which has a wonderful base in Prestwick, Ayrshire.

Gerard painted *The Rowan*, the picture which dominates my office in the Scottish Parliament and which has become one of the most famous paintings in the country. I am interviewed in front of it pretty constantly.

In 1998 Gerard was a struggling young artist and schoolteacher who received the commission of his life, the chance to have one of his pictures hung in the new parliament's temporary home in the General Assembly building on the Mound. He put his heart and soul into the work and painted a group of people carrying a huge saltire set against a Glasgow background. The picture is actually about hope and the rowan sprig in the hand of the beautiful young girl in the picture is a symbol of that hope. They are a family group travelling, perhaps to Hampden for a football match (very hopefully) or perhaps to George Square for a peace rally. Wherever they are going they are travelling hopefully.

All of this potent symbolism was too much for the powers that used to be in the Scottish Parliament, and they sent him a letter saying that they no longer required his very big saltire. Since Gerard binned the letter I cannot positively identify the culprit who believed that the artist's national flag was too big for the national parliament. Suffice to say, I have my suspicions.

At any rate the world spun on its axis and Gerard ceased to be a struggling young schoolteacher and became one of Scotland's most successful and most collectable artists. Meanwhile in 2007 I became First Minister and was on the Channel 4 *Morning Line* programme for the Ayr Gold Cup. Alan Macdonald, the owner of Ayr racecourse and a devotee of both Robert and Gerard Burns, had positioned *The Rowan* so that the giant saltire was reflected over the racecourse like a great rainbow. Suitably impressed, I asked about the picture and was told the rather sad story about the struggling young artist who had been so cruelly snubbed by the Parliament.

'Well,' I said, 'we can put that to rights as I have just moved into a new office.' And so it came to pass that Gerard loaned the picture to the government for as long as I was First Minister: a fine and generous gesture, but not a foolish one. One day Gerard will receive back into his possession one of the most famous and sought-after paintings in the country.

I choose the Bute House portrait because the other one, based on a *New York Times* picture, looks a shade on the messianic side. Gerard kindly offers me the messianic one, but in office I can't accept personal gifts. I suggest instead that he donates it to the SNP or the YES campaign, where messianic pictures are in great demand!

Later in the evening I have dinner with Ken Stott who, when portraying the detective Rebus, is a most convincing Hibernian supporter. He turns out to be a Heart of Midlothian supporter like myself – so a Jambo as well as a really interesting guy with a great grasp of politics.

'How do you play Rebus's Hibee football loyalties with such conviction?' I ask.

'It's called acting!' says Ken.

Day Three: Saturday 14 June

I'm hoping that the Commonwealth Games will produce some new Scots sporting greats – like my boyhood hero from the 1970 Games, Lachie Stewart. I meet Lachie and a range of other Games greats when we greet the Commonwealth baton at Meadowbank Stadium in Edinburgh.

I am able to tell him exactly where I was when he out-sprinted the great Oz athlete Ron Clarke and the rest of the field to win gold for Scotland. It was a Saturday and I was a 'junior agent' (paperboy) for the *Edinburgh Evening News*. Our 'senior agent' (my boss) came to collect the money at my pal Alan Grant's house. However, we were all watching the 10,000-metre final and he sat down to join us.

'Have you ever thought of absconding?' I asked him, nodding towards the cash which lay scattered in small denominations of old money on the Grant living-room carpet.

'You mean with someone's wife?' came the enigmatic reply. Senior agents were not recruited for their extensive vocabulary.

Lachie tells me that in those days you just had to fit in preparation for big meetings as and when you could, but normal life had to come first – in his case his work as a dental technician in Edinburgh. In my boyhood there was a character in the *Hotspur* comic called Alf Tucker, who was known as 'the tough of the track'. Alf used to finish working on building sites, eat a quick fish supper and then demolish prima donna athletes (usually very large Germans or very flash Americans) in the big races. Lachie Stewart is the real-life 'tough of the track' and all the more admirable for that.

Ron Clarke, in contrast, was a professional in all but name. He said later that he didn't even know who Lachie was as he sprinted past him. Lachie Stewart is a Scottish hero. Let's hope for a few more in Glasgow.

The mood at the Commonwealth Stadium is great. Lots of families, lots of saltires and lots of fun.

This is the second time this week I've felt a real quickening of the public mood which makes me think that the improved poll position recorded in both Panelbase and Survation may be a bit nearer the mark than the much poorer ratings of System Three, MORI or YouGov. Or alternatively that the nature of the panel polls means that they may be measuring what is likely to happen among the more politically aware rather than what has already happened in the general population.

It's a day of sport, as I then go to Fir Park, Motherwell, to watch Scotland's women play Sweden in a World Cup match. I wanted to support the Scotland women but also thought this might be a convenient place to be when asked if I was watching the England–Italy match. Eight years ago my immediate predecessor Jack McConnell made a complete fool of himself by supporting England's opponents at the World Cup. This has never been my inclination, although I do subscribe to a theory that an extended England run during the tournament would be a big positive for the YES campaign.

Unfortunately, I think there is very little chance at all that the English nation will be led into an overdrive of patriotic fervour. Their team has a dodgy defence and an ageing midfield. The one hope for them lies in their exciting young players, but the pool of talent of first-team, first-rate English players in one of the best leagues in the world is actually small.

The Scotland–Sweden game is great fun and, cheered on by an enthusiastic crowd of 2,000 or so, the Scottish women give a better and bigger team a real game. Ifeoma Dieke, the Scottish number 4, is a truly marvellous player – not hugely quick but a fantastic reader of the game, rather in the mould of ex-Hearts, Everton, Rangers and Scotland defender David Weir. I hope I get the chance to meet her one day – with any luck at the World Cup finals in Canada next year.

On my way to Fir Park I'd heard that the ICM poll in *Scotland on Sunday* has YES at 45, up three points, but, true to their normal dismal form, the well-initialled *SOS* is leading on the idea that families across the nation are falling out with relatives as a result of the referendum process. What utter piffle.

Most papers (around thirty titles in all in Scotland) are hostile to independence because their predominantly London-based newspaper groups judge it to be in their interests to be hostile. Or at least they consider the idea of independence to be against their interests. However, the *Scotsman* and its sister paper *Scotland on Sunday* are on a suicide mission.

Andrew Neil once ran the *European* newspaper on an anti-European editorial and it did not last too long. Similarly, the

Scotsman could survive, indeed prosper, with any editorial line – left-wing, right-wing, Liberal, Seventh Day Adventist, if it wished.

The only thing the *Scotsman* cannot be is unreliable on the national question, and yet that is exactly what it is. The endgame of that approach is certain. The *Scotsman* will disappear from the newsstands and on to the internet before long.

Back home in Strichen I arrive in time to see the second half of a pretty average Italian side cantering to a close (but still comfortable) victory over England. As I suspected YES will have to look elsewhere for a campaign boost!

Day Four: Sunday 15 June

Today I get to do what I enjoy most in politics: talking directly to people.

Taking part in the Colin Mackay phone-in for Bauer radio allows me to break out of the political bubble. That kind of contact is one of the real joys of the campaign. There are a number of points raised about the Health Service. I will make sure that the individual cases raised are properly pursued by my private office.

The *Sunday Herald* and the *Scottish Sun on Sunday* give us a good show on the apparent tightening of the polls. However, most of the papers do a post-mortem of the week's episode of cyber abuse as if it was a YES prerogative. Interestingly, in the entire hour of the phone-in programme nobody wants to talk about 'cybernats' but about the Health Service and the economy. The lesson for the campaign is to keep on our own agenda and our own medium to deliver the message. We must not allow the old press to dictate the themes of this new campaign.

Day Five: Monday 16 June

Up at the crack of dawn. Destination: Orkney Islands. We have chosen Orkney to launch *Our Islands Our Future*.

Derek Mackay, the Minister for Local Government, has guided negotiations between the Scottish government and the three island councils* with skill, and the launch goes extremely well. The document and the process which has preceded it is an attempt to galvanise support for independence in the islands by providing the assurance (and the reality) that the process of local decision-making should not stop at Edinburgh but be community-focused across the whole of Scotland. It is important to the independence movement that we carry support in all of Scotland.

Visited Kirkwall Grammar School as part of the trip. It's a 'school for the future' and I am greatly impressed by staff and pupils.

The new schools across Scotland are going to stand the nation in good stead. Actually they are the same design – for example, Kirkwall Grammar looks to my untrained eye very similar in terms of layout to Lasswade High, in Midlothian – and all the better for that. More than 460 new schools have been built or renovated since 2007 (almost a fifth of the entire estate) compared with just 328 during the first eight years of

---

* Shetland Islands Council, Orkney Islands Council and Na h-Eileanan an Iar (Western Isles Council).

devolution. All of this has been achieved against a huge cut in capital spending and is a triumph of organisation and ingenuity over funding availability.

Day Six: Tuesday 17 June

Worried that Vladimir Putin might cause me problems – but boosted by an Englishman calling for a YES vote.

We were still in Orkney and Donna Heddle, former SNP candidate in Orkney and wife of the council convener, had arranged a lunchtime meeting at virtually no notice – and forty people immediately turn up. A chap, originally from Nottingham, tells me how he and his wife thank their lucky stars every morning for being in Orkney. He is a firm YES supporter but would just like to hear more people with his accent speaking up for the cause.

He is absolutely right!

This came after the first-ever Cabinet meeting convened from a school for the future. The Infant Cremation Commission report from Lord Bonomy was due out. This report follows the discovery that over many years babies' ashes had been disposed of at Mortonhall Crematorium in Edinburgh without the knowledge of parents. I had promised the parents that I would chair the Cabinet that discussed the report. I was determined to keep my word and therefore I chaired the Cabinet over Skype from Kirkwall Grammar while my colleagues were in Edinburgh. High-tech stuff from a school for the future.

I hope to progress this sensitive issue through building on the excellent work of former Lord Advocate Elish Angiolini. As in everything she does, Elish has adopted a model approach and has earned the confidence of the parents affected by Mortonhall, where this depressing lack of humanity and dereliction of duty were discovered. If we can apply her comprehensive look across all of Scotland then we might implement Bonomy's recommendations and secure the information, explanation and apology that the parents are due for their own treatment at the hands of officialdom.

This would avoid the long process of a public inquiry which can seldom, if ever, provide a satisfactory explanation for individuals as opposed to key investigations of policy. What public inquiries do provide, however, is a dripping roast for less than scrupulous legal companies.

Now to Putin. Flew back to Edinburgh to hold a meeting with the Ukrainian Community. I'm expecting a difficult discussion, since some had taken severe umbrage at an interview which I had conducted with Alistair Campbell for *GQ* earlier in the year.

In it Campbell had trapped me into saying what I 'admired' about Vladimir Putin. In fact I had been rather judicious in what I said, but that is not how it was reported. At any rate I needn't have worried. The meeting goes well and we all part firm friends.

Day Seven: Wednesday 18 June

I was only here for the beer. Not drinking it but spreading the word about the exceptional entrepreneurship of a couple of lads from Fraserburgh, James Watt and Martin Dickie, who employ hundreds of people producing and selling great real beers with their firm BrewDog.

They're giving a presentation at the Scottish Economic Forum and I find out that they have a bar in São Paulo, Brazil.

This is a great way to kick off the forum. Firstly I say it is nice to know that Scotland will be represented at the World Cup in some capacity, and secondly that it is reassuring to know that supporters of every nation – none in particular, mind – will be able to drown their sorrows in excellent beer now brewed in Ellon, Aberdeenshire!

I also raised a laugh by describing my recent visit to the Coca-Cola factory in East Kilbride which was celebrating its fiftieth anniversary. One of that plant's many achievements is to take charge of most of the commemorative bottles that Coca-Cola produce for the World Cup and the Olympic Games. Thanks to Coca-Cola executive Jim Fox they even produced one for Scotland's Homecoming in 2009, when Robert Burns became the first person in world history to feature on the famous bottle.

In the presence of the company's top executives I was taken around the impressive plant in a golf buggy by one of the workers, John McCafferty.

As we passed the World Cup bottle line, McCafferty said: 'As you will know, we in East Kilbride produce the commemorative bottles. You will also know that Scotland, as a nation, decided NOT to participate in this year's World Cup in Brazil. However, such is our generosity of spirit here in East Kilbride that we still produce the bottles for the rest of the planet.'

One of the Coca-Cola top guys turned to me and asked: 'Is that right? You guys decided not to go? Was it a protest?'

'Let's call it East Kilbride irony,' I replied.

Day Eight: Thursday 19 June

Everyone's getting their knickers in a twist about the cost of setting up the governmental structures of an independent Scotland.

Professor Patrick Dunleavy, of the London School of Economics, has been at loggerheads with the Treasury over the past few days after they claimed that it would take £2.7 billion and attributed that figure to his research.

Patrick is not a man to be trifled with or to have his work traduced. He immediately blogged that their figures were 'bizarrely inaccurate' and 'badly misrepresented' his key data. He accused them of being out by a factor of twelve. The Treasury Permanent Secretary has even admitted to 'misbriefing'.

Tory leader Ruth Davidson and the Lib Dems' Willie Rennie pursue me at First Minister's Questions on these set-up costs. Their joint attack badly misfires when I announce that I have already held a meeting with Professor Dunleavy to discuss his work in detail.

This shouldn't really have been too much of a surprise to them, since I had mentioned the possibility two weeks previously – at First Minister's Questions.

Seems like the best way to keep a secret around here is to mention it at FMQs!

Then to Edinburgh's New Club at the behest of the hugely likeable and totally inveterate right-winger Peter de Vink, who has invited me to address the free-market dining group the Tuesday Club – on a Thursday. Peter is totally convinced that, with enough exposure, I can recruit other free-marketeers to support freedom for their country.

It is an occasion to remember, but not so much for my success in recruiting free-marketeers. Rather a young American singer called Morgan Carberry sings 'Caledonia' with Edinburgh Castle as a backdrop through the window of the New Club dining room. 'Caledonia' always makes me cry, but Morgan's story would bring a tear to a glass ee.

She had come to Scotland on a Marshall Scholarship, part of the post-graduation study programme introduced by former First Minister Henry McLeish. She is a graduate of the Royal Conservatoire but now is to be flung out of the country because her personal relationship broke up within days of her qualifying for permanent residence. It is difficult to fathom how anyone could conceive that depriving the country of this intelligent and talented young woman could benefit anyone. It is, of course, exactly why we need our own immigration policy for our own country.

Day Nine: Friday 20 June

Mark Carney, the Governor of the Bank of England, is just about the only public official in London who is playing things with a straight bat.

I have a private phone conversation with him in the middle of a visit to an excellent youth diversionary behaviour project – before heading to the Youth Cabinet.

Mark is a straight down the line sort of guy. I suggest to him that the polls will tighten and that one way to prevent instability in the financial sector is for him to make a 'Whatever happens, I'm in charge' type of statement. That would just reflect reality. Whatever the result, the Bank will have that responsibility at least for the next two years. He promises to think about it and I believe he will.

The Youth Cabinet is in the Scottish Exhibition and Conference Centre in Glasgow and my speech and presentation are starting to catch alight, reflecting the political fires which I think are beginning to burn.

A remark by the late Donnie Stewart, MP for the Western Isles, perhaps reflects best where we are now. He described the political heather as 'not burning but smouldering'.

The golfers in Aberdeen, the families at Meadowbank, these youngsters in Glasgow. The heather is not yet burning but it is starting to smoulder.

Donnie Stewart once found himself, rather unexpectedly, the leader of a band of eleven MPs in a crucial position in the close-run parliament after the October 1974 election. A *Times* journalist was dispatched to interview this hick from the sticks and was clearly not pleased to have been given the lowly task.

In his most patronising tone he asked Donnie: 'And so, Mr Stewart, your outfit seriously believes in independence for Scotland?'

'Nope,' says Donnie, puffing on his pipe.

'Well, Mr Stewart, you do believe in some sort of parliament for Scotland?'

'Nope,' says Donnie, still puffing.

'Ah well, Mr Stewart, you do believe in more SAY for Scotland?'

'Nope,' says Donnie, shaking his head.

'Well,' says the journalist, by now completely exasperated, 'what on earth do you believe in, Mr Stewart?'

'TOTAL WORLD DOMINATION,' came the majestic put-down from the Isle of Lewis!

After the Youth Cabinet I go off to Nairn to join Moira, since we are snatching a couple of days at Castle Stuart near Inverness. I have made up my mind to try and get a minimum of three escapes to golf courses during the referendum campaign.

This is to keep myself reasonably sane and my weight under some control. I need to try and stick to my 5–2 diet.

Moira is a great sounding board for what's really going on in the country. She has been telling me since the spring that the race is tightening. Before that she hadn't said much at all, which I took as a cause for real anxiety.

Moira lunches with ladies in Turriff – at Celebrations, a big concern in the town, where you can buy anything. It's like an old-fashioned emporium, although certainly not old-fashioned in style, and it acts like a magnet. People come into town for it, and that has knock-on benefits for the rest of the high street.

These ladies are a diverse group – farmers' wives, nurses, young mums and the like – and they meet for charity fashion shows and so on. And Moira takes the temperature.

We chat about the latest soundings over dinner at the Classroom restaurant in Nairn.

I meet an American party of golfers who are in high form and high jinks having played Nairn Western. One of them tells me that he has been doing his own opinion polling as he goes around the great links courses of Scotland.

According to him everyone in St Andrews is voting NO and everyone in Nairn is voting YES.

He suggests that I should be in St Andrews!

Day Ten: Saturday 21 June

Hundreds of people turn up for the YES Scotland's Inverness office opening. An incredible crowd given that it was arranged online in a few hours.

I cut the ribbon in the company of the wonderful Julie Fowlis – the singing voice of the Disney movie *Brave* – and that fine man John Duncanson, the former news anchor of Grampian Television.

Golf calls and we travel to the Castle Stuart links. I play not too badly in tying the game. Round in 88, which for me these days is pretty good. I am now within 29 shots of shooting my age.

A quick drink at Nairn Western golf course, where they were opening their own halfway house – not devo max, but a whisky oasis for those who wish to recover from (or forget entirely) the first nine holes.

On arrival, I hold a conference call to make sure that we are properly equipped to respond to Patrick Dunleavy's report on the cost of government for the *Sunday Post*. The call goes well, as I suspect so will the report.

Moira treats me to the Mustard Seed in Inverness, one of her favourite restaurants.

Day Eleven: Sunday 22 June

I'm back on the links today – but it is Patrick Dunleavy who hits a hole in one and bunkers the Treasury.

His report in the *Sunday Post* has gone well for us and very badly for the UK government. He estimates the initial set-up costs of independence at £200 million – in a different league from the Treasury's overblown estimates which they had claimed to be based on his research.

Earlier, in the summer sunshine of Castle Stuart, I had listened to the BBC's new political radio programme anchored by Andrew Wilson and a Labour activist.

Former MSP Andrew is as witty and engaging a political figure as we have in the country, but this format simply will not do. It is not BBC bias this time, just incompetence. It sounds like they have given two minutes' thought to the format and no training at all to the NO lady. I find myself thinking that it is not fair to her.

Back onto the links where I am playing even better, round in 84 (42–42) with a comprehensive 4 and 3 win. I am now within 25 strokes of shooting my age!

But well as I am playing, the Dunleavy report is playing even better. Back to Strichen on a glorious summer evening.

Day Twelve: Monday 23 June

I'm determined to get the huge tourism potential of the Borders railway line on track.

Staying at the Dryburgh Abbey Hotel because it is near the new Tweedbank Station, the terminus of the Borders railway and the focus of tomorrow's visit.

It has been difficult to get our officials to fully understand the economic potential of tourist rail.

Given that the economics of the line are challenging, Transport Scotland have been giving themselves a mighty and, to be fair, well-merited pat on the back for keeping it on schedule for opening this coming year. Of course the main line will be crucial for economic development and in commuting terms will be a great success.

The more I study this, the more convinced I am that the new 'Waverley Line to the Borders' can become one of the great tourist lines in Europe. The reasoning is clear. There are already highly successful tourist lines in Scotland, such as the West Coast Line, but for most people it takes a day to get there, a day to have a wonderful experience and a day to get back.

What we need is to offer the magic of steam and to offer it, not once every third Sunday, but three times a day in the high season. John Cameron, the 'silver fox' – once the greatest sheep farmer in Europe, and now a steam engine enthusiast – has indicated that he could make available *The Union of South Africa*, one of the great and iconic engines of the age. John has told me, however, that any big steam engine will need a turning circle at the terminus.

In contrast to the West Coast Line, the journey up and down the line to the Borders will take half a day from the busiest railway station in the capital of Scotland. Five million people visit Edinburgh each year. Over 1 million go to Edinburgh Castle. Why shouldn't at least half of that number head off to the Borders to sample the magic of that beautiful undiscovered part of our country? If the average tourist spends £200 on the retail and cultural offerings down the line then we will generate a visitor boom of £100 million for the Borders.

But I want to see Tweedbank Station for myself to establish if we can have that turning circle. I phone Councillor David Parker, leader of Borders Council, who has the rather good idea of making a permanent home for the Great Tapestry of Scotland – at Tweedbank. It could be a great boost to the Borders Railway.

The Great Tapestry – an all-Scotland community project of weaving – has been wowing the masses as it has toured around Scotland over the last year. One Thursday I arrived at Parliament where the queues were out the door and around the block. I thought they were in a line for First Minister's Questions. In fact they were there to see the Great Tapestry.

Day Thirteen: Tuesday 24 June

Today is the day I decide to take a stronger hand in the direction of the campaign.

Kick off at the crack of dawn at Tweedbank station with David Parker. We will make his tapestry idea happen in time for an announcement before the purdah* period in August.

We have agreed to abide by purdah in the run-up to the referendum, and so has the UK government, whose record in self-denying ordinances is not a happy one. I am aware that purdah is unenforceable and that they will likely not keep to it. However, Nicola and I have judged that we are better prepared and focused than the UK government and therefore to embrace a purdah period will be more of a nuisance to them than to us.

A mixed-tenure housing development just outside Galashiels is next on the agenda. I'm pleased to see it because

---

* Purdah is the period before an election when the government, although remaining in office, agrees to take no more directly political initiatives.

I think that the new railway will open up all sorts of possibilities for the Borders – and it's really important that all of the new housing isn't just aimed at high-salaried Edinburgh commuters but at ordinary Borders folk.

The Cabinet is held in Selkirk's lovely Victoria Halls. If you can't speak there then you can't speak. The event goes well. The Borders will be the toughest area of Scotland for the YES campaign and I am determined that our dedicated band of Borders campaigners, including my wee sister Gail and my nieces Karen and Christina, will have the maximum support possible.

Then a quick visit to Spark, a challenger electricity company headquartered in Selkirk with 200 people in their facilities centre. They specialise in providing services for tenants, and the fact that they are still running into regulatory trouble for offering tenants lower bills sums up everything that is wrong with the muddle-headed regulation of the electricity markets, which presumably should be aimed at bringing bills down.

On my way through to Kilmarnock, where I am cutting the first turf at the new college, I stop off in Edinburgh to chair the campaign meeting.

The atmosphere is still downbeat, which is pretty infuriating, given that in my best estimation we are doing pretty well. Indeed we could even be doing very well. I decide to take a much stronger hand in the direction of the campaign.

The cross-party YES campaign has had a number of issues in its organisation. In 2012 I chose Blair Jenkins as Chief Executive. He in turn appointed a range of people to lead directorates. Blair, a former head of news at BBC Scotland, had fulfilled an outstanding role in heading up the Scottish government's broadcasting commission. As lead spokesperson for YES he is performing impressively.

However, getting the disparate organisation to reflect the cohesion of a political party is proving much more problematic. Some things have worked really well, such as the launch of grassroots groups, the public meetings around the country, our social media offerings and the celebrity endorsements arranged by my former Special Adviser Jennifer Dempsie. But inevitably a cross-party YES board has found it difficult, even with great goodwill, to provide coherent strategic direction.

It is that strategic direction – the ability to take decisions on the focus of the campaign and to see them implemented – which wins elections and referendums.

I have therefore moved the decision-making to mimic SNP election organisation. Round the table, apart from Blair and Tasmina Ahmed-Sheikh from YES, will be Nicola, SNP chief executive Peter Murrell, my long-standing press adviser Kevin Pringle, Geoff Aberdein, Stuart Nicolson, the political strategist Stephen Noon, and SNP Westminster leader Angus Robertson. These are the battle-hardened group who planned and executed the resounding SNP success in 2011.

I have decided to move the meetings to Thursdays, which make a lot more sense for the campaigning rhythm of the week, and I have asked for proper information on our intelligence from the doorstep and also online, so that the meetings can take strategic decisions based on up-to-date information.

Staying at the Racecourse hotel in Ayr. Over dinner with prominent YES campaigners Marie and Drew Macklin, I recieve the very sad news that David Taylor of UEFA has passed away.

On Saturday I intervened to help David's family get him into the Western Infirmary in Glasgow, transferred from Turkey, where he had taken ill on holiday.

David was one of the finest administrators that Scotland has ever produced. I had dinner with him in Bute House a couple of months back and he was ready to come out for YES. A great, great loss to the campaign and to Scotland.

Day Fourteen: Wednesday 25 June

Beginning to think this is the campaign I've been waiting to fight all of my life. And it's down to the public I meet around the country – including the lovely crowd today at the ground-breaking of the new Kilmarnock College.

I had agreed to do an interview in front of an audience with former BBC reporter Derek Bateman in pretty relaxed fashion – a sort of *Desert Islands Discs* without the discs.

But it is the depth of the questioning from the people who have turned up, their perceptions, that really impresses me. Everyone is really getting into this battle.

These are the most informed audiences I have ever spoken to. I had questions lobbed at me such as 'See on page 26 of the White Paper ...'. This is third degree politics at an advanced level, active citizenship. Whatever happens now we will be dealing with a changed people.

Later it was time to prep for FMQs before a productive dinner with major Scottish entrepreneur (and former Labour MP Mohammad Sarwar's brother) Mr Mohammad

Pervaiz Ramzan, his sons Amaan and Nabeel, and son-in-law Rahan.

These are seriously bright, positive people and totally engaging. What a pleasant contrast with the time-servers and dimwits who occupy the CBI in Scotland, most of whom have never run a business or would even recognise an entrepreneur.

They could play a key role in the campaign and the future of the country. We go to Ondine, one of the best fish restaurants in Scotland, run by celebrity chef Roy Brett. I judge my Muslim friends could use a good feed before the onset of Ramadan.

Day Fifteen: Thursday 26 June

My chiropodist treated my toenails – and gave me some useful insights.

I've known Leslie Grant for a long time (he used to look after my mum's feet too). Leslie chats with his patients and his hill-rambling pals.

Both groups are heavily underrated political communities – perhaps not right up there with taxi drivers, but in a position to have lots of conversations.

Leslie confirms what I suspected: there is movement for YES up in them thar hills, but among his corn-ravaged pensioners of Falkirk things are not looking quite so promising.

FMQs has an end-of-term atmosphere and is generally acknowledged as a good send-off for the troops.

Day Sixteen: Friday 27 June

Meet Morgan Carberry again – and invite her to sing at Edinburgh Castle for the Chinese.

The American Fulbright scholar still faces getting her marching orders from the country.

I have agreed to intervene in her case with the aptly named Home Office Minister James Brokenshire, but have suggested to her that some publicity might help her cause. Indeed it might be the only thing that could help her cause short of immediate independence and a rational immigration policy.

Since it may well be a valedictory performance, she has agreed to sing a song or two for a Chinese investment group organised around the energy giant Petrochina.

The evening goes superbly well and by the end of it memorandums of understanding for £5 billion sterling have been signed and sealed (although it is fair to say that if there is many a slip between cup and lip there is also a difference between signing an MOU and delivering hard investment). Nonetheless a very good night's work.

Morgan, whose singing in the New Club was beautiful, but who has a big voice for a small room, is in her true element in the Great Hall of the castle and steals the show with an impromptu performance which leaves ne'er a dry ee in the house.

Day Seventeen: Saturday 28 June

A warm reaction for me today – and a cool one for Cameron.

We are both in Stirling for Armed Forces Day, a Gordon Brown notion as part of his reinforcement of Britishness campaign of a few years back. This year, the Tory government, aided and abetted by their Labour allies in Stirling Council, decide to hold it in Stirling on the same weekend as the Bannockburn celebrations of the 700th anniversary of Robert Bruce's famous victory.

My young advisers (and some of the not so young ones) are very wary of Bannockburn, since they believe it offers the 'wrong image' for modern Scottish nationalism. I disagree.

You would have to have a dead soul not to be inspired by the stand taken by Bruce and his army – and foolish indeed not to see the analogies with the current political struggle.

Bruce had first tried to reach an accommodation with Edward Longshanks to become his vassal king and then, when forced into open rebellion, had avoided pitched battle knowing that, castle by castle, town by town, victory would be his and Scotland's. However, his headstrong younger brother had created a position where the showdown took place on midsummer's day 1314.

I had tried to reach an accommodation with Cameron, tried to move the Parliament and the country forward, power by power, competence by competence. However, my inability to get traction after the 2011 election on a devo max proposal from enough people and organisations across civic society in Scotland created the circumstances where a showdown would take place on 18 September 2014.

Like Bruce, we are engaged with a force of awesome power. Like Bruce, we are faced with a pitched battle not completely of our choosing, and like Bruce, we have to gamble to win the day.

In any event, on Armed Forces Day the UK government's best-laid schemes gang agley. Cameron's all too blatant attempts to play politics rebound pretty badly.

Although the military crowd reaction is not unanimously favourable towards me it is still positive: indeed warm. The reaction to Cameron is decidedly cool.

Why should it not be, since they are predominantly a crowd of working-class Scottish families on a day out and Cameron is a Tory toff on a day trip?

Meanwhile at Bannockburn, where the organisation is struggling with the surge of the great crowd which has turned up, the reaction towards me is both unanimous and hugely favourable.

Dougie McLean in concert tops the day off nicely.

Day Eighteen: Sunday 29 June

Great reception on my home turf when Moira drags me down to a local garden centre.

We just got back home in the very wee sma' hours.

The *Sunday Herald* has run a very nice piece on Morgan, with a superb photograph that well depicts this vibrant and talented woman who is about to be kicked out of our country. If a picture tells a thousand words then this picture summarises what is wrong with the lunatic UK immigration policy.

To one of Moira's favourite garden centres, White Lodge, near Turriff, where she has decided to invest more funds in her favourite hobby. It is not often that I have any time to spend on her interests, so I take it all in good part, even when we manage to drop the car keys in one of the plant carts and spend half an hour or more looking for them!

Again I am interested in the crowd reaction, which is according me rock-star status. Elvis Presley's ancestors came from nearby Lonmay and the Commonwealth Games baton has been touring locally, but by and large Turriff is not normally known for flashmob events like today. Especially at the garden centre.

I have always been popular in my own area and particularly in Turriff. There is however a degree of evidence piling up – for example, Kilmarnock College, Armed Forces Day – where crowd reaction tells me that something is on the move.

Whatever is happening it is not being fully recorded in most polls which, after moving in our favour, have broadly stabilised. That does not make the change unreal, just unrecorded or still to come.

Day Nineteen: Monday 30 June

Back to Bute House for Royal Week. I've tracked down one of my old professors for help with some historical rough justice.

I've asked Bruce Lenman for a quick opinion on the Appin trial. There is a petition before the Parliament – from a Campbell no less – asking for a Royal pardon for James Stewart.

Devotees of Robert Louis Stevenson will recall that Alan Breck Stuart (who bore a king's name) may or may not have shot the Red Fox at Appin. What did happen for certain in historical terms is that his stepfather James Stuart was strung up by a majority Campbell jury with a Chief of the Clan Campbell on the bench just to make sure that there was no mistake.

Cases such as this are usually turned down, for fear of opening a can of worms and setting a difficult precedent. However, I have decided to make a check or two with Frank Mulholland, the astute Lord Advocate, before we decide on this one.

It is not often in life that you get the chance to right what seems a clear historical wrong. Hence I have asked my old history prof for an informed opinion.

On the subject of history, the *Scotsman* seems grievously disappointed that the Bannockburn event was sold out and decided that the key story was the queues to get in.

I phone the editor, Ian Stewart, whom I have always found a thoroughly decent guy. That makes the suicidal direction of the paper all the more inexplicable. Is it possible that the few remaining readers of his paper probably want to feel good about their country rather than bad?

In truth, Ian sounds like a man at the end of his tether.

Day Twenty: Tuesday 1 July

Meet the Queen for an audience which includes discussion about Normandy and Armed Forces Day. This is probably the first time we don't also chat about her horses, which is probably just as well given that Estimate was pipped at the post for the Ascot Gold Cup, rather than winning it like last year.

Having said that, it is part of the quality of the Queen that she has the ability to take triumph and disaster with equanimity.

No doubt this is due to her long experience as a reigning monarch – or perhaps to her long experience of owning racehorses.

The Garden Party has the sun shining on it, unlike last year when it tipped down. Normally, although not this year, we have a small dinner for guests back at Bute. Last year even the irrepressible Scotland football manager, Gordon Strachan, refused to get out of the minibus, so rough were the conditions.

Day Twenty-One: Wednesday 2 July

Mrs Salmond insisted on a trip to Dumfries House near Cumnock for the grand opening of the gardens by Her Majesty the Queen.

Being a political spouse is undoubtedly the worst job in the world – all of the intrusion and irritation with absolutely none of the glory.

For more than seven years Moira has put up with it all with grace and forbearance. Therefore when there was a rare opportunity to combine my business with her pleasure I did my best to accommodate. Moira approves of Dumfries House and indeed approves of the Duke of Rothesay's* grand design of the gardens.

It was one of my first decisions as First Minister to kick over the civil service traces and back Charles's plan to save this great property and its unique contents. This was partly to support his ambitious idea but also, I confess, to make a democratic point to the civil service who had recommended very strongly

---

* In Scotland, Prince Charles's official title is Duke of Rothesay.

against. It was a very early opportunity to establish the correct relationship between ministers and officials.

At any rate, the Duke of Rothesay's persistence is paying off handsomely, with a remarkable series of developments now taking place near Cumnock.

I recall, back in 2007, going with the Prince to make the announcement. A large crowd had gathered outside Cumnock Town Hall. Charles was really interested in why people had come and how and what they knew of his plans.

I replied: 'I doubt if they all know WHAT is happening but they are all really glad that SOMETHING is happening in Cumnock!'

A good day ends on a downer with Andy Murray getting knocked out of Wimbledon. Moira will have to put her saltire away for another year.*

Day Twenty-Two: Thursday 3 July

An exchange with Director General Tony Hall of the BBC on the way to Edinburgh.

I have growing concerns about the approach of the BBC to the referendum. Part of my planning for the campaign is the assumption that, while the press will be totally biased, the television will be balanced, at least in the campaign period.

However, BBC Scotland suffers from a fundamental short age of journalists, just as the network BBC probably suffers

---

* In 2013, in the royal box at Wimbledon, Moira famously produced from her handbag a saltire to wave in celebration of Andy's victory. This caused a furore, but Moira had kept the same flag and planned to do it again this year.

from having too many. Professor John Robertson of the University of the West of Scotland produced a detailed assessment earlier this year and concluded that there is a clear bias running through broadcasting. He detected issues in the STV news as well, but that has not been my impression. The problem essentially is that, without the journalistic resources to pursue many stories on their own account, the BBC relies on reports led by a partisan print media. They then 'balance' their report by allowing the YES campaign the right of reply to the latest scare story.

I try to keep things on an even keel with the DG, relying on the point that as a distinguished journalist he will appreciate my concerns at a lack of real journalism by our 'national broadcaster'. A reported 1,500 people had gathered spontaneously this week outside the BBC in Glasgow to vent their concern about perceived bias in the BBC coverage. I make the point that the equivalent crowd across the UK would be 15,000. If a crowd of that scale had been demonstrating outside Broadcasting House in London then the BBC would be in crisis mode trying to understand why a public service broadcaster had lost the confidence of a large section of the community.

There are still tensions in the YES team with the key polls showing us making little further progress. Despite the wealth of information people should have from their own contacts, even our campaign team tend to believe whatever the latest poll says.

I try deliberately to capture the spirit of 2011, when we took on and scaled a political summit of similar size. There are some positive signs tonight, with a renewed focus on key issues such as the health service and a determination to move away from the agenda as set by our opponents.

Some good news coming through suggests that the *Scottish Sun* is moving onside after a meeting in London and despite the efforts of the former Scottish editor, and convinced unionist, David Dinsmore, who believes that YES will score 40 per cent at very best. He is wrong.

Day Twenty-Three: Friday 4 July

Independence Day (for America!) at a ceremony with my dad to float the UK's latest aircraft carrier, HMS *Queen Elizabeth*. And I am reminded that a Second World War German pilot is responsible for me being alive at all.

The day out in Rosyth is a trip down memory lane for Faither. He is probably unique among all of those attending as being someone who has actually been shot at on a carrier (although, to be fair, we are sitting immediately behind Prince Philip, who also saw action at the same engagements as my father in the Med). Faither was a petty officer on the fast carrier HMS *Indomitable* when a Junkers dive-bomber put a hole in its side during the Sicily landings in 1943. As one of only two fast carriers in the fleet this was a big setback. However, much to the relief of my dad and his shipmates, they didn't sink but managed to reach Gibraltar under their own power.

The good news continued with the revelation that the *Indomitable* was bound for Norfolk, Virginia. However, my dad's run of luck seemed to have come to an end when his air squadron was reassigned to the escort carrier HMS *Hunter*, a converted freighter with a flight deck stuck on top.

But the story does not end there – as it might easily have for me. The *Indomitable* crew was compulsorily screened for TB on US entry – and the disease was found on board. With exemplary efficiency the Navy screened the previous ship's complement. Faither's test was positive and, according to his own account, he was hauled off a football match at half-time when playing for the Navy in Belfast.

In those days TB was virtually a death sentence, and he spent the next two years in sanatoriums cheating the Grim Reaper by the skin of his teeth. In other words, if the Junkers hadn't put a hole in the *Indomitable*, the crew would not have been screened, my dad's condition would not have been picked up, he would have met his maker and I would not have become First Minister of Scotland – or anything else for that matter. You could say the Scottish referendum is taking place because of a German pilot!

Dad enjoys himself enormously, playfully saluting assorted admirals and offering his services as an experienced carrier-hand when he finds that the *Indomitable* had three times the crew complement of the *Queen Elizabeth*.

'I hear you are short-handed,' he tells one startled senior officer. But his quote of the day comes during the really silly speech from the First Sea Lord about a new Elizabethan age.

'I thought you telt me that the ship had no planes,' he says, nodding at the nose of a jet hanging over the flight deck.

'It's a model plane,' I explain, as I know the Navy has spent some thousands of pounds building fake planes to make the ceremony look better, given that they don't have the money for the real thing. Faither's one-word response speaks volumes.

'Whit!' he scoffs.

The whole event goes pretty well. Some of the press later suggested there was booing when my picture came up on the big screen. It must have been so half-hearted that no one could hear it from where we were, and it was apparently matched by some equally unenthusiastic booing of pictures of Cameron. In reality, I spent a lot of time signing autographs for the Babcock workers present from all around the UK.

Given the set-up and nature of the crowd this was a good day, and I end it by taking Dad to Gleneagles for afternoon tea. I was touched by his reluctance to leave and, given that he has not too many of these kinds of days left in terms of what he remembers, this day went really well.

P.S. Did an early morning radio interview down the line from Bute House with James Naughtie – in my pyjamas. I remind him he had expressed his opinion yesterday that the Royal Navy would not order from Scottish shipyards post-independence, as if it were an established fact. I point out that, if the Navy can order tankers from South Korea, then it could probably manage to order destroyers from the Clyde!

Day Twenty-Four: Saturday 5 July

This could be really naff, I thought. The publicity arrangement for the day was to 'introduce' the Ryder Cup to the Commonwealth Games baton.

However, it all turns out rather well, with the baton parachuted onto the King's Course at Gleneagles, greeted by lots of people and then being carried up to the hotel by Scottish champion golfer and Major winner Catriona Matthew.

In truth, everything at Gleneagles works. Even little bits of subterfuge.

I have a little smile to myself each time I visit the Dormie House beside the courses. On the left hand side as you go in there is an imposing cabinet which displays the solid silver Ryder Cup putter. Each tournament host presents this prestigious object to the next venue – so we will hand it on to Hazeltine National, Minnesota, in September. The putter in the cabinet is the real McCoy, but the more eagle-eyed in the television audience might have wondered why it doesn't look exactly like the one which appeared live from the closing ceremony in Medinah, Illinois, in October 2013.

A simple explanation. Just before the ceremony, the organisers who, ever gracious even in the face of an unexpected and dramatic defeat, were informed that such was the security around the putter, and in the absence of a decent joiner, they couldn't get it off the clubhouse wall. The committee were in a bit of a flap and therefore were pleasantly surprised when I said 'Fine, we'll use our own silver putter.'

In the Scottish pavilion, we had club-maker Hamish Steedman from the St Andrews Golf Company, the oldest club-maker in the world. As luck would have it, in addition to their traditional hickory-shafted clubs they had been displaying all week the prototype of a very special solid silver putter.

Thus the club I brandished in front of a live audience estimated at 600 million was this prototype, rather than the real deal.

After the ceremony we all agreed not to mention this small and innocent piece of subterfuge. Of course, once they got back to St Andrews the bold club-makers were perfectly entitled to promote their club as '*the* Ryder Cup putter' complete with pictures as proof positive. This exquisite product, inlaid appropriately enough with Alexandrite, is now available at a cool $60,000. The other one will be sent on to Hazeltine – assuming we have a joiner on hand to remove it from the cabinet!

We leave the Ryder Cup and follow the baton to Bridge of Allan, Stirlingshire, where it is being presented to the Scottish athletics team training camp.

We have assembled the greatest Scottish squad in history, an army of 310 athletes, and I meet a good number of them, including our youngest squad member – thirteen-year-old Shetland swimmer Erraid Davies – and her mum.

The location is perfect – in the very shadow of the Wallace Monument. And I'm inspired to make a rousing address to the squad and their support teams, including the family members. The atmosphere is electric. It is a proud moment for all concerned and the applause is thunderous.

I am particularly impressed by our young female wrestlers and judo players. They sound like they mean business. To paraphrase the Duke of Wellington: 'I don't know what they will do to the other teams but, by God, they frighten me!'

Back home via Gleneagles.

Day Twenty-Five: Sunday 6 July

Good rest on a day mostly spent watching the racing on the telly. Alistair Darling [leader of the NO campaign] gets a soft time on *The Politics Show* – but still ends up looking hot, bothered and a mite flustered.

Contrary to what must be the general view, I like Andrew Neil, the BBC's demon interviewer. Apart from being rather good and very bright company, I like the fact that his bias is not unconscious (like most of the London operation) but very conscious indeed.

Day Twenty-Six: Monday 7 July

Preparing for the Aberdeen Asset Scottish Open at the magnificent Balgownie links of Royal Aberdeen, I'm minded of a Saturday night call from the estimable George O'Grady, of the European Tour, three years ago. He was concerned they were about to lose the Barclays Scottish Open sponsorship and wondered if I could attend the final day of the tournament at Castle Stuart, which had suffered a flood of biblical proportions.

I spent the best part of the Sunday talking to Bob Diamond, CEO of Barclays, who, when we weren't talking about golf, spent most of his time talking about Bob Diamond.

The locals at Castle Stuart had responded to the flood with a human miracle, mobilising the local farmers to respond to the thousand-year weather event and the landslip which had befallen this gorgeous golf course. And, lo, there was golf and even a rainbow on the final day.

I made the point, rather movingly I thought, that given the heroic local efforts to save the tournament it would be fair-minded to give the North of Scotland a second chance to stage a major tour event. The last thing Bob said to George and me was: 'See you next year.'

A few weeks later, he cancelled the sponsorship. A year later, a fresh Barclay's financial scandal cancelled Bob.

With the tournament in real jeopardy I phoned ten top companies to make a plea to consider sponsorship. The austerity autumn of 2011 was not an ideal time to be embarking on such a task. But, while it seemed a disaster at the time, it was all very much for the best. In the 2012 tournament, if Barclays had continued their sponsorship, no one could have made use of corporate hospitality because the lead sponsor would have been totally immersed in the Forex scandal. The Lord does indeed work in mysterious ways.

At any rate the only person in 2011 with the guts and gumption to pick up the sponsorship was Martin Gilbert, of Aberdeen Asset Management. Over the last three years the tournament has advanced from strength to strength and is well on its way to becoming the second-biggest links golf tournament in the world and the only European tour event, outside the Open itself, to be on American network TV.

If I were to pick up the phone today, then perhaps eight out of these ten companies would grab the opportunity to sponsor. But Aberdeen Asset are set to keep the prize until at least 2020, and deservedly so.

Day Twenty-Seven: Tuesday 8 July

The Canadians arrive with plans that could relieve the pressure on Aberdeen's overheated hotel market. I join them for the launch of plans for a 220-room, 4-star Sandman hotel in the Granite City. It's very good news – but will hardly compensate for the impending closure of the Marcliffe at Pitfodels, due to Stewart Spence's upcoming retirement.

The Marcliffe is to Aberdeen what Rick's Bar was to Casablanca, with Stewart cast in the Bogart role. All human life is there: from oil executives recovering from the night before, to ladies who lunch, and from liaisons dangereuses in the afternoon to the very best and plushest functions in the country of an evening. And over all of this presides Stewart Spence, completely in his element.

To Royal Aberdeen for lunch with the men's and ladies' captains to discuss public and press relations for the biggest golf tournament in the history of the city. The issue is a reasonably delicate one, since both Royal Aberdeen and Aberdeen Ladies are effectively single-sex clubs. However, both have full playing rights over the links, they share facilities and are jointly organising the members' substantial role in the tournament. That puts them in a very different position from the men-only Muirfield and I think, on balance, there is enough press goodwill for mischief not to be made.

Arrive back at the Marcliffe for dinner with Geoff Aberdein and the *Scottish Sun*. Editor Gordon Smart is becoming increasingly hopeful that he may get the green light for nailing the paper's colours to the YES mast.

Day Twenty-Eight: Wednesday 9 July

Part of Team Mickelson today – battling a gale with America's No. 1 box-office golfer, Phil.

First, spend the morning at a Club Golf event at Aberdeen's Murcar course with four hundred enthusiastic youngsters, plus the exceptionally pleasant US player Ricky Fowler and some very helpful Scottish professionals led by our former

Open champion, the North East's own Paul Lawrie, and Scotland's best hope for the Gleneagles Ryder Cup team, Stephen Gallacher.

Club Golf was originally devised when Scotland bid for the Ryder Cup under former First Minister Henry McLeish, and I have nourished and expanded the concept. At its simplest, the aim is to put a golf club in the hands of every nine-year-old in the country. At its most ambitious, it is Scotland's none too secret plan to dominate world golf in around ten to fifteen years' time.

We have never quite managed every school, but this year we are pushing 85 per cent. Over the last few years we have introduced 350,000 youngsters to the game. Of course golf is more than a game, more like a code of living in which you learn to cope with success and failure – and the only person you can cheat is yourself.

Murcar, the adjoining club to Royal Aberdeen, are most welcoming, and one of the positive aspects of this referendum campaign is that I am piling up invites to play golf. Whatever happens, this will stand me in good stead for 2015.

For the pro-am in the afternoon I am (once again) partnered with Mickelson. 'Lefty' is a class act, and due to his interest and generosity of spirit he has, more than anyone else, established the Scottish Open as the upcoming major tournament in Europe with the best-quality field bar the Open Championship itself.

Despite his status in the game, the great man asked for no appearance fee, which means we were able to turn down all other such requests and devote the sponsorship of Aberdeen Asset and the contribution of the Scottish government to developing the tournament, its prize money, and its support for Club Golf and its facilities for the paying customers.

I ask Ted Bishop, from the PGA of America, and Marcliffe owner Stewart Spence to make up our team of four – Team Mickelson. Stewart is there in recognition of his contribution to Aberdeen over many years, and he uses his local knowledge as a Royal Aberdeen member to devastating effect. It's blowing a hooley with a punishing left-to-right wind which makes the first nine just a tad short of unplayable. Not for Stewart, however, who plays like God's anointed … gammy leg and all.

Ted and I just about survive the opening nine, but Phil and his caddy and friend Bones find the wind a real challenge. Although it means Team Mickelson will not be troubling the leader board, the great virtue of playing with Phil is that he actually relishes the challenge. While other great players get grumpy at gusting wind and chance bounces, he embraces the essential injustice of links conditions. It was learning that lesson which has made him both reigning Scottish Open and Open champion and one of the greatest natural golfers of all time.

Coming up the last, Phil points to a bunker which a member had told him was only recently introduced – which on the Balgownie Links probably means in about 1950!

He says: 'I really don't like that bunker. It's wrong for the course. You are the First Minister. If you get it filled in I will declare for Scottish independence.'

'Done deal,' I reply, and we knock knuckles.

'First Minister, you don't understand,' he says. 'You have to fill it in by tomorrow, for the start of the tournament.'

'I understood you the first time,' I say, and we knock knuckles again.

Day Twenty-Nine: Thursday 10 July

Golf is a serious business. Indeed, it is a forum where you can do some very serious business.

Geoff Aberdein has been very nervous of my presence at golf tournaments given the obsession of the *Daily Telegraph* with the Medinah Ryder Cup of 2012. He thinks they will monster me for playing golf instead of attending to business. I have explained many times that it doesn't matter what we do. If I walked on water, they would accuse me of Christ impersonation and blasphemy. However, Geoff is keen that we can defend my week in Aberdeen to all-comers and therefore sets out to demonstrate that the business of golf is the business of Scotland.

So my private office staff have taken up his injunction perhaps a tad enthusiastically and arranged no fewer than forty-three business meetings over the week. A big golf tournament is the best kind of boardroom – everyone comes and everyone is keen to see you.

We start today with the opening of P2D, a very interesting oil supply company. The ancient Chinese used to pay doctors when they were well. This preventative company operates on the same principle with oil and gas pipelines.

Then back to the 'boardroom' for a meeting with BrewDog. I introduce the braw lads from the Broch to Aberdeen Asset's Martin Gilbert, who wonders at first why I have introduced him to a pair of ragamuffins. He then fires a series of financial questions at BrewDog's Martin Dickie, who knocks them out of the park; the clincher is that they had 4,000 people at their AGM, have never paid a non-liquid dividend and still own 78 per cent of their company.

'Good funding model,' says an impressed Gilbert.

Back at the golf, as Rory McIlroy shoots a fabulous round in tricky conditions (he might be worth a bet for next week), we head across town for a meeting of the Energy Advisory Board, to consider some key reports on the future of the energy markets and the oil industry.

The day is rounded off with some cheering poll news from the *Daily Record*: YES on 47 per cent and the SNP a mile ahead on the party ratings. I still think Survation is probably overrating us, but it's a good poll nonetheless.

Day Thirty: Friday 11 July

Have a bit of a sparring match on TV with Danny Alexander on oil. It reminds me of how long I have been debating the value of the black, black gold.

First to Aberdeen Chamber of Commerce for a referendum presentation. The Chambers have been excellent throughout the debate, fair-minded and balanced, and this is an excellent meeting.

I meet an old school chum who turns up to tell me he wants to vote YES but worries about 'layabouts' in Glasgow. I tell him that in Glasgow they are probably worrying about rich folk like him in Aberdeen!

The debate with Alexander is against the backdrop of the Office for Budget Responsibility making an oil forecast for the next thirty years. This was interesting, since they have been totally incapable of forecasting it for the last three years.

Thirty years ago I was forecasting the value of oil and devised the Royal Bank index still in use to this day. Along with Dr Jim Walker of the Fraser of Allander Institute, I wrote the seminal paper on the economic consequences of the single-dollar oil price of 1986 and also explained why the price and the industry would recover. At that time the Treasury believed (or at least they said they did) that the industry would be scraping the very last barrel by the year 2000, and Danny Alexander was still years away from starting his one and only job outside politics as head press officer for Cairngorms National Park.

In those far-off times I used to like to tell a story which is still pertinent today. Albert Einstein arrives at the pearly gates and places the divine bureaucracy into one almighty fankle. The problem is, as Peter confides to Gabriel and to the Lord God Almighty, that there are very few in the entire heavenly host who can match or even approach Einstein's intellect when it comes to offering companionship or conversation. Heaven is faced with total humiliation unless rapid action is taken.

They enlist Heaven's three most intelligent angels to be the great man's companions – angels with IQs of 159, 160 (Einstein's own IQ) and finally an angel with a mind-boggling, record-breaking IQ of 161.

Speaking to each in turn, Einstein approaches the third-most intelligent angel first: 'Delighted to meet you, together we will develop further my theory of relativity.' Then to the second-brightest: 'Delighted to meet you, together we will work on the true meaning of the creation.' Finally he turns to his intellectual superior, the brightest angel in heaven and the most intelligent entity on heaven or earth. Einstein looks at her and simply says: 'What's the price of oil going to be next week?'

The point is no one knows what the price of oil will be in the short term, but over the long run the price will trend towards the cost of a replacement barrel. The key to oil wealth is the extent of the long-term recoverable resources in the waters around Scotland, which on the modest forecast of Oil and Gas UK are up to 24 billion barrels.

The press attention to Danny's musings is much greater than that accorded to Professor Donald Mackay, someone who actually knows what he is talking about. Mackay, who wrote the authoritative book *The Political Economy of North Sea Oil*, dismisses the bleak Treasury/OBR account of the future with the words 'No black hole but missing black gold'.

Day Thirty-One: Saturday 12 July

Should I kiss ass or kick ass with The Donald or, better still, just leave well alone?

Hostile press commentary is affecting the psyche of even the most experienced BBC London correspondents. Between meetings at the golf course, I'm interviewed by John Pienaar for 5 Live. I like John, who is as fair-minded as they come, but even his questions are tainted by commentary from most of the rest of the media: for example, a two-point rise for YES in the *Record* poll becomes a two-point fall. The London media, by and large, believe we will be beaten, and beaten badly. They are wrong.

Not that press bias is restricted to London. In the *Herald*, the revelation that Sir David Edward – former judge of the Court of Justice of the European Communities – is a NO voter is splashed as if it is a devastating problem for the YES campaign. In reality the entirely reasonable and rather positive views of Sir David on the position of Scotland and the European Union were given additional strength precisely because he was always a NO voter.

On a brighter note, the spectacular coverage of Royal Aberdeen continues, with TV images of the oil and gas city, the Buchan hinterland and the Aberdeenshire seascapes. I appear as a guest on the international commentary with Dougie Donnelly. One of the television shots shows a supply boat being 'escorted' out of Aberdeen harbour by a pod of dolphins.

I remark: 'It took six months to train them and another six months to paint the Aberdeen Asset logo on their backs!'

End up partnering Phil Mickelson again, this time as guests at Martin Gilbert's birthday party. Despite my coaching earlier this week, Phil's not going to win the tournament – but he has become something of an enthusiast for Scottish independence.

He also wants to broker a peace between me and Donald Trump, whom he likes, but doesn't agree with on issues such as offshore wind energy. The proposals for a wind demonstrator in Aberdeen Bay have been reported as a spectacular falling-out between Trump and Salmond. I suggest that, in pure electoral terms, fighting with Mr Trump is far more beneficial than a reconciliation. In any case, the Lord Advocate would take a dim view of my even speaking to someone who is currently suing the Scottish government – albeit The Donald is losing and losing badly.

Day Thirty-Two: Sunday 13 July

Officially announce Gullane as the next venue of the Scottish Open – but I fear I may have blown the 'secret' a couple of weeks ago.

It's no great surprise to the press corps when the course is revealed, because Martin Gilbert and I had played the outstanding East Lothian links just a few weeks ago. It is undoubtedly the right place to play the tournament – a community-orientated club without a whiff of gender discrimination and a flourishing junior section. It also boasts an outstanding traditional course with one of the most breathtaking seascape views of Scotland.

It is reasonably certain that Martin has come under a fair bit of pressure to take the tournament further along the coast to Renaissance, the new and hugely impressive development near North Berwick, but at nearly £100,000-a-whack for family membership it would not communicate an ideal message about Scottish golf being open to all.

Complete my last eight business meetings and the tournament ends triumphantly with record crowds, a fine champion in Justin Rose and good Scottish performances from Stephen Gallacher, Marc Warren and Scott Jamieson.

Celebrated with a meal at the Marcliffe. My team have done well in a great but exhausting week. And I have almost forgiven them for totally filling my diary with business meetings.

Day Thirty-Three: Monday 14 July

The golf's not quite over. So, back to the 'boardroom' to complete my last three meetings by playing foursomes at Royal Aberdeen. This is more like it. I team up with Ian Donnelly, Babcock Energy and Marine Services MD, the best player of the four. Between us we keep our noses in front for a pretty convincing three-and-one triumph in tricky conditions.

I am playing not at all badly, albeit there is still room for improvement. I take the opportunity to ask Ian about the story in the *Sunday Times* that 'Babcock aimed a broadside at Salmond.' He denies all knowledge and blames the press.

The defence company's jitters actually come from direct pressure by the MoD ministers, as was exposed by the *Financial Times*'s excellent journalist Mure Dickie last February.

Ironic, since Channel 4's *Dispatches* programme last week claimed intimidation from the SNP government, ludicrously citing the unctuous ex-Scottish Whisky Association Chief Executive Gavin Hewitt. This is totally bizarre, because our battle of the booze has not been over independence but on our plans for minimum pricing for alcohol, which the SWA have been blocking and tackling through legal manoeuvres despite the clear health and social benefits.

Day Thirty-Four: Tuesday 15 July

The proposed deals involving Chinese energy firm Petrochina are still bubbling away – and I travel to London to meet company director Mr Bingjun Si for the first time since our dinner at Edinburgh Castle. He is impressed by a letter I received from Premier Li Keqiang, which is couched in extremely friendly terms towards Chinese investment in Scotland.

As Vice Premier of China, Li Keqiang came here in 2011 as part of his preparation for moving into one of the most powerful jobs in the world. In a reception in Edinburgh Castle's Great Hall, he endeared himself to the audience by opening his graceful speech with the words: 'It is wonderful to be in Scotland – the land of invention.'

The evening went rolling on towards the early hours, with the mighty Lothian and Borders Police Pipe Band beating the retreat inside the Great Hall itself. The then Vice Premier performed the ceremony of the quaich having previously demonstrated considerable knowledge at a whisky tasting. A very good time was had by all and the Vice Premier created a favourable impression of the new Chinese leadership.

The following evening Li attended a much more formal white-tie affair hosted by the Foreign Secretary in Lancaster House. For the first half of his speech the Vice Premier told his London audience what a great place Scotland was – then ended by raising his glass with the enthusiastic toast 'Slainte Mhath'. Most of the audience were ever so slightly bemused. Our Permanent Secretary, who was attending the dinner, was totally delighted.

The unemployment figures to be released tomorrow cause me a bit of concern with an unexpected rise. However, closer examination shows people are flooding back onto the labour market, employment is rising quickly and – best of all – Scotland's GDP has returned to pre-recession levels, one quarter in advance of the rest of the UK. This rather confounds the

Chancellor's claim that even the very holding of a referendum would damage the Scottish economy.

Day Thirty-Five: Wednesday 16 July

Breakfast meeting with the irrepressible Lord Dafydd Wigley, the most successful politician in the history of Plaid Cymru. That may not sound too impressive, but Dafydd is a top-flight politician and a real force of nature. It is impossible not to like him.

I tell Dafydd we can win the referendum, but he really doesn't believe me and is more interested in my 'back-up plan'. The trouble with Dafydd is he thinks I'm just as sleekit as he is – that my real game is to bounce Cameron into devo max. I tell him that, even when a punter places an each-way bet, they still hope their horse is going to win.

When I was a young candidate in 1987, Dafydd campaigned for me at a Peterhead engineering company. As we walked round the shop floor, he said: 'I'll speak to the management, you speak to the workers … and I mean every single worker. Do not miss anyone out!'

Obeying Dafydd's instruction, I spoke to every engineer behind every machine until I passed by a workman about 30 feet up, painting a gantry.

'Go and speak to him,' ordered Dafydd. Thus I duly climbed the ladder until I reached the startled painter. 'I'm Alex Salmond, the SNP candidate. Are you going to vote for me?' I gasped.

'Definitely not,' came the answer and then, seeing my disappointment, he followed up: 'I canna vote for you, ma loon. I'm fae Aberdeen. Howivir, if I did cum fae Peterhead, I'm jist daft eneuch tae vote fer a daft bugger like you!'

Later I meet the new CEO of Diageo, Ivan Menezes, a pleasant enough guy and genuinely interested in the referendum debate. He tells me they are not going to sell Gleneagles, or at least that they have 'no plans' to do so, which is not quite the same thing. He seems reasonably keen on my idea of having a special tournament to capitalise on their prize estate being established as the epicentre of the golfing world after September.

He is also relatively receptive to the concept of supporting a leisure and business development in Kilmarnock – where the former Johnnie Walker plant had been located – with the local council. We agree not to speak about the minimum pricing on alcohol legislation as it is still before the courts.

The jarring note in the meeting comes when I lob in a question about why the ex-Secretary of the Scottish Whisky Association, Gavin Hewitt, was making claims of Scottish government intimidation, which border on the ludicrous. It's pretty clear that Ivan does not have the slightest idea what I'm talking about, but on the way out one of his colleagues whispers conspiratorially: 'Not us. UK government. Gavin is ex-Foreign Office.'

Lunch in the city at Aberdeen Asset, where Martin Gilbert has assembled a very varied cast. The meeting is successful and we are not totally devoid of either support or sympathy from some of the brighter lights of the financial sector in London.

Arrive in Liverpool after a train journey south. I manage (at the third attempt) to stick to a diet day. After months of faithful adherence to my 5–2 diet (one day consuming fewer than

600 calories, two normal days, another 600-calorie diet day, and then three normal days before starting all over again) I have successfully shed more than two stone, but I am finding it harder and harder to sustain in the campaign schedule. Some in my private office say that it is easy to tell a diet day because it makes me crabbit. Others swear they can't tell any difference whatsoever. I'm not sure which is the more favourable assessment!

Day Thirty-Six: Thursday 17 July

Meet Peter Kilfoyle, a first-class guy and a real Labour member for Liverpool Walton for the best part of twenty-one years. Peter is deeply disillusioned with Labour nationally, and in Liverpool in particular, and is endorsing a YES vote in Scotland.

We take a ferry across the Mersey with Brian Taylor of the BBC, who is interested in this support for independence from Liverpool. The affectionate reception accorded to Peter from the public on board is the mark of a fine MP. I get a pretty good response too, but I usually do in Liverpool. I watch the interview between Brian and Peter. They could be doubles.

I remember being on the *Question Time* panel in Liverpool during the election campaign in 2011. On the subject of the health service, I got stuck into the three Westminster parties, much to the delight of the Merseyside audience. As we approached the very end of the programme, an Irish Liverpudlian announced that I should be local mayor, to rapturous applause.

I thought to myself 'what a great way to end the programme' when, just as David Dimbleby was winding up, the audience member launched into a vituperative attack on Liverpool Football Club and their treatment of the residents of Anfield Road. To illustrate the point he marched down to the panel to remonstrate further. After a minute or so we persuaded him to go back to his seat on the promise (which I kept) of hearing his views at length after the show.

However, by then the spell had been broken and another demonstrator, this time against Ryanair, marched down to take his place with a big banner and plonked himself in front of the panel. As we explained that neither protest would be broadcast, since there is a delay in the live transmission to cope with exactly this sort of thing, the fracas was peacefully brought to an end.

It meant my nomination for mayor of Liverpool by popular acclaim was never broadcast. A pity, since I would have done a lot better than the present Labour incumbent, Joe Anderson, who remarked that he thought Peter Kilfoyle was 'dead' in reaction to his intervention in the referendum campaign. Peter's response was that it was better to be just thought dead than to be barely alive and brain-dead like the local Labour Party.

After the interview, I'm on the menu at the *Financial Times* lunch as part of their International Festival for Business. I keep thumping away at the theme that independence will change the economic centre of gravity in these islands and that will be to the general good.

Back in Edinburgh to chair a campaign meeting, I find that my previous tub-thumping is beginning to pay off.

The meeting follows the normal pattern of its mood being too readily influenced by the latest opinion poll. However, this time the news is good – a TNS survey indicates a substantial number of Labour voters is moving to YES. Furthermore, the Committee is starting to gel.

I set up a debating team with former MSPs Andrew Wilson and Duncan Hamilton for the upcoming TV debates.

On a more sombre note, the news breaks that a Malaysian jet has been shot down over Ukraine with pro-Russian rebels the most likely suspects. This seems likely to dominate the news for some days, as does the escalating crisis in Gaza.

McIlroy is doing well in the Open, which is no great surprise to me given his form in Aberdeen. My trio of bets on Mickelson, McIlroy and Gallacher looks to be in with a shout.

Day Thirty-Seven: Friday 18 July

I will be minded to resign if we don't win the referendum.

Today is the first time I have confided that to my deputy Nicola. The only other people who know my view are Moira and Geoff Aberdein. This is not a discussion against the backdrop of an expected defeat. On the contrary, I say it during a conversation in which I stress that we could well achieve victory.

I'm in Glasgow for the last meeting of the Strategic Group, the committee in ultimate charge of the Games. But it gives me the rare opportunity to call on Nicola at her home for a heart-to-heart. We see each other virtually every working day, but time to ourselves is at a premium. We talk about how the campaign is going.

She is an extraordinary young woman. I have never seen a politician master at an earlier age the range of political arts with a more assured step, and seldom have I seen anyone better under pressure.

Back in 2004, after I was persuaded to come back to lead the party, I approached Nicola to run on a joint ticket. She was losing the contest, not through lack of talent but through lack of years. I rather expected that she would embrace the idea with open arms. Instead she coolly weighed up her options for twenty-four hours and kept me hanging on. I think at the time she thought I was put out. I wasn't. I was impressed.

Our partnership has proved successful, indeed unstoppable, for ten years – and whatever happens she will prove formidable for many more.

I tell her I believe we can win and that we now have the first solid indications that the grassroots and internet campaign is starting to count for YES. However, we have to move the focus of the campaign away from fire-fighting the chosen unionist scare stories to the opportunities on jobs and health that would come from independence.

She agrees on both counts and says the vibes from Glasgow are particularly promising. However, I also tell her I think that I should take responsibility for any defeat, so the Party can then move forward and make the best of whatever is to come. My decision will depend on the exact circumstances at the time. Nicola, in very typical fashion, tells me to concentrate on winning the referendum and stop blethering about something which is not going to happen.

Earlier, there was a photo-call at Kelvingrove with the Pakistani triples bowlers – or at least the two-thirds of them who travelled a full three miles from Glasgow's Battlefield Road to compete at the bowling. Chico Mohammed and Ali

Shan Muzahir run the Alishan restaurant. They are very decent bowlers and are representing the country of their birth at the greatest sporting event Scotland has ever seen.

I have known Chico and Ali for many years and, when not dieting, I am a regular at the Alishan. They are on a high about their selection. The one drawback is the non-appearance (as yet) of their team-mate from Pakistan, whom they have never met. I offer to stand in if he doesn't turn up and they both look resplendent in their Pakistani shirts and kilts.

The Strategic Group meeting takes place in the Hydro, which must be the best-value facility venue in the history of the construction industry. It has paid its way already with sell-out concerts and will be a major driver of the hospitality economy in Glasgow.

I declare that I am giving our Commonwealth Games a gold medal before the event even begins. It is going to be a great Scottish success: unique among major sporting events of recent years. We are now confident it will come in under budget and everything about it will display the very best of Glasgow and Scotland. Our undeclared aim is even more ambitious. We intend to restore it as one of the world's great sporting events.

Securing the games in Sri Lanka in 2007 was one of my first jobs as First Minister. We ran the operation as if it were an election campaign, as indeed it was. Our rival, the Nigerian capital of Abuja, was tough competition and many people's favourite for success. Their bid was not well organised but it was well financed and carried the great emotional attraction that Africa has never held the Games. And here was a serious African bid. My key allies in the Scottish bid were Steven Purcell and Louise Martin.

Steven was the hugely talented Labour leader of Glasgow City Council. Until he fell by the wayside in 2011, he would undoubtedly have offered Labour a new leadership prospectus in Scotland.

Louise Martin, luckily, is still going strong as perhaps the most popular delegate to the entire Commonwealth Federation. It was Louise whose contacts supplied us with the key information which allowed us to outsmart the Abuja canvassing operation as we vigorously and successfully strove to keep claims of Nigerian inducements out of the press. We knew we could win and win well on the strength of our bid and the overwhelming desire of the delegates to have a Games venue that they could absolutely rely upon to deliver. Nothing sours relationships for the future more than claims from rival camps about underhand behaviour – something which the losing bids for the World Cup could have borne in mind.

Once the Games were won for Scotland my key appointment was Robert Smith to chair the Games Company and, after a false start or two, he appointed exactly the right people to carry Glasgow 2014 forward. If there is a better corporate chair in the entire country than Lord Smith of Kelvin then I have yet to meet them. The Scottish government deployed a strong team of civil servants, led for the most part by my former principal private secretary Francesca Osowska, while George Black, Chief Executive of Glasgow City Council, provided a secure and steady hand at keeping council and government aligned.

Despite that line-up and a performance of real strength, the Scottish press were well capable of picking the best-laid schemes apart if we had given them the slightest opportunity. However, in truth, the Games had a charmed existence – apart from occasional blips like the madcap plan, attributed to Bridget McConnell, to demolish the Red Road Flats during the opening ceremony. Fortunately I managed to persuade Police Scotland to insist on the rather obvious public safety issues, Robert Smith swung the committee and a publicity disaster was averted.

After thirty meetings or so, the Strategic Group are finally on the finishing straight. Before we wrap up the final agenda, there are two key matters to deal with. First, the outbreak of norovirus. It turns out to be the result of a temporary toilet without a hand-washing basin which had slipped through the cleaning contracts. Luckily the source of infection is not actually in the athletes' village itself. We have also brought in environmental health and the health service people, who know their business, and I wheel them out at the meeting to put the situation into context.

Second, we have to ensure that the communications team of the best financially run Games in history is up to the job of fending off the entire press of the Commonwealth. I insist we will use the meeting to highlight that the Games will come within its £575 million budget. Front-foot-confident, proactive assertion of what is important, and we will sweep all before us over the next two weeks.

Talking of which, I take considerable pleasure in phoning *The Times* editor John Witherow, to talk through their assertion that the athletes' village is about to be closed, based on the comments of a London doctor who seems to be an adviser to travel companies.

Having had the briefing from environmental health, I know I am on strong ground and demand to know why his paper is trying to sabotage the Commonwealth Games. John, a South African with some Scottish connections, assures me there is no such agenda. This is interesting, since the pretty obvious anti-Scottish bias in the paper must be coming from somewhere.

At any rate, the exchange might help them keep their mitts off the Games, and I really do enjoy having a whinge about something which isn't directly connected with politics.

I then have a tremendous time at the Scottish Youth Theatre, where they preview an excerpt of *Now's The Hour*, their show about the referendum.

The idea of writing a letter to your future self is a pretty well-worn dramatic device, but this performance is both moving and very powerful. It captures something of the spirit I have detected over the last few weeks and I tell them that they will take the Edinburgh Fringe by storm.

Day Thirty-Eight: Saturday 19 July

Golf takes a back seat as I fulfil my pledge to open the New Deer show in my constituency.

New Deer is the friendliest of the agricultural shows and, I am reliably informed by those in the know, the very best for showing animals. We have an excellent day and, since the heavens open at noon, I stay until 1.30 p.m. to formally open the show.

This leaves only an hour or so to watch the Open when I get home to Strichen. The Royal and Ancient decided to change the times of the Championship to ensure they finished the day rather than let the Hoylake thunderstorms force their hand.

It means the golfers finish just when they should have been starting. But just about everyone says the R&A acted quickly and effectively, especially when the bad weather arrives on cue at 4 p.m.

I disagree. Golf is an outdoor sport. It is there to be played in all weathers and should only be suspended for lightning, flooded courses, or when balls do not stay stationary on greens because of the wind. Otherwise, they should, in the words of my father, 'play the ball as it lies'. Mind you, my view on this is rather coloured by not getting to watch it.

There is also, of course, the substantial irony of an organisation which has yet to admit women departing from tradition because of a spot of rain.

McIlroy meanwhile has the tournament (and my investment) in safe-keeping.

Day Thirty-Nine: Sunday 20 July

The *Sunday Post* was once a great Scottish tradition – a newspaper with couthy content, the truly excellent Oor Wullie cartoon strip and no malice whatsoever. Now it has an added touch of malice.

Today it attacks me – in a splash, no less – for international junketing. The junkets in question are staying in three-, four- or even five-star hotels on international trips. In principle, it would be possible to meet company CEOs or international dignitaries at the local Holiday Inn, but I'm not sure how well that would work for Scotland's benefit. However, the day I see our press run a story exposing which hotels Cameron stays in is the day I will believe the *Post* has not succumbed to being just another member of the depressing anti-independence pack.

Meanwhile, at the Open, McIlroy has defended his lead and secured a two-shot victory – a decent result for my bank balance and an important one for Scotland. It means the last four Open champions have played in the Scottish Open the week beforehand. This copper-bottoms the quality of the field for next year.

Day Forty: Monday 21 July

An intensive run-up to the Games has begun and Team Scotland are under starter's orders. But other business has to be dovetailed into this busy period, and on our way to Glasgow I call in at the Old Course Hotel in St Andrews for a meeting with a delegation from the Chinese airline Hainan.

For some time we've been trying to interest the Chinese in viewing Prestwick Airport as a potential hub. It has long runways, lots of airspace, plenty of groundspace, a strategic location and is ideal for private jets. As long as the airport does not develop a strategy of direct competition with Edinburgh and Glasgow, then the Scottish government's decision to purchase it to prevent closure will be vindicated, not immediately perhaps but over a period of time. The meeting goes well.

Out to Scotland House, the Team Scotland headquarters for the Games. The venue is well chosen. It is the old Fruit Market building in the heart of the cultural merchant city. That is where the celebrations were held when the news came through from Sri Lanka that the Games had been won. Everyone is in good spirits, and on talking to the team they are all in confident mood. Our team has come to play.

The day's rounded off at an audience with the Duke of Rothesay at Holyrood Palace.

From time to time, stories surface in the UK press about how Prince Charles writes to government ministers and how terrible that is. Well, he does indeed write and has views on all sorts of subjects – and it's not terrible at all. Indeed, most of his opinions are pretty sensible, and ministers can either accept or reject them as they wish.

The work of the Prince's charities is particularly impressive and Charles is constantly looking for funding from public and private sources. At breakfast in Birkhall, his residence near Balmoral, in 2011, I had to break the news that the cupboard was bare – there were no public funds available to further help their excellent work.

'However,' I said, 'I think I know how we could raise a quarter of a million or so.'

This clearly commanded the Royal attention.

'Well, there has never been a Royal race meeting in Scotland. If we were to arrange one at Perth, for example, then we could raise that sort of money.'

Charles, who is not really keen on horse-racing, inquired whether he would be obliged to attend. Camilla, who is very keen indeed on horse-racing and a very practical lady, quickly set him straight.

And so, on 20 August 2011, the racecourse at Scone held the first Royal meeting in its illustrious 400-year history. Thanks to the tremendous efforts of Sara Cornwallis, Samantha Barber and the racecourse general manager Sam Morshead, the target was duly reached and a great day was had by all.

One small blip almost occurred near the end when the Prince's minders decided he should not do the live interview on STV, which had covered the meeting as their first race day for a generation. This was unfortunate, since I had promised the broadcaster the interview in return for getting them to Perth, which was in turn important to the sponsors.

My solution was a bit of direct action. As part of the proceedings, I was due to introduce the Duke in the paddock to present the Cup to the connections of Overturn, the winner of the £40,000 Scottish Hydro Summer Champion Hurdle (and my 4–1 nap of the day in my guest racing column in the *Courier*). Instead, I just announced that someone wanted to say a few words and handed a startled Prince the microphone.

He handled it very well, delivering an amusing and well-received impromptu speech, much to the delight of the crowd and to the relief of STV, who covered the whole thing.

Day Forty-One: Tuesday 22 July

Pretty sure I got one over on John Humphrys after he tried to corner me.

We're at one of the launch events for the Games – a joint conference with the UK Department of Business at Glasgow University. The delegates are from companies from throughout the Commonwealth and we have a non-aggression pact with the UK government – we won't do the politics if they don't.

I make a decent speech about trends in the Scottish economy, praise Lord Smith to the skies, compliment the University Principal, Anton Muscatelli, and have some fun with the delegates.

Humphrys, of BBC Radio 4's *Today* programme, is chairing the event and his first question is along the lines of: 'All the delegates are dying to ask you about independence. What can you say to this business audience about the uncertainty it creates?'

My reply excites a fair bit of enthusiasm. I point out that, of the seventy-one nations and territories that will be competing over the next ten days, the vast majority have become independent from Westminster. Therefore there is probably no audience anywhere who are more familiar and more relaxed about the process of independence.

I'm in a similar barn-storming mood in an interview to the *Evening Times* in which I predict that Glasgow will become known as 'Freedom City' after it votes YES in the referendum. Later, in a press conference primarily for the international media, I take the opportunity to announce a politics-free zone from the opening ceremony to the closing bell.

I tell them:

> I've taken a kind of self-denying ordinance to concentrate on the Games over the next ten days. I think that's what the people of Scotland want.
>
> We have ten days here; we are going to concentrate on presenting Scotland to the world. We have plenty of time when the Games are over … to get into the thick of the referendum debate.

This, of course, greatly upsets the *Telegraph* and the *Mail*, but their questions are batted away simply enough. Once the Games are under way they will generate a momentum of their own. This is particularly the case with the Scottish media, since we have done our best in the scheduling to front-end some of our best Scottish gold chances. This is largely the work of Michael Cavanagh, Chairman of Commonwealth Games Scotland. Michael, a former wrestler, has been successfully wrestling with the Games programme to get some of the Scottish best hopes out first.

A good example of what we are dealing with from the London media comes in an interview with *The One Show*. They ask me how I will respond to booing at Celtic Park during the opening ceremony (they mean of me). I say the crowd will be good-natured and give the English team a generous welcome!

When we get to Celtic Park for the rehearsal we have a real issue to deal with. Malaysia's Prince Tunku Imran (Pete as he insists on being called) expresses the wish for a minute's silence out of respect for the Malaysian air disaster over Ukraine, given that the day of mourning in the Netherlands is taking place tomorrow. It is clearly the right thing to do, but Pete does not want to announce it himself, as that might be seen as abusing his position as Chair of the Commonwealth Federation.

After a rapid consultation with the show producer, David Zolkwer, we decide that I will do it and weave it into a sequence which starts with a tribute to Nelson Mandela, moves on to the South African singer Pumeza performing Hamish Henderson's 'Freedom Come All Ye', then has the incomparable Nicola Benedetti performing 'Loch Lomond'. Then the speeches begin, with Yours Truly holding half a minute's silence for the plane disaster and giving the welcome to Scotland, followed by the council leader, Gordon Matheson, and his welcome to Glasgow.

At least that's the plan.

David Zolkwer is someone I have come to respect a great deal. At first I had doubts about the opening ceremony and how we could compete with Danny Boyle's exuberant London 2012 Olympics production and do so on a mere fraction of the budget. However, the more I found out about David's plans, the more confident I became.

A few weeks previously he had asked me if I knew 'Freedom Come All Ye'.

'Know it?' I replied. 'I once sang it on top of a double-decker bus in front of twenty-five thousand people in the Edinburgh meadows beside Hamish Henderson.'

'We will not be asking you to sing it again, First Minister. Do you know it's in Scots?'

'Yes, David.'

'Could we translate it?'

'No, David. Believe me, it just wouldn't work in English.'

'Fine, First Minister. Then I will get someone to sing it well.'

But politics are never far away when we later go to the University for a series of diplomatic meetings, including one with the very impressive Joseph Muscat, Prime Minister of Malta. He offers to sponsor Scotland's case for immediate entry at the European Council in the event of a YES vote.

On to a speech at the business conference reception, also attended by the Earl of Wessex. But a briefing on a number of Games issues prevents me from attending the event's family dinner. They range from airport security to a few minor incidents at the athletes' village. On the first we have to balance the need for proportionate security with the importance of not frisking our guests from around the planet the moment they set foot in Scotland. On the second we have to keep a sense of perspective about the very occasional bust-ups between highly strung athletes.

Keeping on top of the variety of potential problems is threatening to become a full-time occupation.

Day Forty-Two: Wednesday 23 July

After seven years of preparation, the big day is finally here. But the pressure is substantial – much worse than any election.

We're confident that everything is set for a celebration of sport and a demonstration of Scotland's ability to host great events. But, with the reputation of the whole nation hanging on it, I am determined that nothing should go wrong. The problem is, you're not as in control of something like this as you are, at least to some extent, of an election campaign.

As it turns out, the only problem I didn't anticipate was the one befalling Pete, my Malaysian Prince chum.

In between a host of diplomatic meetings, I meet Bank of England Governor Mark Carney, who I've invited to tonight's opening ceremony. I thought it would give us an opportunity to meet outwith the public gaze. There is no better or more secret way to meet people than in the middle of a huge public event.

I press the issue of a Bank of England statement on their ongoing responsibility for monetary stability regardless of the vote. Carney cautions that an unexpected statement might actually provoke the market stress on the commercial banks which is precisely what we are trying to avoid. I argue that there must be a suitable opportunity or method of making a statement, without it being perceived as a response to pressure. His attention is captured when I say I'd like to make an appointment for a Chair of a Monetary Institute immediately following a YES vote. Securing the services of a hugely authoritative financial figure might be effective in calming market fears. Carney makes the point that this person would have to be carefully chosen, as their every utterance would be seen as a potential policy commitment during sensitive negotiations. I reply that he seems to manage that successfully. We speak a great deal about the aftermath of the referendum and I repeat to him that he should disregard the media commentary. My instinct is that the polls will tighten.

Carney, like his predecessor Mervyn King, is a thoroughly decent sort. He tells me that he hopes to see this referendum take place in an atmosphere free from economic fear. That is a notable contrast with those who seek to engender fear and enlist it as their ally. I am hopeful that he will make a suitable statement at the right time.

Straight after meeting Mark, I see the Spanish Ambassador, Federico Trillo-Figueroa. He assures me of his government's continuing wish not to take a position in the referendum. I assure him of my government's continuing wish that this is his government's continuing wish!

At a reception at Scotland House, Prince Imran (Pete) tells me he has been practising opening the baton that secures the Queen's message. He explains that, within the intricate design, there is a knack to twisting it open – but that he has mastered it.

With Moira at the opening ceremony. I have always been pretty confident about how it would go, but even I have my expectations surpassed. David's quirky asides – John Barrowman's gay kiss, the dancing Tunnock's teacakes, the Scottie dugs leading the teams – all work brilliantly, as does the designer Jilli Blackwood's Scottish team costumes, which had previously taken some panning in the press. Seen in their proper ceilidh context they are brilliantly and colourfully cool.

However, the highlight is, without question, the sequence towards the end starting with 'Freedom Come All Ye'. David tells me that Pumeza has practised her Scots pronunciation for a fortnight to get it right – and she puts in an extraordinary performance.

With all going so well surely nothing can go wrong, until … Prince Imran can't get the baton to open!

I'm sitting beside Prince Philip, and when Pete has trouble getting the message out, His Royal Highness's reaction is priceless and his language choice. I'm sitting there thinking: 'Pete, you did it this afternoon, you showed me how to do it.' I wonder if some evil person has superglued it. Mind you, I suppose it's one thing practising behind the scenes. Repeating it in front of a worldwide audience of pushing a billion is another matter.

But we get there. Thanks to the joint efforts of Pete and Sir Chris Hoy, the message is retrieved and the moment of drama passes. Indeed there have been so many send-ups in David's production that a good part of the crowd thought this was just part of the show! However, what is less visible is that the Queen uses her prompt sheet to read the message without missing a beat – a really composed and professional reaction.

Pete tells me afterwards that he cut his finger in the debacle and declares: 'I now have bled for Scotland – just like William Wallace.' Truly a prince among men.

Day Forty-Three: Thursday 24 July

Whistle-stop tour of the Games venues this morning and it proves to be a winning day.

First up is Tollcross swimming pool, where we had anticipated some very early Scottish success. And the crowd are not disappointed with a remarkable Scottish 1-2-3 in one of the early heats, setting us up for great things to come.

News comes through that our Pakistani scratch triples in the bowling are doing remarkable things, taking the lead against the world champion Australian team with a few ends left. The world looks like it could turn upside down, but then the Australians clean up the last few ends for a 19–12 success.

I decide to pay my friends an impromptu visit at Kelvingrove, where we fancy great success from the Scottish team. When we get there, I can see why Ali and Chico are doing well. It must have been hotter than Karachi in the centre of Glasgow. Our very earnest prayer for great weather has been answered.

Go to the Scottish Exhibition and Conference Centre just in time to see Edinburgh judoka Kimberley Renicks winning Scotland's first gold in the women's under-48kg class with victory over an Indian girl. As I detected when I visited the training camp, the Scottish team mean business and the judo players are the most confident of all.

A quick meeting with the President of Singapore before watching Aileen McGlynn and her pilot Louise Haston scoop silver at the Velodrome. Louise Renicks, meanwhile, follows her sister with a gold – I doubt the achievement of two sisters winning gold on the same day has ever been equalled.

By the time the sun sets on the swimming pool, Scotland has soared to the top of the table with ten medals, including four golds. I do love it when a plan works out!

End up in Jambo heaven at a Business Scotland event where I have the great pleasure of sitting next to Ann Budge, the fairy godmother of Heart of Midlothian football club.

What a splendid woman she is and what a splendid day this has been.

Day Forty-Four: Friday 25 July

I detect a real change in the air. Perhaps it is best summed up by a comment I get during a visit to the Games.

I'm touring Glasgow Green, where we're holding the Games Festival which lets tens of thousands of people try out all the Games' sports and much else besides. I playfully have a go at the boxing, gloves and all, with Labour councillor Archie Graham, a picture that the photographers lap up. The event is being staged by a club from Glasgow's east end.

One of the instructors takes me to one side and says: 'I'm Labour, but I'm Yes – de-fin-ate-ly.'

It is exactly this kind of response which is giving me increasing confidence, and that's what I tried to impress on the campaign committee at a meeting this morning.

There has been no YouGov polling for some three weeks – the last one showed us stuck at the wrong end of a 60–40 result. Our own canvassing is showing some further movement, but not enough to break the predominant press view that the NO campaign has an unassailable lead. I told the meeting that in order to win we must come in very strong and very late.

I know the Games are generating a very particular atmosphere in Glasgow, but there is something else. Our opponents are growing complacent. Their campaign is losing its edge due to its negativity. They have played the fear card far too often and far too early. Scaremongering campaigns are most successful when they are played out very close to polling day. When people have the chance to rationalise fear they tend to disregard it.

We have also just emerged triumphantly from a key day for Scotland; a demonstration that we can stage a major event, with our country sitting on top of the medal table. If confidence is important for the YES campaign then we now have it on a supercharger.

I'm greatly impressed by Pride House – a focal point for the LGBT community during this fortnight. There have been a number of suggestions from equality organisations as to how we can respond to the fact that some of our Commonwealth colleagues do not share our views on the acceptance of human sexuality – some wished to express their point through protests, bans, demonstrations, etc.

But as organisers we don't need to protest: these are our Games and it is for us to set the context in which they are presented. Thanks to the ingenuity of David Zolkwer we made our point in a joyous and celebratory way. The Pride House initiative is a further indication that our Games are for everyone to enjoy and experience on the basis of equality. The real warmth of the reception at this opening is an indication that we have judged the issue correctly. People feel good about our Games.

The Festival at Glasgow Green is a chance for people to experience the atmosphere and try their hand at some of sports. It was in the spirit of unity that I attended with Councillor Graham, who is Labour leader Johann Lamont's husband and who serves on the Strategic Group with Council Leader Gordon Matheson.

Archie is an amiable sort and he and I make an excellent double act as we tour around, having a go at virtually everything. I think he is genuinely touched when I insist that we appear in all photos together. In truth we could have easily spent the entire day there, and my security team led by John Buchanan and the rest of the staff worked overtime with an entirely positive and very enthusiastic crowd.

Eventually I have to tear myself away to the more sedate surroundings of the women's netball at the SECC. Or at least I thought it would be sedate until I got there. It is a much more physical game than I was expecting and much, much faster. I see Scotland beat St Lucia, a better side than perhaps anticipated. Our netball officials are really pleased because the Scottish team would have qualified for Delhi in 2010, but were bumped by home country preference. This time they qualified again, although the same home country rule would have taken them through regardless.

Just time to dash into the boxing in the pavilion next door, and I'm very glad I do. I sit beside the Welsh delegation who expect an easy victory for their top flyweight, world No. 1 Andrew Selby. Instead we witness an extraordinary performance from the young Scot Reece McFadden. Facing a much more experienced opponent, he takes the contest by sheer force of will. The Welsh are stunned but gracious in defeat.

At 7 p.m. I'm put on display – or rather my portrait is. I attend the Gerard Burns exhibition in the Clydesdale Bank HQ, where my Bute House image and those of thirteen other prominent Scots have gone on show. Spend time with Neil Lennon, the former Celtic manager who is also one of the fourteen.

Gerard has produced a really outstanding portrait of Neil which portrays some of the rage within this highly intelligent, complex and thoroughly likeable character. Neil tells me he's a YES supporter, but my immediate attempt to get him to help publicly meets with a cautious reaction. He has hopes of a media contract, he explains.

Having completed my first three days at the Games, I set off for a few days' holiday up at Castle Stuart, the only chance I'll get this year. I had imagined in my innocence that once the Games started it would just involve a procession around various sports. It is turning out to be a bit more exacting than that.

Nicola will take over for a few days.

I round off the day on a call with Nicola and John Swinney to discuss the prospects of an investment in Grangemouth. Great news for the economy if we can pull it off.

Day Forty-Five: Saturday 26 July

Renting a cottage at Castle Stuart for a few days. I do not have a good record on holidays. The last serious one we had was in 2010, for just five days or so.

Still have work to do though, and phone Congressman Mike McIntyre, who is the retiring co-chair of the Scottish caucus in Washington. I'm testing the water for a suitable resolution in Congress, as we know the UK government are actively trying to recruit more US support following the Obama intervention. If Mike and his colleagues can table a favourable motion with substantial backing then it will snooker the Foreign Office. Mike is sympathetic and confident that something appropriate can be arranged.

Day Forty-Six: Sunday 27 July

In my naivety, I assumed that once the buildings were built, the budget adhered to, the athletes had arrived and the Games were under way, then my job would be done – apart from cheering from the stands.

It is not turning out quite like that. Not because people are not doing their jobs. They are – and they are very good at them. However, there is an all-pervasive sense of responsibility to make sure the Games stay on track. Today is a case in point.

After seven years of effort, remarkable preparations and almost universally positive publicity (the abortive blowing up of the Red Road Flats aside), the Games get their first adverse front pages and blow-by-blow tweets as people are stranded at the park and ride, apparently due to a lack of buses. In reality there are plenty of buses, just a lack of drivers, who have been transported to the wrong place by a sub-subcontractor. It could become a case of for the want of a driver the bus was lost, for the want of a bus the people were lost, for the want of the people the Games were lost!

I phone Tim O'Toole, Chief Executive of FirstGroup, from the balcony of the Mustard Seed restaurant, and adopt a tone of controlled menace. It is probably a good job for the digestive tracts of the other diners that I am on the balcony.

The conversation is greatly helped by Tim's tone of total contrition. He assures me that his entire management team are en route to Glasgow and that additional resources are on the way even as we speak. He guarantees that if anyone sneezes in Glasgow they will be placed on a bus and taken to buy a paper hanky.

It is now boom time for buses at the Games. The huge success of the Rugby Sevens also helps turn the publicity around. I am told that people leaving Ibrox stadium on Sunday evening were placed in buses whether they wanted to go in them or not!

Day Forty-Seven: Monday 28 July

The only work for the day is a phone conference on banking issues with special advisers and government economists.

The subject matter is how we persuade the Bank of England to assert its position as being responsible for the stability of the financial system and to make progress with the names of those who would serve on a Scottish Monetary Authority.

The first of these is important in securing the continued neutrality of the Scottish banks in the referendum campaign. The second will become important if we win the referendum.

The background to the issue is worth considering. The Scottish banks have been making appreciable efforts to stay out of the referendum and adopt a proper and responsible position of neutrality. However, both Lloyds and RBS are coming under considerable political pressure, since both have substantial public stakes controlled by the Treasury, and while the Bank of England is playing things with a relatively straight bat, the Treasury bat is as crooked as they come.

The issues are more apparent than real. There is no substantive issue at all for Lloyds, who own the Bank of Scotland. It is true that the registered office of the banking group is on the Mound, but that is nothing to do with the history of the Bank of Scotland and has no operational significance whatsoever.

The reason that the registered office is in Edinburgh at all is because Lloyds took over the privatised TSB in 1995 after it was stolen from its depositors in the 1980s. There had been an existing guarantee that the TSB Group would be registered in Scotland, and that guarantee was inherited by Lloyds when it took over. The headquarters of Lloyds banking group is 25 Gresham Street London and has been for many years since they moved from Birmingham.

This factual timeline renders ridiculous reports that Lloyds are considering moving their 'headquarters from Glasgow to London'. It is hard to move something from Glasgow when it has never been there and hard to move something to London when it is already based there.

The Royal Bank's position is more complex and it is more vulnerable. It is not rational, but irrational forces are not necessarily unreal ones, particularly where markets are concerned. The Royal Bank has two head offices, one at Gogarburn outside Edinburgh and one in London, where the top officials spend the vast bulk of their time. The registered office is neither of these but at 36 St Andrew's Square in Edinburgh, where I used to work.

The reason that the fears are not rational is simple. If there is a YES vote and I am right about the UK government agreeing to a banking and currency union, then there is no issue – the registered office will remain in Edinburgh. Even if I am wrong then there will be at least an eighteen-month period in which the Royal Bank can make alternative arrangements. Therefore there is no risk. Moving a registered office has limited or no impact on real banking operations. In addition, regardless of the outcome, the Royal Bank is 80 per cent owned by the UK government, and therefore the Bank of England has no alternative but to stand behind it under any and all circumstances.

The pressure the Royal Bank feels comes from its vulnerability to the way its debt is rated by agencies, given that much of its business is still in recovery mode. The Royal Bank is therefore very keen that the Bank of England should assert that it will remain in charge regardless of circumstances in the immediate aftermath of the referendum.

Day Forty-Eight: Tuesday 29 July

I can't resist a wee pop at The Donald – just like I can't resist my golf.

Playing a round with Hamish McColm, son of general manager Stuart. The young lad comes roaring back in 36 to secure a well-merited victory. But I play pretty well. I do love this golf course.

Castle Stuart is the antithesis of the Trump course at Balmedie, Aberdeenshire. Mark Parsinen, the American designer and co-owner, is a committed golfer, who dreamt of producing a great Highland golf course. He's done that at Castle Stuart. There the resemblance with The Donald ends.

Mark is west coast, The Donald is New York. Mark loves golf, The Donald loves himself. Mark worked with the local community, The Donald didn't. Mark's course has staged a major tournament, The Donald's hasn't.

The Castle Stuart course also has big plans for a hotel which would be seriously good news in Inverness. Hotel occupancy is almost as high as in Aberdeen and a development like that is exactly what Castle Stuart needs to move things to the next level. The Donald's hotel development at Balmedie has stalled.

Day Forty-Nine: Wednesday 30 July

More golf and a stooshie about Usain Bolt.

We nip up to Fortrose on the second last day of the break. The town has a remarkable golf course of 125 years' vintage, built by James Braid on a sandbank promontory right across from Fort George. Unfortunately they are in danger of losing the sixth fairway into the firth, and the club captain, Phillip Thorn, is keen to secure support to protect this little gem (and the coastal path with views of dolphins) from the elements.

They run a truly admirable Club Golf programme and are a great example of an outstanding community course. I draw the game and play not too badly on the back nine in pretty tough conditions. Of course it is possible that the captain was making great efforts not to win!

The Times, true to form, causes a stir about the Olympic 100-metre champion Usain Bolt, reporting that he claimed the Games were 'a bit s***'.

They used to say about Lloyd George: show him a belt and he would hit below it. Show *The Times* a Scottish parade and they will attempt to rain on it.

Day Fifty: Thursday 31 July

Last day of the break – but I'm still pushing Mark Carney to make a statement.

I have another call with the Bank of England governor in an attempt to get him to go public on contingency plans and a reassurance that the Bank will remain in charge, no matter what happens in the vote.

The aim of the NO campaign has been to spread fear in the financial sector in case of capital or deposit flight due to denominational risk – this is when people see a risk to their asset values through an exchange-rate depreciation. In other words they think that the pound in their pocket or in their purse or in their bank account might be worth less. This is why

I have been so keen to stress that Scotland will use the pound sterling full stop.

Meanwhile, *The Times* helpfully publish a transcript which, to my mind, helps clear up the Bolt issue. It seems perfectly obvious, to me anyway, that when someone is glancing up to the heavens when uttering the word 's***', it is probably the weather they are talking about. At least that's what I do!

Later, there is a practice for Tuesday's TV debate. It goes OK, but I'm not happy about the ring readiness of our debate team and in particular about the unanimous advice to tone down my debating style. With the benefit of 20:20 hindsight it might have been better to have left a gap between the Games and the first debate. I've asked for a full dress rehearsal this Sunday.

Driven back to Strichen by special adviser Alexander Anderson. Alexander is the government's transport specialist and this will give him a fine opportunity to look at the rigours of the A96 close up. Security officer John Cooper is in tow in the car behind. Later, at home, I'm cheering at the telly when Eilidh Child wins a fine silver medal in the 400m hurdles at Hampden – a great achievement given the additional pressure of being the Games' poster girl.

I also catch the end of a Sky programme on the life of boxer 'Smokin' Joe' Frazier – and really like a quote from his fierce rival Muhammad Ali, whom Frazier never really forgave for his merciless taunting. Ali said: 'When the last trumpet sounds and I'm called up to God's army, then the man I would choose to be fighting at my side would be Smokin' Joe Frazier.'

Day Fifty-One: Friday 1 August

I find it totally extraordinary as I wheel round Games venues today to see how the event is changing attitudes, and therefore changing lives. It is good to be back amid the hurly-burly.

At Glasgow's Mitchell Library I talk to some of the youngsters involved in a broadcasting coverage initiative called Future News. A South African lad watched the opening ceremony at home, and he tells me the sequence from the Nelson Mandela tribute through 'Freedom Come All Ye' to the silence for the Malaysian airliner was the most moving thing he'd ever watched on television.

With our youngest competitor, Shetland's Erraid Davies, at the diving competition in Edinburgh later. I had taken her as a treat to celebrate her success. As we sit watching an exciting contest, I ask Erraid if, having just won an amazing bronze swimming medal at the age of thirteen, taking part in the diving might be an option for the future.

'No,' she says firmly. 'The pool in Shetland isn't deep enough. I'd hit my head!'

Day Fifty-Two: Saturday 2 August

Bit hoarse today. Probably down to over-enthusiasm. And no wonder. I'm in Glasgow to take in events I'd missed, as well as going back to the boxing, which I'd really wanted to see as they have transferred the finals to the great Hydro arena.

But first to the athletes' village – and I'm highly impressed. It's my first time back since the place was a building site. Meet members of the Scottish team, who are all in high spirits, and renew some acquaintances with the judo players – or, as I call them, the 'Bannockburn bunch' … 13 competitors 14 medals, 1314! The military guys in the team are keen on getting into the venues to cheer on the competitors who are also in the services, and under all the circumstances I instruct the arrangements to be made. Then lunch with the Canadian women's hockey team and some African weightlifters. On balance I reckon the hockey team are tougher.

I've now been to all the sports apart from the athletics, shooting and rugby. But, back to the boxing. An amazing atmosphere and, within ten minutes, two of our fighters are roared on to gold medal success.

This is when I notice my voice going, so it's probably just as well that I have to rush to our closing reception rather than stay for two renditions of 'Flower of Scotland' in quick succession.

Back in Edinburgh to take the salute at the Tattoo, and Zulu warriors present me with a ceremonial spear. Could come in handy over the next few weeks! This Tattoo has the best production values to date and Alasdair Fraser, the celebrated composer of fiddle music and film scripts, is suitably impressed.

Tattoo Chief Executive and producer Brigadier David Allfrey is understandably pleased to get praise from such a respected source. I am just pleased that at last we get to sing 'Auld Lang Syne' standing up. It is really the only way to sing Burns's international anthem, but in previous years the rickety old seats dictated that everyone had to stay seated. The substantial investment of the Scottish government and the Tattoo in comfy stands is worth it for this fact alone.

He's an interesting character, the Brigadier: totally immersed in army tradition, and yet with a streak of unconventionality which is reflected in the ever more adventurous and successful Tattoos.

Also present as a guest is Lieutenant Commander Colin May, a senior Naval intelligence officer at the submarine base at Faslane. Colin is from the North East and knows Angus Robertson, the SNP leader in Westminster and MP for Moray. He tells me that he retires this coming Friday and will no longer be bound by Queen's regulations. He intends to declare publicly for YES at that point.

All back to Bute House, where Alasdair and friends put on an amazing impromptu performance lasting well into the wee sma' hours. Despite my faltering voice, I insist on a rousing rendition of 'Freedom Come All Ye'.

Day Fifty-Three: Sunday 3 August

I feel this powerful, almost overwhelming, sense of relief that the Games have gone well.

It's the final day and I wake up to find that my hoarse voice is actually a nasty throat and chest infection. I cram myself with antibiotics and gargle enough salt water to record a voter registration message in a dozen languages. My Italian is particularly good apparently!

TV debate preparation has to be shortened to dash back to Glasgow for a closing Games press conference. It's a fairly simple matter – despite my throat – as there are few, if any, negatives from the journalists. I bat off questions about the referendum by suggesting they interview me tomorrow. I'm diplomatic about my advice to the Australian Gold Coast (hosts of the 2018 Games) and lavish in my praise of Lord Smith and Louise Martin.

At supper with Scottish Enterprise and guests before the closing ceremony, the good mood is contagious, with everyone telling loads of Games stories and looking forward to the big event.

I've written a note to David Zolkwer with some modest suggestions for the finale which involves community singing (just about the only thing the opening lacked) and ask for a reprise of the wonderful 'Freedom Come All Ye'.

He does both, with the Pipes and Drums of the Edinburgh Festival coming on to play the original pipe tune of 'Freedom Come All Ye' and glorious all-stadium renditions of 'Caledonia' and 'Auld Lang Syne'.

David is a marvel, while Prince Pete of Malaysia endears himself to everyone by declaring the Games 'the best ever'. Robert Smith makes a fine speech and well deserves the resounding applause he receives. He and I take a moment together at the close of the ceremony. It has been a long journey. Our joy is born of mutual relief.

For four years, I had been teasing him about the previous closing Commonwealth ceremony in Delhi. The mayor of Delhi and the prime minister of India received rapturous receptions. The organiser (Robert's equivalent) was roundly booed and subsequently sent to jail. Luckily for Robert, such has been the success of the organisation that Barlinnie, Glasgow's famous prison, was not required to provide secure accommodation for Lord Smith of Kelvinside! Back to Scotland House for a late night and raucous celebration with

21 March 2013: The date of the referendum fashioned by apprentice welders at Steel Engineering Ltd in Renfrew.

11 April 2014: With Nicola, my deputy, on the opening day of the SNP Spring Conference in Aberdeen.

7 May: With SNP candidate Tasmina Ahmed-Sheikh, campaigning at a bus stop in Portobello for the European Parliament elections.

6 August: At the Business for Scotland conference in Edinburgh, the morning after the first televised debate with Alistair Darling.

25 August: What a difference a debate makes. Taking charge of round two.

18 August: St Andrew's Parish Church in Arbroath, with members of the Cabinet, for a public question-and-answer session.

24 August: Responding to actor James McAvoy's call to take part in the Ice Bucket Challenge campaign to help raise awareness of the disease amyotrophic lateral sclerosis.

3 September: On the campaign trail at Browning's Bakers in Kilmarnock.

4 September: Ten years as Leader and Deputy Leader of the SNP – with Nicola and campaign activists in Buchanan Street, Glasgow …

… and surrounded by the media afterwards. There were almost fights between the photographers and the TV crews.

6 September: 'Bu chòir' or 'We should' – an endorsement in Gaelic in Inverness (*above*) and a visit to a mosque in Inverness (*below*).

10 September: A supporter at the Team Scotland Unites for YES event in Edinburgh.

14 September: With Amy Macdonald outside Usher Hall in Edinburgh, which that evening would host the concert A Night for Scotland.

17 September: One final speech to a rally in Perth on the eve of the referendum.

19 September: Anticipating the result in the early hours of the morning in Edinburgh.

19 September: At Bute House for an afternoon press conference to announce my resignation as First Minister (*left*), and, a short time later, with Moira, in a helicopter on our way home (*below*).

16 April 2015: On the campaign trail with Tasmina Ahmed-Sheikh, SNP candidate for Ochil and South Perthshire, in Milnathort.

18 April: Nicola and I pose for a selfie in Inverurie town square.

28 April: Visiting Clovenstone Boxing Club with local SNP candidate Joanna Cherry and boxer Craig McEwan.

2 May: Campaigning in my 'snappy bus' in the final week before the election.

11 May: 'The 56' assemble for a photocall outside the St Stephen's entrance of the House of Commons – a proud moment.

27 May: Breenging through the doors to the Members' Lobby before the Queen's speech.

21 July: The SNP occupy the Labour benches on the final day of the parliamentary session.

our athletes and, ironically, something finally goes wrong when a false fire alarm sends us all into the street.

Moira and I take the opportunity to slip away. Indeed, I suspect she may have set the alarms off, because she is none too pleased about the hectic schedule I have been keeping. She does not think it possible to sustain this pace up until the referendum.

Day Fifty-Four: Monday 4 August

Rehearsal for tomorrow's TV debate with Alistair Darling. Things are not right.

The format is not what it should be, neither is there agreement on strategy. However, I have accepted the prevailing view that I should tone down my normal combative style.

The day starts with a beautiful service in Glasgow Cathedral to commemorate the Great War. The logic being that Commonwealth representatives would find it easier to attend the day after the Games.

I sit beside Kate Adie, who performs one of the readings, a good choice given that she has seen the reality of conflict close up in a way in which very few politicians have.

I believe the UK government is in for a well-merited disappointment in the impact of these commemorations over the next four years in terms of Scots' attitude to the union. In a supremely crass comment in 2012, Cameron described the anniversary as an event to be celebrated 'like the Diamond Jubilee'. For most people – indeed just about everyone with an ounce of sense – this is no celebration and it is not at all like the Jubilee.

Crasser still, Downing Street briefings of the time directly related the commemorations to the referendum. For example, Patrick Wintour's report in the *Guardian* described the government view of the anniversary as 'another chance to commemorate Britishness'.

The Scottish government have planned an appropriate and respectful series of commemorations for the next four years which try to reflect the horrendous cost to Scottish communities of the Great War, as well as the bravery of fighting men and the sacrifice of individual families. Decimation literally means removal of one-tenth. In many Scottish rural communities, the men of the official fighting age of eighteen to forty were decimated three or four times over.

The anniversary is being studied in schools across the country, with close emphasis placed on local and personal connections. Whatever the impact on this new generation, as they understand the full horror of the Great War, it will not be gung-ho for the union. If an appreciation of Britishness depends upon commemorating this bloody carnage 'like the Diamond Jubilee' then the unionist cause is truly and irrevocably finished.

Day Fifty-Five: Tuesday 5 August

The first TV debate. I lost.

It could have and should have gone better. We've had set-piece leaders' debates in Scottish politics since 1992 and I have won every single one … until now.

The reason? I allowed myself to be persuaded to act out of character.

My team had been concerned that my debating style was not First Ministerial enough and they wanted a more controlled performance. It was felt that to make further progress we had to reach out more to the undecideds and women voters, who, it was argued, are not much impressed by strident debating.

There is a moment at the start of the debate which should have set alarm bells ringing. As I move to shake hands with Alistair Darling, he says something like: 'This is the bit where we pretend to like each other.' I doubt if Alistair will ever win a prize for effective 'trash talk', but it does indicate that he was also being advised to act out of character. He was being pumped up. I was being calmed down.

In addition to style there were things I should just have done better. When challenged by Alistair on a currency 'Plan B', I should have counter-attacked at once, pointing out that it is impossible to stop any country using a tradeable international currency. My own questions to Darling should have been on issues that directly matter to people, like jobs and health, rather than more political debating points, which we had devised immediately before the debate. I am really annoyed with myself about that, since the concentration on issues that really matter is exactly what I've been advocating at campaign meetings for the last few meetings.

I decide to make a change for the last sections of the debate. Too late to alter the overall impression but still important to do. And for that I owe a vote of thanks to a mystery audience member. After the second part of the debate and during a break for adverts, I chatted to a man in the audience in the front row. He was clearly a convinced YES voter but not happy with the way the debate was going and suggested I got 'stuck in more'.

That spurred me on for the final section. I came out from behind the rostrum to answer the audience questions. It had a great impact and helped connect with people.

Afterwards, in the tiny green room, the campaign team are pretty downhearted. In contrast, Clare Howell, my 'lifestyle coach', is positive. 'You will find the ratings are fine,' she predicts.

I smile: 'So, what you are saying, Clare, is that my positive-thinking guru is thinking positively!'

When the figures do come through, Clare is justified to a degree. The ICM snap poll shows Darling ahead, but not by much. Indeed it shows that women and previously undecideds are rather favourable to my more restrained style. In addition, the post-debate poll records only a 52–48 margin for NO – exactly where it was before the debate started.

Geoff Aberdein cheers up a bit: 'The third part of the debate did go well. It's something to build on for next time.'

There is a problem, however. The debate is meant to give the campaign additional momentum, but this one won't. On the contrary, the Scottish press will take every opportunity to stick the boot in.

If there is one lesson it is this: in the second debate I will make sure there is different preparation and a very different First Minister will turn up. After all it was an Englishman who put it best: 'To thine own self be true.'

Day Fifty-Six: Wednesday 6 August

A diary mix-up means I appear late for a Business for Scotland conference at the Dynamic Earth venue in Edinburgh. Bit unfortunate given the press smell blood after last night. The line is that I slept in/was frightened to face them/was closeted away in a crisis meeting/have taken to the bottle – perm any of the above.

In fact I am fine. One of my best qualities is determination in the face of adversity and the ability to put mistakes behind me to do better next time. Luckily, I'm in good form in front of a sympathetic business audience and get stuck into the ludicrous argument that we can somehow be prevented from using sterling. I also point out that, on my way to the conference, I passed a new prestigious office block in St Andrew's Square financed to the tune of £75 million by Standard Life Investments – not the most obvious actions of a company about to flee the country.

I tell the TV interviews that what journalists see as wins and losses in debates are not always what the people see, citing the post-debate polls. In terms of Alistair's souped-up performance I cite the immortal words of Zsa Zsa Gabor: 'Macho men ain't mucho!'

There is nothing which unites the SNP parliamentary group more than the hostility of the Scottish press – I am reminded of that at the parliamentary group meeting at lunchtime today. I am impressed by one story from the doorstep canvassing in Edinburgh, where the campaign team presented arguments in the form of positive questions such as 'What do you like about the YES campaign?' I think there is a lot in this approach of positive rather than defensive thinking.

A late lunch at Bute House with David McAllister MEP, former Minister-President of Lower Saxony and newly elected to the European Parliament on top of the Christian Democratic Union party list in their system of PR. It is entirely possible that David might at some point become the first-ever Scot to be Chancellor of Germany. With a Scottish father and a German mother he is likeable, smart and very electable. He is fiercely proud of his Scottish heritage, even campaigning under the slogan 'Ich bin ein Mac' (I am a Scot). JFK eat your heart out.

David tells me he understands Angela Merkel has refused a direct request from Downing Street to intervene on the side of the union, preferring to steer the normal neutral course in other country's affairs. It seems that the German Chancellor has more gumption than the American President.

I call Lord King later about the position with the financial sector. Mervyn, when he was Governor of the Bank of England, and asserting his independence from the UK government, agreed to 'technical discussions' between Scottish government economists and the Bank of England. He is one of the few senior UK public officials to approach the Scottish question with proper impartiality. He once memorably told a Commons committee that the Bank was the Central Bank of Scotland as well as of England and he would answer accordingly. Even more significantly he once told me in private about the sterling debate: 'Your problem, Alex, is what they [Westminster politicians] say now is entirely different from what they would say the day after a YES vote.'

I call this piece of wisdom the 'King dictum' for shorthand. He is, as always, well worth listening to and gives wise advice on how to tackle the currency question.

Day Fifty-Seven: Thursday 7 August

I am seldom disappointed by the predictability of Johann Lamont and Ruth Davidson at First Minister's Questions. And I'm not disappointed again today when they reprise Alistair Darling's currency argument from Tuesday.

However, the format is not the same and that sort of question is easily repelled. In addition I have done a fair degree of preparation. I quote for Johann's benefit Gordon Brown's doubts about the NO campaign's veto on the currency. Even better, I am able to quote Ruth against herself, since she had revealed to the *Sunday Post* that if currency union were in the interests of Scotland, she would argue for it. As I point out, this is a tad less dramatic than her own deputy Jackson Carlaw, who once said that in the event of independence he would 'man the barricades' to save the pound. Ruth makes the fatal mistake of trying to deny her own quote. Never something you should do when your opponent has the last word, as is inevitably the case in First Minister's Questions.

The relative ease with which the opposition leaders are seen off cheers up the back benches and gives me further resolve that we will deal with the question effectively come the second debate. It will be done on the front foot not the back foot. However, the issue kick-starting the campaign is more complex than giving good answers to bad questions. It is about seizing the initiative and dictating the agenda and moving the independence debate onto jobs and health.

This is the message I take to the campaign meeting, which today includes Andy Collier, the former political editor of the *Scottish Sun*. I use my experience at the STV debate to ram the point home: 'We have to break out of their old press agenda.'

In the evening I speak to a very enthusiastic audience at an Asian event in Edinburgh's Jewel Miners Club in Musselburgh. It's my first public meeting since the Commonwealth Games and Asian audiences are generally sympathetic. There is a very positive and confident response.

Day Fifty-Eight: Friday 8 August

The business of government goes on even as the future of the state is debated. I hold an early Resilience meeting in Bute House to address the impact of the developing trade war between Russia and the European Union.

Unfortunately for Scotland, the biggest single commodity affected by an import ban is pelagic fish. Scotland exports substantial quantities of herring and mackerel to Russia. It is a very big business indeed and impacts on one of the most successful parts of the fishing industry. We produced a framework for action which looks at the possibility of developing alternative markets and boosting the home market – perhaps using the expansion of school dinners as an opportunity to introduce young people to the delights of mackerel. It will make them brighter and probably live for ever if some of the research on omega and oily fish is to be believed.

The Resilience Committee is Scotland's equivalent of Westminster's Cobra. It used to be called the Emergency Room, but I didn't think it helpful to have the equivalent of a red flashing light over the door when you are trying to reassure the country that all is well. Thus it became the Resilience Room and Committee.

I prefer to have a very active Resilience profile, using the committee not just for flu pandemics or weather emergencies but to bring focus and attention to subjects requiring urgent action. Hence this meeting on the Russian import ban.

Meanwhile, the business of being a local MSP goes on even as the future of the State is being debated and I later hold a local surgery in the Town House in Strichen. In this I am in the very capable hands of Lisa Gordon, one of my constituency team who keeps my feet firmly planted on the Buchan earth on the basis that all politics is local.

Day Fifty-Nine: Saturday 9 August

The *Daily Mail* has the first post-debate poll, apart from that immediate snapshot.

Survation shows a 4 per cent swing to NO, leaving a gap of 57 to 43. Our estimates are just below these figures, but show us steadily gaining ground as opposed to losing it. The *Mail* is gleeful, believing the game is over. I think there is a long way to go.

Later, with a new member of my constituency staff, the former journalist Ann-Marie Parry, I go to a homecoming in Inverurie for our local medallists, swimmer Hannah Miley and wrestler Viorel Etko. There is a huge town centre reception followed by dinner at the legendary Mitchell's dairy and grocers. They've painted the coo outside the shop golden in honour of Hannah's success.

Who needs a golden post-box when you can have a golden coo! Ann-Marie gets some great copy for her first constituency assignment.

Day Sixty: Sunday 10 August

The first of our Scottish commemorative events for the First World War with a Drumhead Service on Edinburgh Castle esplanade. It's a moving and effective start to the programme.

However, the weather turns and the wreath-laying at Holyrood Park takes place in monsoon conditions. Despite that the old soldiers battle on. There is a noticeably favourable response to the fact that I am there in the downpour with them to lay the Scottish wreath.

After drying out, I take a phone call from Scotland's most celebrated historian, Tom Devine. I'm interviewing him at the Edinburgh Book Festival tomorrow and want to touch base. Tom confides that he is moving towards a YES declaration, but will not be announcing it tomorrow.

The latest YouGov poll shows NO at 60 to our 40 – no change from the one before the Commonwealth Games. On the one hand it doesn't show the same trend as Survation, on the other it means that, since the White Paper launch, we have only reduced the NO lead from 30 per cent to 20 per cent.

And we only have 40 days left.

Day Sixty-One: Monday 11 August

Another sell-out appearance at the Book Festival – and raspberries for the Queen.

The Festival is held each year directly opposite Bute House – in Charlotte Square, which is turned into a literary tented village. In my first year as First Minister I promised the then Director of the Festival that I would conduct an event every year. This is remarkable, since I have never written a book; loads of pamphlets, speeches and White Papers, but never a book. However, thanks to the ingenuity of the current director, Nick Barley, we have always managed to produce a sell-out event. My interviewing of key authors has been one of our démarches, and Tom Devine is good box office.

He talks well about politics for a historian. I speak well about history for a politician. Afterwards at lunch in Bute, Tom tells me he now intends to declare for YES, but on his own terms and probably in the *Observer*, where he respects the journalist Kevin McKenna. He also says he thinks the race is tightening considerably, fuelled by contempt for Westminster politics and the suffocating negativity of the NO campaign.

Moira and I go straight from lunch with Tom to dinner with the Queen at Balmoral. The weather is still ropey and we have to make a substantial detour to avoid the flooding, coming into Balmoral from Stonehaven.

I have never been late for the Queen before, and so, as a brainwave, we stop at Longleys Smiddy near Meigle, where Raymond and Sandra Norrie have produced the best berries in Scotland for many a year. Her Majesty is very understanding of our tardiness, noting that the Dee has risen to its highest level since 1914.

But what do you take as a gift for the woman who has everything? A few punnets of raspberries grown near Glamis Castle, the late Queen Mother's family home.

Her Majesty is delighted. We eat them for dinner.

Day Sixty-Two: Tuesday 12 August

Breakfast at Balmoral then back to business.

John Swinney chairs the Cabinet and leads the parliamentary debate on the economics of independence.

I meet the German Ambassador, who assures me of Teutonic neutrality, and then get together with the government economists, and Nicola and John, to discuss the release of the final report of the Fiscal Commission.

The Fiscal Commission working group is a committee of the Council of Economic Advisers, an idea I borrowed from America. Due to the work of a hugely talented young American special adviser, Jennifer Erickson, it was set up early in my first term of office. It combines business and economic expertise – all members give their time freely to advise on the Scottish economy. They have included no fewer than three Nobel laureates in economics and a number of other top-flight economists and business people. I often joke that Joseph Stiglitz chaired President Clinton's Council of Economic Advisers, but only gets to be a member in Scotland!

The Fiscal Commission includes both Stiglitz and fellow Nobel laureate James Mirrlees as well as the respected economists Andrew Hughes-Hallett and Frances Ruane, of Ireland's

Economic and Social Research Institute. It first presented the case for a sterling union in 2013 and this final report is the response to the various contributions which have been made.

In contrast to the serious work of the Commission, most, but not all, of the attacks on currency union have been low-grade and empty nonsense. A case in point is the attempt to compare the advantages or otherwise of a currency union between two countries of virtually identical productivity with the stresses and strains of maintaining a monetary union between totally divergent economies such as Germany and Greece.

A much more substantial criticism is whether being in a monetary union is compatible with national sovereignty or whether there is enough 'economic freedom' in a currency union to justify the process of becoming independent.

On this the Fiscal Commission has helpfully published a long list of economic powers that are unavailable to a devolved country, but available to an independent state – even one in a monetary union. These include fiscal policy, social security, competition policy, energy policy and a host of other key powers. In a celebrated exchange at First Minister's Questions earlier this year Labour leader Johann Lamont referred to these key economic powers as 'the wee things'. In economics, as in life, the wee things can often be important.

Day Sixty-Three: Wednesday 13 August

Looks like Scotland is about to pull off a successful double with the Games and the Ryder Cup. It would be nice to make it a treble in the referendum!

Attend the Ministerial Steering Group of the Ryder Cup at Gleneagles. It is to the Cup what the Strategic Group was to the Commonwealth Games. But it's an easier event to organise, largely because our partners in the European Tour are experienced at running dozens of events a year. Not on the same scale, of course, but nonetheless, under the likes of George O'Grady, James Finnigan, Richard Hills, Scott Kelly and tournament director Ed Kitsen, they are a highly professional outfit and a real pleasure to deal with.

At the meeting the Police Scotland representatives bask in the afterglow of a highly successful Games from a security perspective and give an upbeat assessment of preparedness. The electronic infrastructure, my key concern after the experience of Medinah, is near completion. On the last day at Medinah the information platform froze at key moments due to overload. I am determined that we avoid this in Gleneagles and just make the assumption that everyone will have a handheld device. The transportation arrangements, which everyone else has been worried about, are looking good, with Transport Scotland doing their usual sound job.

For the referendum to also hit the standard of the other two great events we will have to change both the focus and pace of the campaign.

I explained to the backroom team last week that it is not enough to be batting off fears about sterling and deposit flight from banks. We have to be talking the language of jobs and the health service and the difference it can make to control these things ourselves rather than being at the mercy of austerity and privatisation agendas set elsewhere.

With that in mind, I intend my set-piece BBC interview with Jackie Bird to launch this approach. As luck would have it Mark Carney chooses today to make his contingency assurance in terms of the role of the Bank of England. He does so in response to a question from the BBC's Kamal Ahmed. The press will interpret this negatively for YES but they are entirely wrong to do so. In fact the Governor is making explicit what was already implicit: the Bank will still be in charge on 19 September and has appropriate contingency plans.

However, despite this, I manage to pull off my objective in the interview. I embrace the Governor's comments, allocate responsibility to the NO campaign for the fears of the financial sector on capital flight, and spend the bulk of the interview explaining why the Health Service is under real threat from the Union and therefore why we are offering the constitutional guarantee of health care free at the point of need.

The real credit for this new approach on the health service, which I think will impact strongly in the campaign, should go to breast cancer surgeon and political newcomer Philippa Whitford, who first articulated this argument in a YouTube broadcast which has become an internet sensation. It is an argument that Health Secretary Alec Neil is already taking forward to full effect.

Day Sixty-Four: Thursday 14 August

First Minister's Questions are a rerun of the currency debate with the added spice of Mark Carney's 'contingency comments' and the financial meltdown headlines of the unionist press.

I clutch the Governor warmly to my bosom and accuse the Better Together alliance of promoting instability, while the Governor promotes stability – citing the very helpful comments of Anton Muscatelli, Principal of Glasgow University, who described the claimed currency veto as 'economic vandalism'.

In the afternoon, I meet US ambassador Matthew Barzun, and to make him feel at home I ask former American SPAD Jennifer Erickson to join us while she's on a visit from the United States. With reference to Obama's comments and his faltering backing for NO, I ask the ambassador directly how he would feel if I were to appear in the United States at the next presidential elections and declare for either the Democratic or Republican interest in a rallying call to Scots Americans.

I also point out that, given the substantial contribution, in terms of intellectual weight, made by Enlightenment Scots to the American Declaration of Independence, and the contribution in blood shed by Scots in the American Civil War, it seems poor treatment by an American administration towards a small country that has always been a staunch ally.

To make the point I take him on an impromptu visit to Calton Cemetery beside St Andrew's House, where next to the tomb of David Hume is the country's only statue to Abraham Lincoln, erected in memory of Scots who fell fighting in the Civil War.

I end the meeting by inviting the ambassador to the Ryder Cup and we wager a bottle of malt against bourbon on the outcome, of the Cup not the referendum!

Then up to the Marcliffe Hotel in Aberdeen for a YES fund-raiser. Thanks to the work of Elaine C. Smith as auctioneer, Stewart Spence as mine host and businessman Harvey Aberdein – Geoff's uncle – my messianic portrait by Gerard Burns is successfully auctioned. The event (not just the portrait) triumphantly raises £120,000.

Day Sixty-Five: Friday 15 August

On my way to Glasgow for the Team Scotland reception, I make a whole string of calls to sympathetic businesspeople to gather declared support for the campaign, buoyed by the success of the business dinner.

One of the most significant is Ralph Topping (recent CEO of William Hill and indeed Chief Executive of the Year). I've known Ralph as the independent chair of the Premier League in Scotland – he is straight and forthcoming. Now that he has retired he says he'll be delighted to speak up for a YES vote.

I also call Philip Grant of Lloyds to talk about the Governor's statement, since the CEO, Señor Antonio Horta-Osorio, is on holiday. We agree that it is a positive move and should help calm things down, at least in the absence of further political mischief-making.

The event at Kelvingrove for Team Scotland goes well, with vast crowds turning up to cheer the team. None of the squad can believe it is almost two weeks since the Games – they're all still walking on air.

I meet with Kenyon Wright at the Grand Central. Kenyon, who did more than anyone else to hold together the Constitutional Convention of the 1990s, is now a convinced advocate of independence. The father of devolution has become the grandfather of independence and understands probably better than anyone the difference between devolved authority and sovereign power.

The day ends with United Wholesale Grocers turning out a huge assembly of their customers and suppliers in the Kabana in Glasgow. It is a truly formidable display of YES support from the Asian business community. Mr Ramzan, as company chairman, makes a powerful and impressive speech. He is, it should be said, a decidedly better speaker than his brother, Mohammad Sarwar, Governor of the Punjab and former Labour MP.

Day Sixty-Six: Saturday 16 August

Get stuck into Australian Prime Minister Tony Abbott in a BBC interview. Of all the world leaders that Cameron has begged for support, Abbott is the biggest plonker.

This morning he suggests the 'enemies of democracy' worldwide would celebrate a YES vote. This is a barefaced cheek coming from the leader of a country which itself became independent from London. And in any case, Scotland is enjoying a festival of democracy.

Since I believe these interventions from the stands actually help the YES campaign, I'm usually pretty measured in my response. But I make an exception for this fawning Oxbridge-educated misogynist and let him have it with both barrels. It is after all the Australian way!

On the way up to Aberdeen on the train with Lorraine Kay I'm able to get a fair bit of work and a lot of thinking done. It's perplexing that we haven't as yet seen the same movement in the polls that I'm detecting on the ground. My hunch is that things are now closer than 60–40 and I'm waiting for MORI, System Three and particularly the next YouGov poll to start showing us closing. Perhaps it will require something like a big win in the BBC debate to get the polls really moving.

At a constituency barbecue in Inverurie later, hosted by Hamish and Mo Vernal. Hamish is the SNP Group leader on Aberdeenshire Council. The mood among our campaigners is increasingly optimistic. These are people who have been out doorstepping for the past two years and getting more and more encouraged by the reaction.

Day Sixty-Seven: Sunday 17 August

Happy with my performance on another talk-in show with Colin Mackay on Bauer Radio. Wonder if Alistair Darling is? He was on immediately before me and started fighting with the callers for no apparent reason. Perhaps the adrenalin they pumped into him in the first debate has its drawbacks.

Another interview, this time with STV, about how we're faring.

Our campaign meeting is still somewhat subdued but buoyed by news coming through of an 'interesting' YouGov poll tomorrow.

Day Sixty-Eight: Monday 18 August

It's the movement we have been waiting for. The first full YouGov poll since the debate shows a seven-point closing of the gap in less than two weeks – to 13 per cent.

And I'm in the perfect place to hit this result hard: the historic setting of Arbroath – 'as long as but a hundred of us remain alive we shall never submit to the domination of the London media'! The Scottish government events team led by the ever-resourceful Scott Rogerson have played a blinder.

I play foursomes at bowls with Commonwealth gold medallist Darren Burnett at the Abbey Bowling Club, the ancient ruin providing a dramatic background. The secret of winning bowling games is to pick your partners well.

We do the full round of interviews with the entire media pack in train – but they are much less impressed by the polls than I think they should be. The difficulty, of course, is that there have been a number of polls – Survation, Panelbase – which have shown closer figures. However, to my mind the YouGov poll is much more significant – showing movement in a poll which has not seriously shifted since the start of the year.

We hold the Cabinet meeting at Arbroath's St Andrew's Parish Church and a public discussion in the church hall. The metropolitan media should have stayed to watch the event. It is hugely well attended and very optimistic. YES supporters have their tails up but, even more significantly, loads of people just want information or reassurance about the prospects for an independent Scotland. The *Scottish Sun*'s Andrew Nicoll is one of the few journalists who stay. Not one of life's optimists, even this hugely experienced journalist is seriously impressed by the meeting.

I had asked David Middleton, the chief executive of Transport Scotland, up to Arbroath. I give him a lift back to Edinburgh so that I can speak to him directly about the need for his officials to grasp what a tourist opportunity the Borders Railway presents. David, whose team has enjoyed substantial success in great projects such as the Queensferry Crossing, takes it very well. We finish with a quick whisky toasting the painting in Bute House of Walter Scott's drawing room at Abbotsford. The toast is the new Waverley Line to the Borders.

Day Sixty Nine: Tuesday 19 August

A full breakfast meeting with chair of the Council of Economic Advisers Crawford Beveridge, John Swinney and Scottish government economists Professor Gary Gillespie and Graeme Roy. Graeme is flushed with his success as a key player of the Field Marshal Montgomery Pipe Band which has carried off the world championship laurels to Northern Ireland, yet again.

Crawford is launching the final report of the Fiscal Commission in the form of a lecture at Glasgow Caledonian this evening. He is composed and confident about the event and we run through the likely questions.

Off to the Dryburgh Abbey Hotel for dinner with Mike Cantlay, of VisitScotland, Councillor David Parker of Borders Council, and Peter de Vink, an independent Midlothian councillor as well as free-marketeer. Subject: the launch of our ideas for the Borders Railway. Mike is a good ally in getting government and agency enthusiasm behind the proposal, and we come up with a strategy which will have Scottish Enterprise convene a group, including VisitScotland and the Council, to drive this forward to success.

News comes through that Crawford ran into a spot of turbulence at his lecture in Glasgow. On being briefed on what he actually said it hardly justifies the puerile excitement of the *Telegraph* and *The Times*.

Day Seventy: Wednesday 20 August

Phone Crawford Beveridge to console him on some of the usual suspect press headlines and point out that his television interviews were excellent. Crawford, a hugely respected former chief executive of Scottish Enterprise, is apologetic, but has no reason to be. We are long past the stage where the looking-glass world of the unionist press can have much impact.

I embark on a series of announcements which is appropriate for the last day before purdah. The Borders Railway launch goes very well and, given the enthusiasm, commitment and knowledge of those assembled, I am sure it can be made to work.

Later, in North Berwick, East Lothian, we announce that, in combination with Aberdeen Asset, we are moving the Scottish Women's Open onto the same basis as the men's. That is, the Scottish tournament will take place on a fine links course the week before the Ladies' Open Championship. Highly appropriate given that the Scottish Parliament debate today is 'opportunities for women'.

As I play this fine old course, news comes through that Sir Ian Wood has unburdened himself of some pessimistic views on the future of the North Sea. Ostensibly his complaint is that the Scottish government has relied on the findings of an organisation called N24, which had released a very bullish report stating that North Sea reserves were underestimated.

However, although N24 is certainly run by YES sympathisers it is not a government organisation. The government view has always been to rely on the UK Oil and Gas estimate of 'up to 24 billion barrels' of recoverable reserves from the North Sea. This selfsame figure is quoted in Wood's own final report on North Sea oil, on page 7, where he suggests that if his conclusions are implemented there would be a 'low end' figure of 15 billion–16 billion barrels recoverable and a 'high end' closer to the 24-billion-barrel potential. This makes the sudden intervention of this respected businessman surprising to say the least.

I make two key phone calls. The first to Professor Alex Kemp, who is the real guru on oil and someone who I know considers the UK Oil and Gas estimate entirely reasonable. The second to the former BBC Europe correspondent Angus Roxburgh. I want Angus's help in preparing for the second debate.

Day Seventy-One: Thursday 21 August

I have an idea to save the threatened Ferguson Shipbuilders – and have been working on it with two of the shop stewards, Alex Logan and John McMunagle.

Blair Nimmo, of KPMG, has been appointed administrator for the Clyde's last commercial builder. He posted online a helpful comment last night and I want him to indicate that he would prefer bidders who intend to keep the yard working as opposed to those who might find the assets and the name of Ferguson useful, but wouldn't want the workforce. In particular I want his permission to visit the yard personally and see the workers. I need to assess their determination to save their plant. I have seen many industrial closures and some great successes. The one consistent factor about those that survive to prosper is that they have the ability, when faced with adversity, to still think like winners.

In preparation for First Minister's Questions, I take a call from Blair this morning to find out what the timescales are to pull a viable bid together. FMQs concentrate, predictably enough, on oil. But I have some good stuff, including material from BP expecting up to 27 billion barrels and from Alex Kemp predicting 16 billion–17 billion barrels over the period to 2050 – but also saying that 24 billion in total, including the years beyond 2050, is 'entirely plausible'. In that light, it doesn't seem unreasonable for the Scottish government to quote an industry estimate of up to 24 billion.

The afternoon provides a rousing end to the session. I propose the motion on independence, Nicola sums up and the debate ends well. Labour are reduced to near-hysteria as I spell out the argument that privatisation of the health service is a threat, not just to the English health service, but to Scotland. Malcolm Chisholm, normally a thoughtful MSP from Edinburgh Leith, suggests that no UK government would be elected on a programme to privatise the health service or introduce charging. The trouble is, this is exactly what Labour is alleging that the Tories are doing south of the border. I do hope that Alistair Darling takes this line on Monday.

The Scottish Parliament approves an independence resolution by 61 votes to 47. NBC describes this as a 'nominal vote' – an interesting choice of language when a national parliament passes a resolution supporting national independence!

The end-of-session Group meeting at 5.30 p.m., right after the debate, is an emotional and positive event. The MSPs are energised by the thought that the next time we meet in the Parliament, it could be in the wake of a YES vote. It is an inspiring thought to take with us out onto the campaign trail – that the next time we gather in the national parliament it will be to prepare for a free Scotland.

Reports from round the constituencies suggest that the canvassing is on a strong upswing and the YES campaign is taking off at local level.

Later, at the inaugural dinner of Business for Scotland in Glasgow, Gerard Burns's portrait of me raises an incredible £50,000 for the children's cancer charity CLIC Sargent.

Day Seventy-Two: Friday 22 August

I am able to give the Ferguson workers some real hope today.

They assemble at the Port Glasgow yard for a meeting where I can tell them that there are at least three bids for the yard – and I know that one of them has every intention of taking it over as a going concern.

I am also able to reveal that, within his terms of reference, the receiver has indicated that he will favour bids which maintain employment in the town. The shop stewards Alex and John are steady and impressive. One is a Celtic fanatic, the other favours Morton and Rangers, but they are holding their men together. The mood is sombre, but determined. In saying that, there is a fair amount of shipyard and graveyard humour on display. They're a really likeable bunch of people and I'm determined to do my absolute best for them.

I get a tour of the yard and go into a shed where the lifting cranes date from the early 1920s. It is a near-miracle that skilled men can turn out quality product with these machines. I remark that we'll need plenty of TV coverage to secure the yard.

'How about *The Antiques Roadshow*?' comes the rapid-fire response.

Much the best part of being First Minister is being in a position to occasionally help people who really deserve it. And that position takes several turns for the better during the day. First, the bus company brothers James and Sandy Easdale withdraw in favour of enterprising businessman Jim McColl, whose interest has become public. There are still two other bidders, but neither has approached the government for detail in the upcoming ferry contracts. That would tend to suggest that, whatever else they are doing, they are not considering building ships.

I arrange a meeting between Jim and the shop stewards for tomorrow morning at Glasgow Airport. A great deal now depends on the development of trust between them. If we have that then a solution could well be in reach, particularly as the receiver will be impressed by a serious offer which carries workforce support.

There are differing views on the wisdom of direct political intervention in industrial disputes. I have taken a highly interventionist stance, paticularly when there is the threat of closure. My logic is that you are very unlikely to do harm and could possibly do some good. In any case my experience tells me that market failure is far more prevalent than most suppose, and often there can be a total breakdown in relationships which can be helped by a genuinely honest broker.

As a constituency MP I can point to occasional successes over the years. As First Minister I have a lot more scope to step in and have often decided to do so. A case in point is the Grangemouth refinery. Twice as First Minister I have intervened in industrial disputes when I felt the future of the plant was at risk and the wider economy threatened. The second of these, in 2013, still involves unbreakable confidences. The first, in 2008, does not. The strike began on 27 April 2008 and lasted until 29 April. The fuel supply of Scotland was affected by the strike, as panic buying led some petrol stations across the country to run dry. BP's Kinneil terminal at that time relied on power from the Grangemouth refinery. With the shutdown of Kinneil, 70 North Sea oil platforms were forced to shut down or reduce production. Shutting the pipeline down reduced the petroleum supply and cost the UK economy an estimated £50 million in lost production for every day it remained closed.

As the two-day strike reached the point of no return, with the prospect of days, and potentially weeks, looming before the refinery would be back up and running, both Unite and the chemicals company INEOS showed signs of wanting to talk, since it became clear that union and company, refinery and chunk of the Scottish economy, might go over a cliff together. Tony Woodley, co-convener of Unite, and Jim Ratcliffe, Chief Executive of INEOS, met for the first time secretly in London and, rather amazingly, hit it off. Both from Liverpool, I seem to remember. What they needed was the DTI to stand behind an agreement – no money, just some honest brokerage. What they needed from me was to make this happen.

I contacted the Prime Minister, who gave me short shrift, so I announced a meeting in the press anyway. Under these circumstances Gordon Brown had little choice but to meet, which we did in the PM's office behind the Speaker's chair on Monday 28 April. Gordon spent the first ten minutes of the meeting complaining about the way I had bounced him into the meeting. The next ten were a lecture on why it was best not to intervene in industrial disputes. The final ten were a confessional on how he faced a 'poisonous legacy' (from Blair) and rumination on why I got such great publicity while his was so awful.

Finally, we got down to talking about Grangemouth, and it took a matter of minutes to agree on what needed to be done. The next day UK Business Secretary John Hutton and John Swinney went to Grangemouth and the dispute was settled.

I wasn't unsympathetic to Gordon's view on the 'poisonous legacy' and it was only one meeting, perhaps on a bad day. However, I left the meeting with a firm impression that this man was not in a fit state to be Prime Minister.

Back to the Hilton Hotel for debate preparation. This is a night-and-day difference compared with the preparation for the first debate. We know exactly the points we need to get across and spend our time productively in trying out lines to achieve that. With me are MP Angus Robertson and former MSP Duncan Hamilton, along with Tasmina Ahmed-Sheikh and Kevin Pringle. Also helping is journalist Angus Roxburgh, whose experience and skill take the line on Europe to a new level. It is often useful to get someone from outside to judge the best way to put across the arguments. I'm very happy with the way this is developing. The full dress rehearsal is set for Dundee on Sunday.

Later I meet representatives of the Jewish community who are concerned about a number of anti-Semitic incidents following the trouble in Palestine. The hard evidence is pretty sketchy and most documented abuse low-grade, but there is no mistaking their worries. I make a rapid succession of phone calls to the Lord Advocate, the Chief Constable and Communities Minister Humza Yousaf. These things always require immediate action and reassurance.

Visit my dad at Erskine Home before travelling to Inverness for the night.

Day Seventy-Three: Saturday 23 August

Back on the golf course, but it looks like we may have aced the Ferguson situation. I'm buoyed after taking a call from Jim McColl and the shop stewards. Given that I had spent a fair bit of time during the week promoting the shop stewards to Jim and Jim to the shop stewards, I was hoping they would hit it off. And they have. Big time! Progress could now be rapid towards a good outcome for the yard.

I meet a lovely American couple on the course at Castle Stuart. They're playing with hickory-shafted clubs and playing really well. At the last hole, I ask why my new friends haven't mentioned politics.

'Ah,' says the gentleman, 'we saw you on the news last night at that shipyard, but figured if you wanted to talk politics you would have raised the subject.'

Day Seventy-Four: Sunday 24 August

Full-scale debate preparation, and this time I'm looking forward to the showdown – even after getting drenched in the Ice Bucket Challenge.

It is probably right that we stage the rehearsal in the Apex Hotel in Dundee. We chose it for the convenience of all involved in the team, but I have a warm feeling towards the place, given that our leadership team devised the overall strategy for winning the 2007 election there. And Dundee is shaping up for the biggest YES vote in the country.

There was a key moment in our preparations for 2007 which summed up the change in approach of the SNP. Under Clare Howell's guidance we were having a leadership bonding session. As part of the exercise we all had to nominate who we thought was the most positive person in the room. To a person we all nominated Jim Mather, the party's business spokesperson and later the Scottish government's Business Minister.

Jim, however, nominated me. He confided later that he wouldn't have done it previously. 'You believing we can win doesn't guarantee success,' he said to me. 'But if you don't believe it then it guarantees failure.'

I decided there and then that I had spent too much time in politics behaving like an opposition politician and too little presenting what the SNP would do in government. It was a mistake I corrected and corrected in full.

First, before the debate preparation, we get down to some real business. The Ice Bucket Challenge is proving an internet sensation. Even Alistair Darling tried it at the weekend, though he looked somewhat less than comfortable. Getting dooked in

Dundee offers two great advantages. First a chance to wear my Black Watch polo team outfit – I'd been looking for a use for it since Martin Gilbert sent me it from South America.

Second, I get the opportunity to nominate David Cameron for a soaking, because I know he won't do it, and Nicola Sturgeon, because I know she will. She's there with me and therefore has no choice!

Once we dry out it is time to prepare for turning up the heat on Darling. Round the table are Nicola, her special adviser the enigmatic Noel Dolan, Geoff Aberdein, Kevin Pringle, Stewart Nicolson, Duncan Hamilton and Tasmina Ahmed-Sheikh.

Duncan, the former MSP and talented advocate, plays Darling as we stage a proper dress rehearsal complete with podiums and the likely layout of Kelvingrove. Kevin, our lead press man, who has been with me on this political journey longer than anyone else, suggests with a dry wit: 'Of course, Alex, we all know that you only lost the first debate to win the expectations game for the second one. In terms of press expectations, we are now in a great position!'

The rehearsal goes well. Tasmina, who has substantial film experience, is first-rate with advice on style, camera angles and presentation. We decide to incorporate the best things from the first debate with a distinct change of strategy for the second. Thanks to Angus's work on Friday, I have worked out a crisp line on Europe. However, the most important aims to come out of this rehearsal are to seize the initiative on currency very early to unsettle Darling, and to nail his defence of the Tories on the health service as being a more general indication of the Better Together, Tory/Labour establishment alliance.

On the former Duncan is brilliant. On the latter, Nicola and Noel are very effective. Kevin and Stuart want me to pin down Darling on job-creating powers for the Parliament – a simple enough question which they believe he will be incapable of answering.

This is going to play out well (I hope).

Day Seventy-Five: Monday 25 August

It plays out very well indeed! Perhaps down to Lucozade. I go in swinging and Darling ends up on the ropes.

The Kelvingrove in Glasgow turns out to be a magnificent venue. It always looks great, but normally it is a challenging place to speak because of the cavern-like effect on sound. To be fair to the BBC technicians, they had it sorted by creating a *Question Time*-style audience space in the heart of the main hall.

The audience starts out opinion-poll-balanced, but ends up very heavily pro-YES. The key to the debate is my seizing of the currency issue from the very first question – on the economy. I go straight out from behind the lectern, leaving Alistair stranded like a beached whale. It was the tactic which worked well in the latter part of the first debate, and this time I pursue it from the off, and I quickly establish a rapport with the audience.

After my comprehensive explanation on the currency, every time Alistair subsequently pursues it he comes across as a one-trick pony. The audience eventually start groaning when he raises it, while his admission that 'of course you could use the pound' provides the icing on the cake. With his best lines preempted, Alistair can't do anything right and comes up with precisely nothing. The longer the debate goes on, the worse things become for the Better Together game plan.

By the time we get to job-raising powers he is blethering, and the more agitated he gets the more the fingers start pointing and the worse his body language becomes. He even starts petulantly fighting with the audience. His attack on our health service argument comes across as a defence of Tory stewardship. When a lady starts to question him on his paid speeches for private health contractors there is no hole big enough in the Kelvingrove into which Alistair can dive.

During the debate I am conscious that this is now more than a contest between two politicians. At stake are two different attitudes towards Scotland. Alistair is in the same country as that Labour canvasser at my father's door all of these years ago, all about what Scotland couldn't do. That is his secure space, but this night in front of this audience that country is no-man's-land. I finish the debate – as we need to climax the campaign – with a positive appeal to Scotland's potential and self-belief.

When we walk off stage and back to the green room Geoff does not say anything. He clenches his fists, hugs me and, after an eternity, lets me go. He is crying.

I took just one artificial aid into the debate with me, Lucozade. When I was a boy singer I used to insist on a copious supply of it to provide instant energy and clear my larynx. I did the same thing for the debate, perhaps subconsciously understanding that this would help generate an inner confidence. When the debate was over I noticed that there was one bottle left and I drank it in a single go. The bottle had a

Lucozade YES logo on it, which caused much hilarity in the campaign team. They duly tweeted a picture of me holding the bottle.

Later at Glasgow's Oran Mor (Gaelic for 'big voice') the YES team gather to watch the debate and I enter – through the wrong door – to a hero's reception. I deliver a rousing rallying call for the rest of the campaign. It is clear the team are on a debate-induced high.

By the time we get to the Alishan restaurant, the ICM flash poll shows a landslide result of 71–29, with women, the undecideds and Labour voters all overwhelmingly favourable. In contrast to the first debate where the NO voters thought Alistair won and the YES voters thought the opposite, this time even the NO voters think we've carried the day.

Result! All is now possible.

Day Seventy-Six: Tuesday 26 August

At Fergusons this morning with the workforce in an exultant mood and think to myself: How I'd love the referendum to take place here and now in this shipyard.

I woke up to a *Good Morning Scotland* interview with Jim McColl, who has been named as the preferred bidder for the yard. Later, during the visit, the workers come out to meet me at virtually no notice. Just about all of them know the score with the shipyard and indeed had watched the debate, and they're on a high. It is quite a contrast. Last Friday I was there keeping the spirits up. Now I am keeping them steady.

This is how the Press Association covers my visit:

Afterwards he [that's me] cautioned there could still be 'anxious' times ahead, adding: 'It will be two weeks at least before work is restarted at this yard. There are a lot of negotiations still to go forward with Clyde Blowers, the preferred bidder.'

But he stressed: 'The government's up for these negotiations, the stewards here are up for these negotiations and the morale of the workforce is moving in a very positive direction. These people have stuck together, they deserve to win and there's every indication that they're substantially on the way to a victory.'

He said Clyde Blowers Capital was a 'great choice' for preferred bidder, describing the firm as a 'company with a great track record of creating jobs in Scotland, building companies up, exactly what's needed'.

Will these fine people save their shipyard? Yes, I think they will. The advantage they have is that this is as steady a group of shop stewards as I have come across. They have as a prospective owner one of Scotland's greatest job creators. I now rate their chances as very high.

Lunch with Moira and Joseph Stiglitz in Edinburgh at Ondine. As well as being a Nobel laureate economist, Joe really is a first-rate guy. He batted off the press effortlessly at an event in the Book Festival. The great advantage of having a first-rate mind is that you can see the trick questions coming before they are even asked. Professor Gary Gillespie, the Scottish government's Chief Economist, gives a humorous account of the intellectual mismatch of the Scottish press corps and this

Nobel laureate. If it had been a boxing match the referee would have stopped the fight after question three!

In speaking to Joe I am reminded of another Joe, NBC's Joe Scarborough, whose morning talk show I appeared on earlier this year. With total American confidence, talk-show Joe threw me by asking the question: 'Why on earth would anyone in Scotland NOT vote for independence?'

Listening to Joseph Stiglitz today is an economics lecture version of the same experience. Scotland, as economics Joe points out, has high productivity, great industries, world-class universities, substantial human capital, an extraordinarily positive international branding and strong natural resources. Clearly we would be one of the top-performing countries in Europe as an independent state. So why on earth would anyone NOT accept that Scotland would be successful economically as a country?

Joe tells us he has been following the referendum debate and wishes us every good fortune, since, he says, we deserve to win. It is probably the first directly political thing he has ever said to me.

I take some time to study press coverage of the big TV debate, which is universally good with the exception of the *Daily Telegraph*, who have decided that their man Darling must have fallen victim to a BBC conspiracy. They're right, of course, that there is a BBC conspiracy – just wrong about its direction.

At the campaign meeting later the atmosphere has now changed totally. Confidence is flowing and a quick-fire range of initiatives is laid out to create the momentum we now feel lies within our grasp.

Day Seventy-Seven: Wednesday 27 August

Sean Connery is in a mood of high excitement when I call him – after he has watched the head-to-head on the BBC.

I had decided to strike while the debating iron was hot and made a series of calls looking for further endorsements and support. Sean would dearly love to make a late appearance in the campaign – and we talk about the possible logistics of that. Sean is always good value, insightful and passionately interested in the progress of the campaign. He speaks about Darling's demeanour as the debate went on and says that 'He looked like he'd lost half a crown and found a sixpence.'

An anti-independence letter from the usual business suspects gets ludicrously big licks from the BBC. Auntie has been under fire from the *Telegraph* and the *Daily Mail* on the silly Better Together line that they had stacked the debate against NO. The over-reporting of this non-news story looks like the BBC trying to get back into the fold. At any rate we'll see how they report the 200 YES business supporters when their counter-letter is released tomorrow.

Two great campaign stories enliven the day. First, perhaps the most disastrous political broadcast of all time: Better Together's campaign advert featuring a hapless woman finding politics all a bit complicated is becoming an internet sensation. It is as distant from modern Scotland and modern Scottish women as dancing around the maypole is to contemporary England. Without their faithful prop of an ever-obedient old unionist press, this campaign of total duffers would collapse in a heap.

Second, news breaks that the CBI have had to cut back on expenditure on alcohol at their annual dinner to stay within the referendum rules given their hokey-cokey support of the Better Together campaign. First they were in. Then they were out. Now they have no permissible expenditure left to shake the booze about at their dinner. It will be Irn-Brus all round!

Day Seventy-Eight: Thursday 28 August

Try to get celebrity endorsements from two key figures in the world of sport and music.

Phone Scotland and Celtic captain Scott Brown, who has developed into a very considerable footballer. Scott normally wears his heart on his sleeve on and off the pitch and is a YES supporter. However, his contract negotiations with Celtic are at a delicate stage and he is under pressure not to make a political declaration.

Equally sensitive is the call to singer Amy Macdonald, who has just moved to a new record label and is also under pressure not to make a political statement. Amy is a passionate YES supporter and tells me the proudest moment of her life was in belting out 'Flower of Scotland' before a Scotland game at Hampden Park.

Both of these people are truly likeable and gifted, and their support would mean a great deal. However, if they feel under pressure, what must it be like for the ordinary Scot? If I had to guess, of the two it will be Amy who goes public. At any rate, Scotland will need every declaration possible over the next three weeks. She needs all her daughters and all her sons.

Where we do have tremendous support is in the breadth of the business community. This is illustrated on a visit to Foxlane Garden Centre in Aberdeen, where I meet some ardent YES backers. Our list of business supporters, led by Brian Souter, Jim McColl and George Mathewson, is impressive – but what is even more impressive is the range and scope of the businesses: from Footsie 100 to the Foxlane Garden Centre.

On every key area we are now starting to function as an integrated campaign.

Later at the Marcliffe Hotel there's a photo-call with Aberdeen (and Rangers, Cardiff, Dundee and Scotland) footballer Gavin Rae. He is an engaging and intelligent man and is off to the Australian Gold Coast for a coaching job. I promise to visit during the next Commonwealth Games. He has become interested in the YES campaign like many of the sporting endorsements through the campaigning work of Michael Stewart, one of the few fitba players to become both a Hearts and a Hibernian legend.

But the best part of the day comes with a visit to Garthdee Community Centre. Garthdee is one of the big working-class schemes in the Granite City. This isn't just so I can sing along with their community choir (and play the drums), but also to get a view of the progress of the debate from the community workers in the centre. One wise lady tells me: 'You do realise that around here at least you are almost home.'

From Aberdeen to Edinburgh …

Day Seventy-Nine: Friday 29 August

Our campaign plan involves moving the focus onto jobs, health and education, and the ambition which independence can unleash in Scotland. Post-BBC debate the dire warnings on currency and Europe look distant and flimsy. The key to winning this is to keep our agenda moving.

Kick off the day with an interview on *Good Morning Scotland*. Gary Robertson is being a bit nippy, but I'm in such a good mood I don't really care. Then on to the *Call Kay* programme where, when the subject of anti-English feeling is raised, I take the opportunity to remind listeners that the BBC had once held an entire phone-in based on a purported tiny rise in anti-English recorded crime. It then turned out the real figures had actually fallen – and it was anti-Scottish hate crime that was on the rise. At that time there was no apology, no retraction, no response from the BBC. They just ploughed on with their own agenda oblivious to the reality of the world around them.

This is the first time this subject of anti-English feeling has been raised with me in the entire referendum, which would suggest that, outside the strange land inhabited by the BBC, it is a total non-issue.

Our theme is nursery education and I visit the TimeTwisters play centre in Sighthill, Edinburgh, to highlight our independence childcare plan which will save families almost £5,000 per child per year.

The media turnout is huge and I take my shoes off to go into the soft play area with the kids. Such is the press scrum that I do most of my interviews and dozens of selfies in my socks!

My passion for nursery education and the reason it appears so prominently in the YES campaign stems from the work of a wonderful feminist economist, the late Ailsa Mackay. It was Ailsa who convinced me that affordable and universal nursery provision was not just a good idea (which just about everyone supports) but one of the essential economic strategies for developed democracies.

Now, when I think about it, the reasoning is so clear and obvious that I just cannot understand why it took Ailsa's persistence to drum it into me. In common with most other developed democracies Scotland faces a demographic challenge. Sometimes this is hugely overrated – a fairly persistent mistake of the Institute of Fiscal Studies – but it is nonetheless a reality for Scotland as for most of Europe. Put at its simplest, the number of people of working age is declining relative to the overall population.

There are a variety of approaches to this, all of which I have advocated. We should have a much more liberal attitude to immigration and we should not just allow but encourage overseas students to use their acquired skills in our economy. We need to raise productivity to make sure that each worker is contributing as much as possible to economic output, and we have to eliminate the scourge of youth unemployment.

However, one of the answers has been staring us in the face: to use all of the skills of our current working-age population. This would lead to a sharp rise in female employment. The key to unlocking this potential is nursery and childcare provision.

The Scottish government has made substantial moves in that direction by increasing the hours of free nursery education available by 50 per cent to 600 hours per year per child, and by a joint campaign with the trade unions in breaking down barriers in the workplace. But what we really need is a revolution: free universal nursery and childcare, flexible but equivalent to school hours, from the age of two. Ailsa herself made a presentation to the Council of Economic Advisers to secure backing for this radical approach. What I didn't know at the time was that she took on this task in the full awareness that she was suffering from a fatal condition. It was simply one of the most impressive and bravest individual commitments I have ever witnessed.

As a result this has become something of a personal as well as a political passion for me. I decided to put it at the centre of the independence argument. The point is that the initiative will be much more affordable when increased revenues from greater economic activity are flowing into the Scottish Exchequer, rather than being sent down south to be wasted by George Osborne.

Early indications from our first faltering steps in nursery education are impressive. Scotland has already soared up the European rankings in terms of female employment. There are all sorts of other benefits from this transformation, including a substantial move to equality of opportunity. However, when the revolution comes, as it will, it will stand as a testimony to the work of Professor Ailsa Mackay.

After being reunited with my shoes I go campaigning in Stenhouse Cross. The weather is awful, but the reception warm, with lots of toots of encouragement from passing motorists and a strong and passionate turnout of YES activists.

Lunch with Pat Cox, one of Ireland's European grandees and former President of the Parliament. Pat is a solid friend of Scotland and one of many European figures who have been perplexed by the Barroso line, and he has prepared a rebuttal. Pat has fought more referendums in Ireland than just about any other politician. His assessment is that ours is now on a knife-edge but that in his considerable experience momentum is all.

He tells me that the word in Brussels is that Barroso had been hopeful of securing UK and US support to become the new NATO Secretary General. Now that the job has gone to Jens Stoltenberg (the former Norwegian prime minister and previous critic of NATO and nuclear weapons), he will show much less enthusiasm for kowtowing to London on Scotland and, indeed, on European policy in general. Pat says however that the key task is for the future, and we discuss our detailed European preparations for a YES vote.

I also meet Tom Farmer, someone for whom I have enormous respect and who carries real authority in the business community. Tom had backed the SNP financially in 2007 when he felt we needed support to even up the battle, but declined in 2011 when he felt we were running away with the election. A long-term devo max supporter, he is on the cusp of a pro-independence declaration. He tells me he has refused all pressure to come out for NO and certainly will not do so. However, he is still swithering about a public declaration for YES.

Day Eighty: Saturday 30 August

Get a sense today of how our activists are building a strong network from the YES shops which are springing up like flowers across the country. These are spontaneous decisions at grassroots level. They are emerging so fast that YES Scotland do not even have a record of many of them. Some have their origins in the SNP but many are a physical manifestation of the social media campaigns led by the National Collective, Women for Independence and the Radical Independence Group.

We're campaigning in Ellon, where the activist base is in great form with confidence flowing like a river. I officially open the YES hub which is one of the SNP-inspired offices.

The council estate in Ellon is rock-solid and hardening to YES. However, when we get to one of the new estates near Inverurie, the response is more mixed. Some real enthusiasm, but also concerns. One worker tells me Charlie Ritchie, owner of Score Group Engineering in Peterhead, had called his apprentices in to tell them that they would all be looking for a job following a YES vote. He then says his grandfather had told him that this had been the favoured tactic of the local lairds with their tenants and farmhands and adds: 'Even if there were no other argument, I'm now voting YES.'

Day Eighty-One: Sunday 31 August

This week we've decided to target undecided voters with a simple tactic – letters inviting them to a public meeting. I'm doing Dundee, Perth, Falkirk and Kilmarnock combined with a sweep through the borders and finishing in Ayrshire.

Today, though, is virtually free and I'm at home in Strichen. I have a two-way interview on Sky's *Murnaghan* with Labour's Jim Murphy, whose sole contribution to the campaign has been to complain about being 'egged'. In Mr Murphy's twilight world, his dry-cleaning bill has become the story of the campaign. In the dungeons of the London media he is their hero of the streets. In reality, if you are not careful he turns up at your local street corner and starts shouting and winding people up. In the interview, Murphy is keen to emphasise that he is 'no coward'. It reminds me of the first meeting I had with him when he was briefly Secretary of State for Scotland and he made a point of saying he wasn't 'scared' of me. I suppose people who are very anxious to say they are neither cowards or scared usually have a reason.

According to my Labour Party friends, Mr Murphy is not really interested in the referendum. He is out of favour in London and is eyeing Johann Lamont's job in Scotland. If so, they are daft. She is worth ten of him.

I take the opportunity to advertise a website I came across the other day called Still Raining, Still Dreaming. It has a hilarious blow-by-blow account of Murphy bawling at Stonehaven. It also carries a football graphic of the line-up on either side of this campaign, which I rather like. On one side there is a combination of the unacceptable establishment and the just plain unacceptable. On the other a combination of progressive parties and grassroots movements for change. All rather appropriate since, for the public meetings this week, I am developing a theme of the 'Hampden Roar' which will shake the establishment to its foundations.

Finally back in Moira's good books as we manage a late lunch at her favourite restaurant Eat on The Green, in Udny Green, with North East fishing legend Willie Tait and his lovely partner Ya Chu.

Day Eighty-Two: Monday 1 September

For the first time in the campaign I'm close to tears after being humbled by an amazing sight of ordinary people queuing in the street.

Headed up to Dundee with my former office manager Lynsey-Anne Marwick, who is quite simply the most positive person I have ever met. She is a joy to campaign with.

Amid all the hurly-burly of the high-visibility campaigning and street responses, I come across something truly extraordinary which encapsulates everything that is happening now at community level.

There's a queue of people waiting patiently for the forms to register to vote. I chat with one guy, perhaps in his mid-forties. He tells me he had never voted, had no interest in voting, thinks politicians are a bunch of complete chancers (that is a translation), but now there is something worth voting for. He says to me he thinks it is one of the most important things he has ever done and that lots of people just like him feel exactly the same way.

As I reflect on this on the way to a meeting in the Dundee Mosque, I consider that this could be my most significant conversation of the campaign thus far. Indeed it could be the most important conversation of my life in politics. For the first time, I feel tears welling up.

It is one of the most humbling moments I have ever experienced.

Here we have ordinary folk queuing up in the sun in Dundee to register for the vote. It is the essence of democracy, the essence of determination: people thinking about something bigger than themselves. At that moment I think: we're almost there. Something special is happening.

At the mosque, I have a question-and-answer session and lunch and then talk to the guys also running a registration stall at the door after prayers. They report a brisk business.

An interesting joint photo-call with supporters of Dundee's two football teams. It takes place in the street between Dens Park and Tannadice, with sports commentator Jim Spence. They are the closest two stadiums in the country and now the YES campaign has united them in common cause.

Back at the SNP offices, I'm scheduled for an interview with the *Courier*, but the people in the factory across the road spot me and ask me to pay their premises an impromptu visit, which I happily do. The Dundee campaign is superbly marshalled by local MSPs Joe Fitzpatrick and Shona Robison, and Shona's husband Stewart Hosie. If the whole country is moving like this city then we are home and dry.

Interview at Radio Tay. The station's Ally Ballingall tells me that, during my last Sunday phone-in which they were coordinating from Dundee, they had an emergency when someone broke in and tried to wreck the station. More a mental health issue than a political one, but a tribute to the professionalism of Radio Tay for keeping the show on air.

This is the first of the undecided voters meetings – in Perth. It's packed to the gunnels, the atmosphere is electric, the questions funny and engaging and the meeting long. It is true, of course, that many committed campaigners joined the uncommitted voters in the audience. However, even if this audience is half and half, then we are well on our way. It would be inconceivable if what I am now feeling on the streets is not reflected soon in the major polls.

I drop Lynsey-Anne off at her mother's house in Tayport, Fife, and head off to St Andrews for the night. As I go into the Fairmont Hotel, the concierge winks at me and folds down his lapel to proudly display a YES Scotland badge.

I'd tried earlier today to persuade Nick Nairn to join us. Whatever else happens in an independent Scotland, we will not be short of a good meal. Just about every great chef in the country – including Andrew Fairlie, Roy Brett, Albert Roux and Colin Clydesdale – has come out for YES. Nick would have completed the nap hand but, despite it having been a sympathetic call, he has just opened a new business and is steering clear of controversy.

The day is topped off when I turn on the midnight *Sky News*, which leads with a 'sensational' YouGov poll.

Day Eighty-Three: Tuesday 2 September

Good news: the sensational poll shows the gap at its narrowest yet for YouGov. Possible good news: Henry McLeish may come over to YES.

The poll is major. In the space of a month and over three polls, the gap has closed from 22 points to 14 and now to a mere 6. I consult with our polling guru John MacInnes. John is quickly onto the trends. He says that the big movement is among women voters and young people. Older voters are still against by large margins but we are not losing ground in any group. He thinks we could hit the front by the last weekend. That trend and particularly that timescale is music to my ears. The poll means there is a formidable press turnout when I go to open the Eden Mill Distillery and Brewery near St Andrews, a fascinating new project which combines real beer with a new distillery. There is also a big turnout of YES campaigners who have heard I was coming to Guardbridge and just wanted to be there. I speak to them before starting my tour of the distillery. Some have been there for a couple of hours waiting for me to arrive.

The BBC has sent Nick Robinson, a sure sign of panic back at ground control, and we do an interview which heavily features sterling – as if the debate with Alistair Darling had never even taken place. If we leave to one side my feelings about the BBC and their demonstrable bias against the SNP and independence, then why do they feel compelled to transport network journalists with inevitably less knowledge when they have in Brian Taylor an experienced political editor who has forgotten more about the Scottish constitutional question than his London colleagues will ever learn? I think Brian would be perfectly capable of explaining matters to a network audience.

The momentum of the day continues with news that Stephen Gallacher has claimed one of the captain's wildcards in the Ryder Cup team. There are moments when you feel that the stars are coming into alignment.

Lunch at the Balbirnie House Hotel, near Markinch, Fife, with former First Minister Henry McLeish after stopping off to meet the people who have set up yet another ad hoc YES shop in the town. Henry has been a model example of how a former FM should behave, always making himself available for chairing good causes and producing excellent reports on subjects as diverse as criminal justice and the future of Scottish football. It was Henry who had first advised that Ralph Topping, formerly of William Hill, would be amenable to backing a YES vote, and today, in addition to discussing a range of Henry's contributions, I want to persuade him to follow suit. I ask Tasmina Ahmed-Sheikh to join us. She sits on the Glasgow Colleges Board with him and carries the trust that might help Henry to declare his hand.

Henry asks for more time to think about things but is clearly torn between loyalty to party and country. He does concede that he is finding the fence an increasingly uncomfortable place to sit on.

After a quick interview with Kingdom FM we drive to Bo'ness for a spot of high-visibility campaigning outside the local YES hub. I delight a large crowd and many passers-by when I tell them that my mother was born in Bo'ness and, despite what they may have read about my attachment to my home town, and their fierce local rivals, Linlithgow, this was really my genuine homecoming. I then announce a competition between Bo'ness and Lithgae on who will achieve the highest YES vote.

Before we leave, the mother of the young YES worker Callum Timms, who had organised the visit, quietly asks for some signed memorabilia for a memory box which she intends to give him after the referendum. She tells me how proud she is of her son.

We drive on to the Park Hotel in Falkirk for another undecideds meeting. YES campaign chairman Dennis Canavan is in charge and totally in his element (this is his old stomping ground). It is another huge gathering. The confidence of the campaign is extraordinary. Health and safety would have something to say about the numbers crowded into the Park main hall.

During the meeting I'm giving it laldy about the queue in Dundee patiently awaiting their registration forms and claiming their right to vote.

'I saw in the great city of Dundee only yesterday something extraordinary, something that I thought I would never see in a lifetime in politics. There in the City of Dundee I saw something unbelievable ...'

'A Tory!' comes a heckle from the Falkirk audience.

Again for an undecideds meeting, there are many people pretty committed, but the feedback from the surveys also shows a big movement to YES.

Following the meeting I leave with Campbell Gunn to take in a photo-call at the *Daily Record*. Up until now the *Record* has not been too unreasonable given that the paper is effectively controlled by the Labour establishment. They need to be careful given the make-up of their readership. At the start of this campaign around 40 per cent of *Record* readers were YES voters. Now it will be over half. It will be interesting to see which way the paper jumps as the polls tighten and things come to the touch.

As part of this more fair-minded approach, editor Murray Foote has asked me to edit one edition while the NO campaign edits another. It is a good and interesting initiative and I accept with alacrity.

After the *Record*, I arrive at the BBC with no time to spare to do a feature interview with BBC's *Scotland 2014* programme. Not a bad interview, and afterwards the chat shows there is a real change of mood among the Beeb journalists. It has finally dawned on them that the game is afoot.

On the way back to Bute, I phone Jim McColl to check that all is moving along with Fergusons. It is.

Day Eighty-Four: Wednesday 3 September

In the Borders, probably our most challenging area. Not because of a lack of SNP voters – there are plenty. It is the lack of Labour voters who are rapidly defecting to the YES campaign that makes the Borders difficult to win for us. So, I'm really encouraged to find enthusiastic crowds gathered outside the new YES offices in Penicuik and Peebles.

In Penicuik, I make two speeches – one inside, one outside – so everyone can hear. I also meet a lovely family. Young Isaac who is fighting leukaemia, his big brother Tadhg and their terrific mum Ruth. They are all totally committed to the YES campaign. I spend a fair bit of time with them. Amid the manic pace of the campaign it is sometimes important to pause and be reminded that if YES stands for anything at all it stands for hope.

On the way to Ayrshire we visit Whitmuir organic farm at West Linton for a different style of campaigning and an interview with Peter MacMahon, of Border Television. Splendid people at a special place which has generated substantial employment in this rural area.

While there, I make a call to Niels Smedegaard, of DFDS Seaways, after getting information that they are about to announce the cancellation of the Rosyth Ferry. I successfully ask Mr Smedegaard for a stay of execution so we and Forth Ports can put together a joint proposal to maintain Scotland's only direct ferry link with the Continent. After some debate he agrees.

Straight to a bakery business in an industrial estate in Kilmarnock where another large crowd has gathered spontaneously. Super photograph of me with two AYE cupcakes for eyes. My view is not to be too precious about these things. When in doubt I look to Allan Milligan, the doyen of the photographers' pack, to give me the nod. If Allan says OK, then I go ahead. In this case Allan nods.

At the briefing I give *Telegraph* journalist Ben Riley-Smith a packet of liquorice allsorts for good attendance at every press event. He always appears with pen at the ready desperately hoping for a mistake to be made. He takes exception so I give them to the campaign kids gathered outside instead. I take his tetchiness as a sign that morale is not as it should be in the *Telegraph* bunker, a subdivision of the NO campaign.

At the Park Hotel beside Kilmarnock FC ground Rugby Park, I tell another huge gathering not to be worried about Westminster claims of a veto on the use of sterling by recounting a true story about a peer of the realm who came to see me in St Andrew's House.

In came the peer of unionist persuasion, but of humble origins, and retaining a tendency for shipyard language:

> You know me, Alex, I am a [expletive deleted] unionist. But, if that [expletive deleted] Osborne says one more [expletive deleted] time that we can't use our own [expletive deleted] pound when we invented the [expletive deleted] Bank of [expletive deleted] England and just about every other [expletive deleted] thing, then I will come and [expletive deleted] join your [expletive deleted] bunch.

This story obviously fascinates a member of the audience since, fully two hours of speaking and selfies later, he comes up to me and says: 'I know who it was.'

'Who what was?' I reply.

'That peer of the realm,' he says confidently. 'It was Willie Haughey.'

'Named that man in one,' I lie!

Day Eighty-Five: Thursday 4 September

Nicola is getting increasingly bullish about the YES prospects in Glasgow. And, after experiencing the street campaigning today, I can understand why.

We meet to discuss our week of meetings around the country. In Buchanan Street a vast number of people formed a giant ring so that they could be addressed by us both. The press contingent was huge too, and the campaign shows all the signs of being on the move forward.

It was a real struggle finding a spot to do television interviews given the hubbub, but we managed to keep it all good-natured and under reasonable control. At least, as far as the campaign is concerned. The journalists got pretty jumpy, with near stand-up fights between the photographers and the TV crews.

While this was going on, further good news was coming through of a YES vote by RMT members in Scotland. It is interesting to note that the unions that have fully consulted their members have either come out for independence, or in the case of UNISON, remained neutral. Perhaps company bosses should take a lesson in democratic consultation from the RMT.

One small incident was of interest as we left. A couple of NO campaigners did some in-your-face stuff with placards. It wasn't a real problem since there were only two of them. However, I found out later that at least one of them was a paid organiser in Glasgow. The point is obvious: when you have to send out paid organisers to attempt to disrupt your opponents' press events, you must be very, very short of people on the ground.

Back to Bute for a Resilience meeting on the raising of the terror level by the UK government. It isn't clear what specifically provoked this step, and after the meeting and briefing I am still none the wiser.

A phone call with Stephen Gallacher to congratulate him on his selection for the Ryder Cup. He is in the midst of a family issue, with his grandmother gravely ill, but still takes the time to speak to me. He will be a fine representative for Europe and Scotland.

The campaign meeting is very happy. The most recent canvassing and online figures show us neck-and-neck with NO – but with the trend moving in our direction. If we keep doing what we're doing and do it well, we should overtake them by the last weekend. By then hopefully it will be too late for them to stop the forward momentum.

Head back to Strichen after a YES fund-raising dinner at the Locanda De Gusti in Edinburgh. Pleasant end to a busy day.

Day Eighty-Six: Friday 5 September

A fishing industry meeting at the Peterhead Port Authority auction hall. The harbour at Peterhead has always been blessed with good and progressive local chairs and chief executives, and John Wallace is very much in that mould.

The industry is by no means unanimous for YES, but there is strong support. Opposition is led by the Scottish Fishermen's chief executive Bertie Armstrong, who is still smarting after being frightfully bruised by the tone of a letter I sent him months ago. Our debate about that and other things lights a spark at the meeting, which turns into a lively affair.

I don't know as much about fishing as I once did when I proudly represented these brave and loveable rogues in Parliament, but I do know more than any other politician with the possible exception of Richard Lochhead, the government's Rural Affairs Secretary. The meeting is very worthwhile. A long time ago, a former chairman of the Port, J. D. Buchan, told me a wise thing: 'Remember the skippers will be divided between SNP and Tory but every crew member will vote for you – if they vote at all.' I suspect it will be something like that in this referendum.

Back to Strichen, then on to the Aberdeen Asset Management Investment Conference at the Ardoe House hotel in the city – a totally different scene. Martin Gilbert has been scrupulously fair in the arrangements. He invited Alistair Darling last year, and me this year.

It goes very well and the questions in particular are pretty disarming for many of the gathered investors. Indeed so great is the declared support, admittedly from people who in the main cannot vote, as they are non-resident in Scotland, that I begin to wonder whether an expanded franchise might not have been a good idea. Perhaps we should have put the question of Scottish independence to everyone across the planet!

In conversation afterwards, the BBC's Andrew Neil tells me London is only just waking up to the reality that they have a fight on their hands. I express to him my hope that they snooze a little longer.

P.S. Make a point of being nice to Douglas Flint, one of the big financial backers of the NO campaign and chairman of HSBC. I want Douglas to realise how confident the YES campaign has become. HSBC is a bank with next to no branches in Scotland. A long time ago the Bank of England effectively blocked a merger between HSBC and the Royal Bank of Scotland because it didn't want this organisation in the Committee of Clearing Bankers.

Day Eighty-Seven: Saturday 6 September

It's the day the polls finally turn – but I worry it's too early for us.

I'm on the course at Castle Stuart to unwind after extraordinary scenes during an Inverness walkabout. I am teamed up with a couple of locals – one YES and one NO. Just as I'm about to tee off, Geoff Aberdein informs me that a *Sunday Times* poll is expected.

At the second hole, Geoff calls again to tell me Rupert Murdoch has tweeted that the result is sensational. I tell him to call the paper and wheedle out of them what is going on.

The third hole is a short par four and I am in high form. My drive just shades off the green before landing in a depression to the left. It is a tough enough shot and I decide to try the flop shot that I saw Mickelson play from the same position at the Scottish Open. I'm lining up when the phone starts vibrating again. It is Geoff, in a state of high excitement.

'The poll,' he says breathlessly. 'It's 51–49.'

'Fine,' I reply. 'Now, I'm turning off the phone. I'll speak to you when I finish the round.'

I'm thinking that's pretty good. Closing to a two per cent deficit. Continued momentum. Couldn't be better, really. However, I still manage to foozle the flop shot.

When I get back to the clubhouse, I have twenty-odd missed messages.

I phone Geoff: 'What's going on?'

'First Minister, I told you. We're in the lead!'

'Damn,' I say, realising my mistake.

'Why damn? It's great,' enthuses Geoff.

'Geoff, it is a week too soon.'

A week too soon, but a tremendous result nevertheless on a day which started with a sweep up the Moray coastline. The street surge in Glasgow had been such a contrast to the Aberdeen Asset investment dinner, although both were encouraging in their respective ways. I was anxious to see what the feeling was in an SNP heartland, but not necessarily a YES stronghold.

What's meant to be a brief stop in Elgin town centre turns into an intense walkabout and event. Lisa Gordon from my constituency office tries hard to keep to schedule but it is impossible given the enthusiasm of the crowd. Families have brought their children to see me and the stop-off turns into more like an hour. The YES campaigners are in buoyant mood and, just as in Glasgow on Thursday, there is a growing expectation of victory.

If Elgin was electric, then nothing prepared me for the reception in Inverness. The YES stall in the city centre is totally swamped. People are up lamp-posts, hanging out of windows, and the mood is exuberant.

The selfie count is off the scale and it is difficult not to be carried away by the passion. I make my favourite stump speech that the Westminster establishment are about to hear a 'Hampden roar' from the 'missing million' and it is punctuated by explosions of applause.

Only once before in Inverness have I experienced this sort of enthusiasm. In 2001 Sean Connery agreed to do a walkabout for our then young candidate, now MP, Angus Brendan MacNeil. I had chosen Inverness as the location to fling the Scottish press corps off the scent, but still made sure the TV cameras were there.

Sean duly arrived at the airport and we headed into the town centre. He then announced that he needed a comfort break, so we detoured to Culloden House Hotel, where the great man inquired of a shell-shocked staff in that familiar burr: 'Excushe me. Can I ushe your toilet?'

Later in town, Sean received exactly the sort of reception which I was to experience again today. Bonnie Prince Charlie famously spent the night at Culloden before the battle. Sean spent a penny before the walkabout.

I have since struck up a firm friendship with general manager Stephen Davies and the rest of the staff at Culloden House and joked that, given they had a plaque to remember Charlie, they should erect another, suitably positioned, to commemorate the more famous, if briefer, visit from Sean.

Day-Eighty Eight: Sunday 7 September

All hands on deck planning our strategy to deal with the astonishing lead.

We expect an extreme reaction from the political establishment as they appreciate for the first time that they are in real danger of losing. Our team realise that we have got there earlier than we planned. However, we aim to keep the momentum of the campaign going. A great deal can be achieved by political momentum.

The reaction we expect is twofold. They will keep doing what they have been doing, but will redouble their efforts. Thus far they have been pretty unsuccessful in their scare tactics. People have become inured to them and they are becoming background noise.

However, we also expect a 'new offer' to be made. The reason is obvious. They are game-planning exactly on the Quebec referendum. Wee Douglas Alexander discovered Quebec about a year ago and thought it would be really clever to translate the NO campaign in Quebec of 1995 to the NO campaign in Scotland 2014. Thus 'Non Merci' becomes 'No Thanks'.

If this doesn't seem all that sophisticated it is because it is not. There are a number of problems with this approach, not least of which is that the NO campaign in Quebec won by a knife-edge 51–49. I would hate to live on the difference. In Quebec there was a 'new offer'. We therefore expect a 'new offer'.

I am reasonably confident about our ability to handle this, since they have a major problem. Indeed it is so big a problem that I can't see them getting around it. The people who could make the offer have no credibility. In the Scottish opinion polls approval ratings, Cameron is around minus 40, Miliband minus 50 and Clegg off the scale of unpopularity. How can people with no credibility offer something credible?

My opinion is strengthened by George Osborne on the *Andrew Marr Show* suggesting a new deal is coming this very week, only to have this immediately denied by Alistair Carmichael, the Scottish Secretary, who looks in an even more desperate state than usual.

So far so good, but we have to believe that they will get their act together before very long. What we really need is a rocket booster, something to take the campaign beyond the reach of the unionists.

I phone Rupert Murdoch to discuss the poll and ask him straight out if the *Scottish Sun* would commit to YES. Mr Murdoch replies, as he always does, that 'it is up to my editors'.

The problem is, of course, that there are two: one in Scotland and one in London.

For such a momentous day, I end it in rather unusual circumstances with a speech to the International Conference of Agricultural Journalists at Raemoir House near Banchory. I have promised to do this for a great friend, Brian Pack.

I end up speaking just as the European championship game – between world champions Germany and the nation who had decided against World Cup participation, Scotland – comes to a climax. Scotland play well but lose narrowly in the end. I tell some delighted German agricultural journalists the result in the middle of my speech. I hope it is not a metaphor for the referendum.

Day Eighty-Nine: Monday 8 September

What we need is Eli Gold, the scheming political campaign manager from *The Good Wife*. Mind you, we do have the next best thing – Alan Cumming, the actor who plays him in the TV series.

Nicola is campaigning with Alan in Glasgow as our main event of the day. He is a gem and deeply interested in politics. I went to see his one-man *Macbeth* in the Tron theatre a couple of years back, and what really impressed me was not just his amazing performance, but the question-and-answer session at the end.

People were invited to give their views on what was really going on in the play, which was set in an asylum as Alan shifted from character to character. Some of the theories were madcap, others profound and some just quirky. Regardless, Alan dealt with everyone with humour and courtesy. He is – although he probably doesn't realise it – a natural politician. Above all, he is likeable – an underrated asset in politics. If people like you then they will forgive you just about anything. If they don't then they will forgive nothing.

The campaign meeting in the Grand Central Hotel, Glasgow, focuses on planning the final week to try and work out how to repel the inevitable counter-attack. In the absence of a daily newspaper campaigning for YES, we have to continue to provide the best pictures, the best stories, dominate social media and take every television opportunity to stay on our campaign themes.

On which subject, I do a late-night TV interview with Bernard Ponsonby. Bernard has been around Scottish politics almost as long as I have, and is a talented impressionist as well as a fearsome interviewer. In conversation afterwards, Bernard confirms the view that the streets and council-housing schemes are YES territory.

Day Ninety: Tuesday 9 September

Things are getting serious.

I take three separate phone calls today from business contacts warning me of a Downing Street summons last night for leading companies, effectively demanding that they call for a NO vote. The phone calls come from those who have refused. One contact, from an energy company, describes the meeting as 'weird'. He says that Cameron was banging on about the war and the Dunkirk spirit. Certainly he was in a bunker.

This type of negative intervention is in complete contrast to the real sense of anticipation among YES campaigners. The atmosphere is becoming infectious.

The day starts in a positive vein too. Had coffee with Pat Cox, the former President of the European Parliament. Pat has come up trumps with a first-rate article in the *Scotsman* and an excellent follow-up of interviews where he proclaims the EU will enable entry for Scotland.

We have, for the first time, really seized the initiative on the European issue.

To make the point I attend a media event in Parliament Square with, not just the world's media, but 'new Scots' of every conceivable nationality – saying YES in as many languages as we can muster.

So today it is a case of oui, ja, si, and the Gaelic bu chòir. Apparently there is no exact Gaelic word for 'yes'. 'Bu chòir' means 'we should'. In any language, it is a good-natured and impressive event, designed not just to show the breadth of the YES campaign but to transmit pictures of energy and diversity.

The media press me to respond to the ludicrous *Telegraph/Mail* suggestions of a Palace intervention in the debate, sparked by Cameron having been at Balmoral over the weekend. The *Sunday Times* coverage of their YouGov poll must have made splendid reading for him over breakfast! My view is that the more they occupy themselves with this stuff and nonsense, the better it is for us.

On the way to a Facebook question-and-answer session at SNP headquarters, I call in at a drinks reception organised by Women in the Business Community. It is coordinated by Kat Heathcote and Dame Mariot Leslie, the former UK ambassador to NATO. I go round the tables speaking to women in groups. We have some formidable support among women professionals. Perhaps one of the positive fallouts of this campaign will be to involve more than a few of these excellent women in the public life of the country.

Day Ninety-One: Wednesday 10 September

The Three Amigos arrive – but does anyone really care?

For YES, the momentum of the campaign seems to be carrying us forward. I am relaxed about the arrival of Cameron, Miliband and Clegg – who are instantly dubbed 'The Three Amigos' by the veteran Scottish actor (and YES supporter)

Brian Cox. Indeed, I think it works for rather than against us, given that it demonstrates how important Scotland has become and how desperate they have become: Prime Minister's Questions cancelled to rush north. However, the most important point is that not one of the three has a shred of credibility. Without that precious commodity it doesn't really matter what they have to say.

As far as I can gather, they came up together and went their separate ways. I pay no attention to what they are up to.

As our counter to the Amigos, we attempt to unite 'Team Scotland' against 'Team Westminster' with a YES campaign gathering in Piershill Square, near Musselburgh, east Lothian. Jim Sillars, Greens leader Patrick Harvie, the Scottish Socialist Party's Colin Fox, Nicola and I march arm in arm to the 'Margomobile', in which Jim has been touring the central Scotland housing schemes. Piershill is bedecked in YES regalia and is a great place to make the point about what is happening across working-class Scotland.

The symbolism of Jim and me campaigning together would be totally lost on the metropolitan media, but well understood by the Scottish journalists. We fell out badly twenty years ago and have barely spoken since. Earlier this year we were reconciled when I went to visit his MSP wife, Margo, in the last weeks of her debilitating illness.

Margo would have been a huge asset to the YES campaign. She was often impossible, but always had a warm humanity and a keen intelligence. That restless mind often got her into deep water with the party but never with the voters. In a pub quiz, if ever asked to name which SNP leader managed to avoid flinging Margo out of the party, then the answer is me.

She resigned under Gordon Wilson and was expelled under John Swinney. Under Alex Salmond she was readmitted.

Margo was successfully elected three times as an independent to the Scottish Parliament. She would have been an enormous positive for YES.

Jim and I burying the hatchet, in the final stretch of a campaign for an objective we have sought for most of our political careers, sends a powerful message. Appearing in front of Margo's bus makes it all the more poignant. This is particularly the case given that the 'snappy bus' was a street campaigning technique which we had jointly devised and used to devastating effect in the Govan by-election, where Jim triumphed for the SNP back in 1988.

After the traditional campaigning event in Musselburgh, I head to Hemma café bar beside the Parliament for a Mumsnet webchat. Alistair Darling is doing a simultaneous one at a separate venue and it is clear, even from his terse answers, that all is far from well in the NO campaign.

The television pictures show me chatting with smiling mums and babies, in contrast to the Better Together image which has Alistair sitting with one glum-looking aide and a poster.

On my way to Glasgow for a final interview with Jackie Bird when I hear that BP have declared officially for NO. This is not just another piece of waffle from the chairman Bob Dudley in his individual capacity, but presented as a company position. There has been, of course, no consultation with shareholders or other interest groups, just the arrogant assumption that a corporation which has enriched itself from Scottish resources for the last forty years has the right to dictate to people in a democracy, at the behest of a desperate PM, how they should cast their vote.

BP are no strangers to using corporate power in their company interest. In 2007 they succeeded in changing the UK government's position on the release of the man convicted of the Lockerbie bombing, Abdelbaset Ali Mohmed al-Megrahi. When Jack Straw became Lord Chancellor in Gordon Brown's administration, he came to see me at Bute House. Over breakfast, he agreed to have Megrahi excluded from the Prisoner Transfer Agreement which was being negotiated with the Libyans. He didn't see any difficulty in the matter at all when I explained Megrahi's inclusion in the PTA would cut across the judicial process in Scotland, as he was then in the process of appealing his conviction.

A few weeks later Straw rang Justice Secretary Kenny MacAskill to say that he could not deliver on his commitment. Kenny reported that it was 'because of BP'. When I called Straw, he told me that BP interests had indeed prevailed upon the UK government. BP were bidding for Gaddafi contracts at the time and the Libyans made it clear that if Megrahi wasn't included in the PTA then there would be no contracts. BP lobbied and the UK government jumped.

I don't know whether BP has been promised anything for its referendum intervention. Perhaps there was a continuation of the 'dialogue' about compensation in the Gulf of Mexico, where Cameron had first refused to intervene but by the end of 2013 was wading in in support of the company with the US President. I have no way of knowing what arrangements, if any, have been made between the UK government and BP. What I do know is that, as the Megrahi case shows, as a company they are perfectly capable of that degree of naked self-interest and political intrigue – a case of perfidious BP.

From the BBC straight to the Central Mosque for an extraordinarily powerful meeting. All of our key supporters in the community are present in a huge gathering of a thousand or so. Then straight from there to the Sichuan restaurant where I'm having a meal with the Chinese community. On the way I take a call in the car – a grave update on the situation with the ISIS hostages, one of whom is the Scot David Haines.

Then at the Sichuan restaurant, all hell breaks loose …

The story is that RBS would relocate its headquarters to London in the event of a YES vote, and Lloyds have also made a statement. Catriona Matheson or Cat – my key aide for the evening – takes the call from Geoff Aberdein. She's standing in tonight on the basis that it will be just a couple of hours and a nice meal at a Chinese restaurant. I leave the room to make some rapid calls, before returning with a brave smile. Cat and I skip the rest of the dinner. I pose for photos and selfies and we leave as soon as we reasonably can.

The news from the banks is dramatic and unexpected given their often-stated determination to stay above the fray and maintain that the vote is a matter for the Scottish people. Lloyds made a statement first, followed by a BBC report on the Royal Bank. On my way back to Bute House, I make repeated phone calls to Ross McEwan, the RBS chief executive.

I reach him just before midnight and he explains that they have held a board meeting which has just finished and that they will be making a market-sensitive announcement. He assures me they are not going to relocate their head office and that he will be issuing an immediate letter to staff to explain their contingency plans and spell out the difference between a registered office and operational headquarters. He says the letter will make it clear that the office of registration is a technical, rather than an operational, issue.

'But Ross,' I say, 'it was on the BBC *News at Ten*.'

'That's impossible,' he answers. 'Our board didn't finish until near eleven. The announcement will be made tomorrow in the proper way.'*

Catriona and I have to completely redraft a speech I am making tomorrow and dictate a letter to the Cabinet Secretary

---

* The full detail of the extent of the Treasury manipulation of the Royal Bank announcement has become clear subsequently: After encouraging a statement from Lloyds to pressurise RBS, the Treasury leaked news of the Royal Bank's intentions before the board meeting to decide its position had even concluded.

In an email timed 22.15 and 34 seconds on the Wednesday night, a Treasury official in an email to the BBC quotes a 'source' saying: 'As you would expect, RBS have also been in touch with us and have similar plans to base themselves in London.'

The Royal Bank board meeting did not conclude until 10.40 p.m. The Treasury were informed by RBS at 10.45 p.m., and the markets were told at 7 a.m. the next morning. Overnight RBS shares moved.

It is as dramatic and clear-cut a breach of confidence in respect of potentially market-sensitive information as you will find but, despite that, neither the Cabinet Secretary nor the Financial Conduct Authority have agreed to investigate. The City of London Police are still investigating, but in the knowledge that civil servants carry protection from the 1993 Criminal Justice Act on insider dealing where an individual is acting on behalf of a public sector body in pursuit of monetary policy – which is what the Treasury claim they were doing. The police would have to establish an offence had been committed that carries no such protection.

The Treasury official immediately responsible for the leak was Robert Mackie, who is, coincidentally, son of Catherine McLeod, former special adviser to Chancellor Alistair Darling, the leader of the NO campaign. Mr Mackie's ultimate boss is Sir Nicholas Macpherson, the man who believes that civil service impartiality did not apply to the Referendum!

demanding an inquiry into what is clearly a Treasury leak attributed to a 'source' by the BBC. If we can make that the issue then perhaps we can turn the tables on the story. Above all, I need a copy of Ross McEwan's letter to his staff, and as quickly as possible. Luckily, Ross is not at all impressed by finding out that his board's decisions have been leaked even before they were made.

We wait for Liz Lloyd, my special adviser in economics, to provide some additional material, and at 3 a.m. I give Cat a guided tour of Bute House, pour her a large whisky and leave her to finish tomorrow's speech.

Day Ninety-Two: Thursday 11 September

I manage to get a copy of Ross McEwan's letter to his staff. It is excellent and puts the question of a registered office in its correct context. I'm ready to go to war with it.

Today is the seventeenth anniversary of the devolution referendum of 1997 and we'd chosen the date for a major press conference for the international media. The plan was to have speaking together Nicola Sturgeon, Green leader Patrick Harvie, the Muslim Friends of Labour general secretary and YES campaigner Anum Qaisar, and Kenyon Wright.

I am in combative mood on *Good Morning Scotland*, robustly defending and explaining the Royal Bank's real position – and posing the question of how such a contingency decision could be broadcast on the BBC before it had even been made.

I know that we are going to face intense interrogation on the matter at the Edinburgh International Conference Centre, but

I am well prepared with Ross's letter, which is very helpful indeed. It makes the point that the location of the registered office is a largely technical matter which he would expect to have no operational impact on investment or jobs.

The speeches at the EICC go well and, when we get to questions, I take a few from the international press before the BBC's Nick Robinson asks his first question, the important one about the Royal Bank, and the tax revenue impact of moving its 'base' from Scotland. He then adds something about why business is all against YES.

He doesn't get the reply he is expecting. I dismiss the practical impact of registered offices, mock the BBC for believing that Lloyds are headquartered in Scotland and then counter-attack heavily by demanding an inquiry into the leak from the Treasury to the BBC. I quote extensively from Ross McEwan's letter, which has come as news to the press conference. I point out that the leak was reported on the BBC the previous evening and I expect that as a public service broadcaster they will cooperate fully with an inevitable inquiry.

In his frustration, Nick gets rather agitated. I suggest he should stop heckling, give him another comprehensive reply and point out again that corporation tax liability is based on economic impact, not on the location of the registered office.

The international journalists are more interested in the knife-edge nature of the campaign and ask a series of good-natured and informed questions. This stands in contrast to the overexcitement of all the London-based reporters.

The general consensus is that, under the circumstances, the conference has gone very well. While still at the EICC, I receive a phone call from a senior contact in the financial sector who gives me an urgent rundown on the key questions I should be asking of the Treasury. He says that in more than thirty years' experience he has never seen behaviour like it from civil servants. I send off the letter to the Cabinet Secretary demanding an investigation into the Treasury leak of the Royal Bank board decision to the BBC.

Lunch with Kenyon and his daughter at Bute. He says he is now at the full disposal of the YES campaign and can't believe the behaviour of the BBC. It is a different world from the one he was familiar with in the devolution referendum.

In the afternoon I hold a round of interviews at SNP HQ for the Sunday papers, but my press team tell me that social media is alive with complaints about Nick Robinson's report on the 1 p.m. news. Incredibly, he claimed on air that I didn't answer his question! He based this on suggesting that his questions had really been about the credibility of business leaders and politicians as opposed to the Royal Bank. Even if that were so, it would not have been true to claim that I hadn't answered his questions. Citing individuals such as Angus Grossart and Martin Gilbert, I had demonstrated that major business figures had said that the Scottish financial sector would prosper regardless of the constitutional circumstances. Worse still, his TV report had been edited in such a way that all mention of the Royal Bank had been removed. This is unfortunate for whoever edited the BBC report because the whole press conference was live-streamed and available for all to see. So I tell the team to put the full live stream of that section of the press conference online in as many forums as we can.

It would not be reasonable to say that the BBC role in the campaign has been entirely malicious. Their current affairs output has produced some substantial debates and some really good programmes, such as Robert Peston's commendable account on the economics of independence. In Scotland James Cook chaired an excellent series of referendum debates in a fair and impartial manner.

However, the news output generally has been disgracefully biased throughout the campaign, as Professor John Robertson identified in his analysis. This is much more a structural question than a particular issue with any one journalist. Political balance is not achieved by first picking up from a partisan written press the latest scare story on independence and then allowing a YES campaigner to reply to that agenda. The problem has been amplified by London heavies rolling into town and repeating, as if new and newsworthy, scare stories that the Scottish public tired of many months ago.

One example of a good programme is tonight's debate in the Hydro with ten thousand youngsters between sixteen and eighteen having a magnificent time with a panel that includes Nicola Sturgeon, Patrick Harvie, Ruth Davidson and some strange guy in a Guy Fawkes hat who turns out to be George Galloway.

Patrick had been so incensed by Galloway being nominated by Better Together that it had taken great persuasion to get him to turn up at all. He need not have worried. Nicola and he make mincemeat of the opposition. More to the point, it is an exceptional demonstration of the wisdom of forcing the issue on sixteen- to eighteen-year-olds voting.

There is the point of principle here. If you are old enough to marry and pay tax then you are old enough to vote. When we embarked on this experiment we were told that young people would not vote and those who did would be voting NO. Both of these suppositions are turning out to be wrong.

The social media generation, free from the bias of the old press and the television, have turned on to YES in a huge way. And as the Hydro debate demonstrates, there is no shortage of interest and there will be no shortage of votes from the age group that have the most personal investment in the future of Scotland. One of the legacies of this campaign must be that youngsters will no longer be denied their democratic entitlement and responsibility.

Day Ninety-Three: Friday 12 September

A whistle-stop tour of Scotland covering seven cities. I'm buoyed by the overwhelming optimism of the crowds.

I take the high road in a helicopter to hit Aberdeen, Inverness and Dundee – with Nicola visiting Glasgow, Edinburgh and Stirling. Then both of us meet up in Perth. But the best-laid plans …

Such a programme is beset with logistical difficulties, not least of which is the haar that descends on much of the east coast this morning, so we travel to Dyce by car instead of taking the helicopter.

We start with some door-knocking near Aberdeen airport, after dealing with the press, who are reasonably keen to pile pressure on the Treasury about the Royal Bank. News is also beginning to leak out about the companies who were summoned to the meeting in Downing Street last Monday. The declarations from ASDA and John Lewis, who have both said prices could go up in an independent Scotland, should be seen in that light. Indeed, the theme that Scotland should not be intimidated by big money, big oil, big supermarkets or big government is becoming a very strong one with significant doorstep appeal.*

While knocking the doors in Dyce, I visit the house of a D-Day veteran, John Johnstone, who my campaign team said was undecided. We have a great chat about his war-time experiences. He went through D-Day without a scratch and then broke his leg in Norway getting out of a commandeered

---

* Since the referendum the whole argument and debate about company positions in politics is still running strong. For example, the Labour Party, who were up to their necks in seeking to egg on supermarkets to declare for NO, were by February 2015 crying like babies with nappy rash when the boss of Boots dispensed his views on Ed Miliband.

The correct position is clear enough. Individual business people have the same right as anyone else to pronounce on politics or to financially back the party or cause of their choice. Similarly it is perfectly reasonable for a company to argue (as the airlines do) for lower air passenger duty or (as the supermarkets do) against a retail levy. This is the case whether in elections, a referendum or just general public debate.

However, to commit a public company to a party political position or to a political donation is a totally different matter. That should require consultation with shareholders and other stakeholders. It is also by and large an extraordinarily foolish thing to do. The pronouncements of ASDA, for example, will do them long-term damage in terms of the attitude of many customers in Scotland. The head of John Lewis was forced into a rewrite of his remarks because of the concern voiced by the employees who are partners in the business. Bob Dudley, who comes from a totally different political culture in America, no doubt thinks he is powerful enough to breeze through democratic niceties. He isn't. At the highest level in BP there was concern not about his personal pronouncement in February that he didn't want to see Scotland 'drift away', but about his arrogance in September in claiming the company backed his position. The company is bigger than Bob.

German staff car. It turns out he was not undecided at all, but a firm YES. However, his lovely wife, Rosalind, has a doubt or two and he wants to enlist me in persuading her over. This I do.

Just as we are leaving there is a loud bang. A young motorcyclist has come off her bike after hitting a car. It is never a great idea to come off a bike, but if you have to, then doing so with a full police security team and a qualified nurse in tow is a good time to do it. The young lady is taken to hospital in an ambulance. We get a later report that she is OK and I send her some flowers.

Fortunately, our pilot for the day is Johnny 'Hydro' McKenzie – so called, not because he works for Scottish and Southern Electricity, but because he has his own hydro-electric plant at his farm near Beauly, Inverness-shire. Johnny is ex-military and a pilot who exudes skill and confidence. If there is a way to get us safely into the air then he will find it.

At 11 a.m. Johnny is able to take off and we travel in the helicopter to Culloden House Hotel, near Inverness. On board, I am joined by *Observer* journalist Kevin McKenna.

Kevin tells me the *Observer* had a long internal debate on positioning for the referendum as he had decided, as a columnist, to commit to YES. He doubts if the process will be as fair-minded or as rigorous in other papers.

On the way we get the latest ICM poll, which has YES on 49 per cent, moving up three points. This is useful because the morning papers had been full of a YouGov poll reversing the YES lead of two to a NO lead of four. This is hopefully no more than statistical variation. That being the case, it still would have been so much better for YES if we had been behind by four last Sunday and up by two today.

The weather clears completely and in Culloden we receive a rapturous welcome in the shopping centre. We then dash to the Mustard Seed for a quick lunch with some very old friends, Dennis and Glynis MacLeod, who have come all the way from Canada to campaign for YES. Then we set off for Dundee.

Johnny Hydro takes us on a small detour to see something he has noticed the previous day. Indeed you could hardly miss it from the air or the ground. As we fly over the Kessock Bridge, there is a giant YES sign, the size of a house.

On arrival at Dundee I take media bids on the tarmac before making a visit to the waterfront café where we are greeted by the actor Brian Cox, who is also the Rector of Dundee University. I am hugely impressed that Brian knows the names of all the campaign team as he introduces me. He tells us it is a skill he has acquired from years of learning lines.

We are now against the clock to get to Perth. We have arranged a photo op with Nicola, but have a tiny window to get there before she has to leave for elsewhere. We make it, but with no time to spare. We arrive on the main shopping street in Perth by walking down an alley, and as we arrive I am taken aback by the crowd – only to realise this is just a small group and most people are further up the street. It is extraordinary. Lots of selfies, lots of signings, lots of excited activists.

We manage some clips for the TV and, watching it later, it looks fantastic. The street is packed in the late afternoon and full of YES signs. The sun is shining.

I see my first NO campaigners for ages at Perth airport – a small knot of people looking glum with their arms folded and holding a clutch of posters. I pass them by with a cheery 'hello'. They still look glum. It seems such a timid show compared with the amazing crowd on the street in Perth.

As we walk in the direction of the helicopter, we hear a couple of men shouting for me. I walk over to meet them. They are from the local boxing club and have written a big YES with a marker pen on the board outside the club. They explain that they had taken the hump at the NO campaigners, who apparently had been waiting for me for hours, and decided to have their own counter-counter-demonstration. I pay an impromptu visit to the club. There are lots of photos, and we chat about the campaign and their hopes for a new boxing school. I arrange for them to get a proper YES banner to replace the one with the marker pen, and a signed bottle of whisky to help with their fund-raising.

We travel on to Gleneagles where we have a splendid view from the air of the preparations for the Ryder Cup. Moira has been monitoring the television coverage of the seven cities tour and fills me in. She is really pleased, as she says that our shots were all smiling crowds, sunshine and optimism.

Meet with Professor John Kay before a convivial dinner in the Dormie House at Gleneagles. John is a brilliant economist, *FT* columnist and a former member of the Council of Economic Advisers. I am having dinner with him to put into place some of our final preparations for the aftermath of a YES vote.

We have been working with Pat Cox on the European dimension, both to ensure that the Commission does not say anything untoward at their Friday press briefing following a YES vote and also to find a venue and timescale for sensible early negotiations. This is all proceeding well and the key people are proving increasingly amenable as the chances of a YES vote grow. For example, the office of the incoming President of the Commission, Jean-Claude Juncker, has put out a firm rebuttal of NO campaign claims that his reference to a five-year wait for enlargement of the EU was relevant to the Scottish position.

I also need to make progress in steadying the financial markets, and one approach is to have in place on the day after the vote the membership of a Scottish Monetary Authority with the prestige and reputation to send the clearest signal that the thinking has been done and all is in hand. This, in conjunction with a firm position from the Bank of England about being in charge throughout the negotiation period, would serve the purpose.

Mervyn King had recommended John. At Gleneagles he accepts the remit and we lay the plans in the event of a YES outcome. This involves the content and timing of the key announcements and the membership of the Monetary Authority. Together we go through a list of specialists with central bank experience and financial technicians with the weight and track record to impress. Over the next few days I will contact them one by one to secure their services.

Day Ninety-Four: Saturday 13 September

I'm told a huge crowd has gathered to greet me in Rosehearty, Aberdeenshire – but it is Rupert Murdoch they get.

I'm on my way from Dumfries to Glasgow by helicopter with the BBC's very professional and very likeable James Cook, who tells me that Rupert has arrived in the North East to take the political temperature personally. As it happens the Banff and Buchan campaign team meet him in Rosehearty, where his great-grandfather had been minister. Eilidh Whiteford, the local MP, quickly realises that it is Mr Murdoch who is arriving and that the STV cameras on location are for him not me.

Rupert understandably enough is not keen on the STV cameras, but Eilidh is able to take him on a tour of his great-grandfather's charge. Eilidh is an indomitable feminist but, she tells me later, they got on famously. In all the London commentary speculating about Rupert Murdoch's views on Scottish independence there is an assumption that it is guided by an urge to get his own back at the establishment. It never seems to have occurred to them that he might have a genuine interest in what is best for the Scottish people and the reason for that might lie in his great-grandfather's parish of Rosehearty.

Had a difficult conversation with Jim Sillars late last night over remarks he made about a 'day of reckoning' for the oil companies who had come out for NO. I pointed out that, however justified the anger, it is a comment you would make only if we were losing, since it is meat and drink to our press and media detractors.

I asked him straight out: 'In your estimation are we losing?'

Jim replied: 'No, we are winning.' This morning Jim went on Radio 4's *Today* programme and told a perplexed interviewer that his remark had been designed merely to secure his appearance 'on their prestigious programme'. I phoned to thank him for getting things back onto an even keel.

Johnny Hydro has spotted a weather window which means we can fly to Prestwick from Cumbernauld. And when we get to Ayrshire, we go campaigning in Prestwick town centre, where the scenes are even more intense than in Perth. I go into a branch of Wetherspoons to do what I think is my first-ever photo-call drinking a pint. This is to celebrate the refusal of thier managing director to bow to Downing Street pressure to line up for NO.

This is by far the best way to deal with these unscrupulous companies. For every ASDA that succumbs to political inducements there is a Tesco that refuses. For every business magnate like Bob Dudley who wants to dispense his opinions where he has no vote there are others like Ignacio Galan of Iberdrola/ Scottish Power who are content to leave these matters to the people. Individual business people are entitled to say what they like and do as they please. However, the business of their business should be business, not politics.

The manager of the local Wetherspoons is somewhat overwhelmed by the intensity of the media scrum but takes it all in good part.

Back in the helicopter and off to Dumfries town centre, after landing at the Mabie House Hotel. Local MSP Joan McAlpine has arranged an extraordinary turnout on the stone bridge across the Nith, complete with a YES swing band. It is one of the best photos of the campaign.

Joan makes a shrewd point that in areas like the South-West, where YES has ground to make up, we are now attracting some of the brightest and best new people into politics.

Back to Cumbernauld airport and then to Prosen Street in the East End of Glasgow. Inevitably, we are well behind the clock and Nicola has had to leave for another engagement. However, the street canvassing is impressive.

One of the guys from the scheme has brought his grandson along to see me. The wee lad is resplendent in his Celtic shirt.

'It's eighty, you know,' says the man as I do a selfie with his grandson.

'Eighty what?' I ask, thinking to myself, 'It doesn't seem THAT warm.'

'Eighty per cent YES round here,' comes the matter-of-fact reply.

Day Ninety-Five: Sunday 14 September

I look at Nicola. She looks at me. We could be but days away from victory. It is the stuff that dreams are made of.

We are meeting at Bute House to survey the evidence. The Sunday paper polls are of little help. ICM in the *Sunday Telegraph* has YES seven points clear, Opinium in the *Observer* has NO four points ahead. Panelbase in the *Sunday Times* suggests a dead heat.

YES canvassing, including the online assessment from a Canadian group of analysts, indicates that we are now in front. Not by very much, but ahead. The Canadians project from their current figures that we'll be at 54 per cent by polling day. Our canvassing is much tighter. The YES people are more motivated, and that should overcome, to a great extent, the fact that our strongest leads are in those parts of the community and those areas which normally poll low. I distrust a purely online assessment. It has the advantage of being right up to date, but there are still many people who don't get their information from social media. They are potentially our biggest challenge.

We don't see what else NO have in their armoury. The scare tactics of this week have reached the point where their impact is limited and the Three Amigos have been greeted with a giant raspberry.

Nicola is normally the most pessimistic of campaigners. The Monday night before the 2011 election she was convinced that she had detected a big swing away from us. We won by a landslide. This time she is very confident. The key is to keep things on an even keel and, above all, polling-day organisation.

There was an indication earlier today that all is not well in the NO camp. I was on the *Andrew Marr Show* with Alistair Darling – the first time we have seen each other in the flesh since the second debate. Whatever their internal polls are showing cannot be good, because Alistair was clearly agitated. After the interview I joined the band which had played out the programme for a photo. Alistair has to be cajoled by his staff into a very uncomfortable-looking pose.

A piece for *Newsround* before the *Sunday Politics* and then Colin Mackay.

I was right about the guts of young Amy Macdonald. She has not only declared for YES, but headlined the 'A Night for Scotland' concert tonight. Took part in a photo-call for the gig outside the Usher Hall in Edinburgh with the bands. We now have an enormous trail of broadcast media, UK and international, following us each day. The young, good-looking, hip bands add lustre to the campaign.

Moira and I – and everyone else – have a great time at the concert. I decide against speeches on the strong advice of Geoff Aberdein and Stuart Nicolson. Apparently we don't want any

Sheffield rally* comparisons. This is a bit rich, since they were both barely out of nappies then. In any case they are right that our pictures of a young, dynamic and above all optimistic YES campaign tell their own story.

Get a message from Johnny Hydro that the helicopter will be grounded due to weather, so we plot out some rapid alternative arrangements.

Day Ninety-Six: Monday 15 September

I was outside my old family home in Linlithgow today – and there were YES stickers all over the windows. My best pal from school, Ronnie Bamberry, excitedly told me the new residents were SNP members. Sadly, they weren't at home – but we posed for pictures outside the house in Preston Road.

Back in my old stamping ground, the reception is incredible – and it is a taste of things to come. I have arranged for Channel Four's Jon Snow to interview me in the housing scheme where I grew up. We are in Councillor Martin Day's house, just across the swing-park from my childhood home. My friend Ronnie takes relish in assuring Jon that he used to thrash me at fitba headers in the garden. Some things in life you can't escape from, regardless of how hard you try. Jon has only been in Scotland for the day, but says he believes we are on our way to victory. He is a shrewd judge and a fine journalist.

West Lothian politics have been moving strongly in the

---

* The rally just days before the 1992 general election when Neil Kinnock is thought to have flung away his chance of victory: probably a myth, but it certainly didn't help him.

SNP's direction under the influence of two of our brightest MSPs, Fiona Hyslop and Angela Constance. We are persuaded by Fiona and her husband, Kenny, to go to Linlithgow Cross, where I address a vast and excited crowd, assembled by Twitter. To a person, they believe that we have the NO campaign on the run. Speaking in my home town under these circumstances is something special. It is one of the greatest moments of my life.

Ronnie and I head to the Star and Garter Hotel, where my Auntie Abby used to work, and which has recently been restored after a disastrous fire. In chatting to the new owners I meet a group of expat Scots on holiday from Australia. They demand that after a YES vote I go to Melbourne for St Andrew's day on an early state visit and assure me that launching the ABA (Anybody But Abbott) campaign will receive widespread support from all those who want shot of their Prime Minister – and not just from Scots Australians!

Earlier, we arranged to use Edinburgh airport as the setting for a photo op with Business for Scotland, with some of Scotland's top business people including Brian Souter, Ralph Topping, Russel Griggs, Marie Macklin and Mohammed Ramzan. This is to highlight that 'Scotland will welcome the world' after a YES vote.

The networks are out in force and things are pretty chaotic. The questioning from the BBC is particularly aggressive about the demonstration in Glasgow yesterday when thousands turned up outside Pacific Quay to protest against BBC bias. The trigger point was the Nick Robinson broadcast but the problem goes beyond a single report by a single journalist.

I wonder if these journalists have no self-awareness. What really worries them is that ordinary people are exercising their democratic right to spontaneously and peacefully demonstrate. However, they are sublimely unconcerned that the greatest broadcasting reputation in the world is being sullied by turning into a state, rather than public service, broadcaster.

Not all of the metropolitan media are blind to the extent of the BBC's bias. Paul Mason, ex-BBC and now of Channel 4, tweets: 'Glad to be out of the BBC, in its biggest propaganda mode since the Iraq war.'

Later, on the way to Stirling, I tell BBC director-general Tony Hall how it is. We are well beyond niceties. I say that they are a disgrace to public service broadcasting, that their replacement of their experienced Scottish correspondents by network numpties reflects a near-colonial attitude. I tell him I now have evidence of collusion with the Treasury officials in terms of the Royal Bank leak, I read him Paul Mason's tweet and suggest that it is now difficult to tell where the network BBC stops and the NO campaign begins. This will do absolutely no good but I really enjoy saying it – self-indulgent, but none the less satisfying.

When we get to Stirling I can hear the crowd before I see it. This was meant to be a rapidly organised bout of street campaigning beside the YES stall. In fact the whole of Stirling is a vast mass of thousands of YES voters and banners. It is a wet day but there is nothing that can dampen the spirits of this gathering.

Winnie Ewing once told me that on occasions like that, you should wave at the windows to see the response. In Stirling today all of the windows are waving back. The crowd starts a chant of 'YES, YES, YES' when they see me but are perfectly behaved and part like the Red Sea to let us through to the

Cross where Bruce Crawford and Dennis Canavan are waiting. We hold an old-fashioned street meeting there and after I ask Dennis if he has experienced anything like it in all his time in politics.

He says: 'I've never seen anything like this in all my time as a football supporter!'

Staring at this massive and buoyant crowd, it is very easy to think, We surely must be winning this.

On the way back to Strichen, I reflect that my only criticism is that our pictures for the day should have been the vast crowds at Linlithgow and Stirling rather than the media scrum at the airport. In truth, it was not one of our more inspired photo-calls of the campaign despite the strength of the business cast we had assembled. However, being able to organise such events at a moment's notice is indicative of the grassroots power of the YES campaign.

Day Ninety-Seven: Tuesday 16 September

Almost at the finishing line, but two matters give me cause for concern: the *Daily Record*'s coverage of the 'vow' to Scotland – and Gordon Brown being wheeled in to replace Alistair Darling in an interview with me.

Unlike yesterday's street campaigning, today is a round of big interviews. Moira tells me I have to get my hair done first though by her hairdresser Siobhan Maguire. There is no way Moira will allow me to make history in an unkempt condition!

We fly to Edinburgh for an interview with David Dimbleby in the Point Hotel. It gives me the opportunity to examine the

Record's front page. Suppressing my anger, I see that it is, technically, a clever job – presenting 'A Vow' to Scotland on medieval parchment gives it a quasi-religious authority. Hackneyed perhaps, but effective. This is the first thing that has worried me about press coverage for some time. The word 'vow' was chosen no doubt because 'pledge' had been undercut by Nick Clegg and tuition fees and by David Cameron and Ed Miliband on just about everything else. Behind all of this was the guarantee, underwritten by Gordon Brown, of 'home rule', 'devo to the max' or, as Brown once said, 'as close to a federal state as you can be'.

My concern increased when I learned that Brown had taken over from Darling in the Dimbleby interview. For reasons I have never been able to fathom, Gordon, despite everything, has a degree of credibility that Cameron, Clegg and Miliband lack – and Darling doesn't have at all. When people thought Gordon had retired this was much less potent. However, he has clearly not retired and even hinted at a comeback in the Scots Parliament. As long as he keeps that door ajar he will retain some credibility.

This, of course, is typical Gordon. Let Alistair do the work, the debates, the heavy lifting, and arrive at the last minute to save the day. That way he risks nothing. If the YES campaign had replaced me for major interviews at this stage, then it would have been presented as being in chaos.

However, an increasingly desperate press will swallow anything from the NO campaign. We now know that the *Scottish Sun* will maintain its position of benign neutrality. In truth we would have needed their support last week to make the big difference.

Dimbleby is an outstanding journalist and a fair interviewer. He regards the campaign with the wry look of the seasoned veteran. Maybe we should make him Director General and reintroduce some of his colleagues to journalism.

In Glasgow for the last of the Jackie Bird series and then for a Sky interview with Adam Boulton at the Premier Inn. One of the waitresses tells me her boyfriend proposed to her because he is so excited about the YES campaign. Scotland is becoming the sort of country he wants to bring up a family in. Who says the YES campaign is not about unity?!

On my way to the Alishan restaurant, I make a series of calls to see where we are and to get briefed on the last day of campaigning. Our own figures from the canvass now show us steady at 52 per cent from the latest sample. Not increasing, but no slippage. We believe the motivation of our supporters will carry us over the line. I'm still concerned that the 'vow' offers the classic easy option, but the general feeling is that people are not in the mood to be deflected. Our finishing slogan, 'Let's Do This', is designed to take people over the line.

Day Ninety-Eight: Wednesday 17 September, Eve of Poll

Today feels like the eve-of-poll tour in 2011. Nick Robinson declares the SNP have 'claimed the streets'.

The last day of campaigning is a predictable race against the clock between my helicopter and the ground organisers' cars.

Multiple visits are interspersed with phone calls as we put the finishing touches to our monetary authority and seek agreement with UK civil servants on the text in the event of a

YES vote. It is important that we have a very early statement repeating clause 30 in the Edinburgh Agreement that both governments will work together to take the will of the people forward. That is now agreed.

Johnny Hydro takes us from Edinburgh's Turnhouse to Strathaven and then on to East Kilbride for a very effective walkabout through the town centre and shopping precinct. In a sense I am mimicking 2011 – good memories never hurt. It all feels fine with the crowd confident and buoyant.

Johnny flies on to Prestwick while we dash to Hyspec Engineering near Ayr, a fascinating company where I get to meet the staff and where a large crowd has gathered outside for selfies and celebration. I do a number of sit-down interviews at Hyspec and then on to an industrial estate in Kilmarnock. On the way I agree to an interview with Ewan Macaskill of the *Guardian*. He is quite surprised at how much time I give him. In truth it is a pleasant change to see a real journalist again.

At Kilmarnock there is the familiar sea of YES activists outside the food emporium that I am visiting. Braehead Food is a good business, but not ideal for eve-of-poll pictures. We need images of enthusiastic crowds, not of supermarket-like shelves. The BBC ask me about a ludicrous piece of *Telegraph* nonsense that is only relevant in this sense: on the day before a knife-edge referendum on the future of the nation the public service broadcaster wants to ask me about a fatuous piece of propaganda in the *Daily Telegraph*. Then again George Orwell did write about the Ministry of Truth on a Scottish island!

Johnny Hydro is getting concerned about timings and when we are in the air he tells me we've lost our slot at the airfield where we are due to land. So he phones Largs Golf Club, and hits lucky with a YES-inclined president of the club. This amazing pilot puts us down in the middle of the monthly medal, by the 18th green, taking a large amount of the sand out of the greenside bunker. As I thank the gathered members for their help and apologise for the denuded sand trap, one remarks that he never liked that bunker anyway.

Finally in Largs town centre we get the shots of the day that I have been waiting for. Huge and receptive crowds, alive with the excitement of it all. I make a particular point of being interviewed by Nick Robinson, who makes the ringing observation that we've 'claimed the streets'.

Back to the golf club and then to Prestonfield House. Again this is a reprise of the Scottish election of 2011. I quickly dash down to the media village outside the Parliament to headline the STV news. I reflect that this is the first time I have been back at the Parliament in weeks, such has been the grassroots nature of this campaign.

Johnny takes his leave and says, given the weather, we will be better heading to Perth by car. We embrace and I promise to sign him up full-time after referendum day. Bite to eat at Prestonfield with Chris and Colin Weir before we head to Perth Concert Hall for the closing rally with Nicola.

By this time it is important to avoid mistakes. The speech written for me lacks punch and so I insert some. Geoff and Duncan are so obsessed by the Sheffield rally! There is a huge crowd gathered outside who can't get hold of tickets. Inside the atmosphere is electric, joyful, complete with a YES choir. Nick Robinson arrives to a chorus of boos like a pantomime villain, but it is good-natured stuff.

Nicola and I get some time to gather our thoughts. Our wait

is nearly over. We hug and I head north to Strichen, she goes west to Glasgow.

Day Ninety-Nine: Thursday 18 September, Referendum Day

It is a strange experience. I've waited for this day all of my life. And it finally dawns, just like any other day. What had I expected? A heavenly host trumpeting in the sky? What I am presented with are YES banners, posters and stickers everywhere.

I can't get my dad's favourite lines of poetry out of my head, from James Graham, first Marquis of Montrose.

He either fears his fate too much,
Or his deserts are small,
That puts it not unto the touch
To win or lose it all.

I start polling day where I have started so many others, at the Ritchie Hall in Strichen. A couple of first-time voters are there to walk in with me. Natasha is a first-time voter because she is only seventeen, and Lia is in her early twenties, but has never voted before. They are excited and full of hope, which helps with their nerves in front of the many cameras.

Lia asks me: 'We are going to win, aren't we?'

'Yes, I think so,' I reply.

The kids from the primary school next door come out to meet me and we pose for some photos with their saltires. A nice way to start a big day.

At Moira's insistence I eat some breakfast and news comes through of a tweet from Andy Murray, who is sick of the negativity of the NO campaign. 'Let's do this,' he says. He'll take stick of course, but it is a brave thing to do, well expressed and right on campaign message. I just wish he'd said it yesterday.

The weather isn't great, but not dreadful, as we head to Turriff for some morning knock-ups. But I reckon it will take more than a spot of rain to stop people voting. I have the *Scottish Sun*'s Matt Bendoris in tow. He can write just a bit and is good company to have around.

First call is to Tesco's where a decent crowd has gathered, then on to one of the older council schemes. This is very solid SNP territory and the response seems good with plenty of waves and thumbs-up.

But there is one incident which gives me pause for thought. A young single mum asks to speak to me, so I go into her small, very tidy but sparsely furnished house. She has a baby, a Scottie dug and very little else. And she is terrified. She's never voted before, and fully intends to this time – but is locked in an agony of indecision in case she does the wrong thing and loses what little she has.

We talk for a while, I manage to allay her fears and she decides to vote YES. She is very relieved and I give her a hug of reassurance. When I emerge Matt asks me why I've taken so long and I tell him everything is fine. She has promised to vote Yes, and I'm sure she will. But I know that there will be others like her and I can't wipe every tear from every person in the country. I just can't.

Later, at the YES hub in Ellon, I find myself regretting not having exit polling. Normally, we'd sample at stations around the country, but it takes up people power and we thought we'd need all hands on deck. The exit polling can't change anything. It is normally a help in judging what the party should say on election night. Tonight will be different though – no party line, just a national decision. Even so, I'd have liked some figures to go on.

However, we do get an early taste of one thing. From the returns at the stations, we know the poll will be very high. Right through the campaign I have forecast a turnout of 80 per cent. It looks as though it is going to be even higher. That must be good news I think.

By 5 p.m. we are in Newmachar, where I have the best polling-day experience. At the community hall it seems everyone is voting YES and the schemes are festooned with saltires and YES regalia. It is very good for our morale.

From there we travel to Inverurie where the entire staff of the Spice of Life Indian restaurant has been out to vote YES. Inverurie is not as solid as Newmachar, but there are still plenty of encouraging signs.

I give one final campaign speech at 9 p.m. to a large crowd gathered in the car park. There is no point in holding back – and some words borrowed from Edinburgh-born Irish socialist leader James Connolly seem appropriate:

> The great are only great when the rest of us are on our knees. Whatever happens tonight we are no longer on our knees and the nation has changed. Changed for the better and changed for good.

Matt and I head to Eat on the Green, where we meet up with Moira. The owner Craig Wilson gives us the private room and access to his office so we can stay in touch with the campaign across the country. The plan is that we will fly to Edinburgh in the early hours.

After all the elections we've been through, Moira still believes I should know the results as soon as the polls close. I never really do, and with no exit poll this time, I am even more in the dark than usual. Every sense I have tells us we are home. My judgement is based on the 2011 election which we won in a landslide. We are much, much further forward than then, with vast sections of our community touched not by politics but by hope. Surely that hope must have prevailed over fear.

'Have we won?' Moira asks. 'I think so,' I reply and go to the office to ensure that all of our plans are laid in the event of a YES victory tomorrow. Statements have been prepared, including a joint statement with the UK government, a financial statement from the Scottish government, the announcement of the Monetary Authority, and the taking forward of European discussions. The key personnel have all accepted their positions. All is ready. All is in place. I learned in 2007 that, in the aftermath of a close-run thing, the man with the plan has a huge advantage. I make the calls because I think they will be necessary.

But I'm also a betting man, and while I am in the office I steal a quick look at the odds on Betfair. They haven't shifted, which is ominous. Even so, we have a great meal and I patiently answer Matt's questions for his article, which will certainly be overtaken by events one way or another.

The first bad news of the evening is the 54–46 YouGov exit poll against independence. YES HQ tell me we are still confident about Dundee and Glasgow, but elsewhere things look ropey. Keith Brown MSP, an experienced campaigner, isn't happy about Clackmannan, the first declaration. And when it comes in at 1.31 a.m. it is against us at 54–46. I know the game is up. Moira asks me: 'How bad is that?' I reply: 'It's only the first result and it's pretty close.'

But I go back up to Craig's office and this time I write a concession speech.

Day 100 (Reprise): Friday 19 September

I add the final sentence of my resignation speech only at the last minute. The version handed out to the press doesn't have the line: 'For me as leader my time is nearly over. But for Scotland the campaign continues and the dream shall never die.'

I take questions and thank everyone for being there. I'm calm. Always am in situations like that. But as I prepare to leave the stage I notice that BBC Scotland veteran Brian Taylor, who for a generation has observed just about everything in the development of our national story, has a tear or two in his eye. I place my left hand briefly on his shoulder as I walk to the door.

It is done. Moira, Lorraine Kay, Fergus Mutch and I set off homewards to Aberdeenshire. When we get to Prestonfield House, Johnny has revved up the 'copter. The entire private office staff and the events team have lined the entrance to say goodbye. It is a nice touch. I warn them that I have checked the civil service manual and there is no overtime for this situation, even on a Friday evening.

As we move to leave I notice a photographer hiding in the bushes. I beckon her out and pose for a photo with Johnny beside his helicopter.

On the way north I post a picture of Moira and me, with our headsets on, onto the parody site AngrySalmond #sexysocialism. This has been a source of constant humour and a fair bit of insight throughout the campaign. I judge it's time it received some official recognition.

Angry has tweeted: 'For the record I never lost. I simply repositioned the location of victory.'

I post: '@AngrySalmond #sexysocialdemocracy … I'll leave that in your capable hands!'

Angry replies: 'I think some universe ending paradox has just occurred. From one reality to another … Believe in SexySocialism.'

It is a glorious September evening as we sweep up the East Coast. Johnny, who has ambitions of entering into shared distillery ownership, points out a new one being built in the East Neuk. As we pass over the YES city of Dundee, into my head comes Robert Burns's reworking of an old Jacobite song, 'Bonnie Dundee':

Then awa' to the hills, to the lea, to the rocks,
E'er I own a usurper, I'll couch wi' the fox!
Then tremble, false Whigs, in the midst o' your glee,
Ye ha' no seen the last o' my bonnets and me.

Epilogue: The Scotland We Seek

At the end of the SNP Conference on 19 November 2014 I discovered the full impact of the change wrought by the referendum. I was in one of the dressing rooms at the back of the Perth Concert Hall, trying to adjust to my first moments of not being the SNP leader, a position I'd held for twenty of the last twenty-four years.

Political conferences tend to be exhausting and I was just expecting an evening with friends and family. But I agreed to go outside for a few moments because I was told some people had turned up wanting to have their picture taken with me.

There wasn't a handful of folk waiting – there were thousands. A flash crowd had gathered in response to a single Facebook message. I spent a considerable time walking through the people and talking to as many as I could, before making a speech of thanks to them, just as they had gathered to thank me.

They were the YES generation, not in terms of age but of attitude. People affected, touched, by the process of change.

A similar experience has been replicated a hundred times since the referendum. A week after the Conference Nicola Sturgeon packed out the 12,000-seater Hydro arena in Glasgow.

There were more people at that single meeting than the Labour Party has members in Scotland. And it could have been filled eight times over before reaching beyond the SNP's own membership.

Meanwhile, a few hundred yards along the road at the SECC, the Radical Independence Group were simultaneously holding a conference with a further 3,000 attending. These are levels of political activism which have seldom been seen anywhere that I know of. Full stop.

On 18 January this year, as the SNP's newly announced candidate for the Gordon constituency, I held a campaign organisation meeting in the Insch leisure centre on a Sunday night. The weather was not auspicious. Indeed it was wild.

These meetings are normally both necessary and necessarily dry affairs – a matter of press-ganging a few people into the key election roles. We were uncertain if we would get a quorum, given the conditions. But 250 people turned up. In a snowdrift. Not the usual sort of organisation meeting, but then these are not normal times.

In the months since the referendum I have talked to thousands of people about the campaign and about the result. Overwhelmingly, they have said two things to me: thank you or sorry. Occasionally both. The 'thank you' is for giving Scotland the opportunity to vote for independence. The 'sorry' is not so much an admission of making a mistake, although occasionally it can be that. It is more often a regret for not being able to vote YES. It is a recognition that political change is a two-way process. Those advocating the change have the responsibility to make their case, and those hearing the argument have the responsibility of being active citizens, not passive in the face of organised intimidation from those with a vested interest in the status quo.

It would be a mistake to believe that only YES voters will be voting SNP at the forthcoming general election. Most YES supporters will do exactly that, but so will a substantial number of NO voters. They will now take the same path to move the country forward and ensure the 'vow' that was made to Scotland is honoured and honoured in full. For the old conventional press all of this is very distressing. For the newly engaged electorate it is all very exciting – a chance not to replay the referendum, but to make a process of change meaningful and substantial.

There have been times like this before in Scotland. I remember, for example, the extraordinary level of attendances at public meetings during the poll-tax campaign, and again in the run-up to the 1992 election. However, the process is now amplified many times over through social media, which gives it a resonance and staying power. Indeed social media provides much more than amplification. It is not just a great advertising board for meetings, it is interactive. It feeds both ways. The audience become the cast.

For example, the week after the Insch organisation meeting we were back in the town doing some canvassing and an interview with Buzzfeed. One of the SNP activists there, Billy Sangster, asked if he could do the same thing on his audio blog. We did this in Dyce the following week. The interview was fun, entertaining, and he duly posted it online. A few days later one of Scotland's leading political journalists asked me for a comment based on it. Billy's blog was making the story for the written press – a case of the new media leading the old.

This flow of information cannot and must not be stopped in a democracy. In addition, the established structures are no longer trusted. 'Auntie Beeb' is now regarded by many people in Scotland as being more akin to a wicked stepmother.

The Scottish referendum was not just a battle between YES and NO. It was not even just a struggle between hope and fear, although it certainly was that.

It was a contest between two types of media. The old established order against the new upstart army. The old media was hostile to independence certainly, but many were just hostile to any change. They live in a world where negativity is king, where debacle, chaos, scandal and crisis dictate every description of every story. The new media is chaotic and even anarchic, but it is also essentially creative and it is much, much faster. It is the place where dreams are allowed to flourish.

The interaction between new media and street and grassroots campaigning is also vital. Many of the YES campaign's most successful events were organised at a moment's notice and we were totally taken aback by our ability to do this. The lesson internationally is also clear. Combine the right social message with the right social media and any established order will have to justify itself to survive or change to sustain itself. Political democracy has just become quicker and smarter and far more equal.

In 1302 the Flemish peasants humbled the flower of French chivalry at Courtrai. In 1314 the Scottish foot soldiers shattered the English heavy horse at Bannockburn. Both battles demonstrated that the medieval world had changed and the established certainties of power altered. Now in the field of modern democratic politics the peasants have a chance of unseating the knights. It doesn't make the contest equal or fair, just more equal and more balanced.

Given the forces arrayed against us, and where we were starting from, a YES vote of 45 per cent could be seen as a triumph. However, it could have been better. We might have won, but only if everything had gone right in content and in timing. 'If only' are the two saddest words in the English language. The key to this referendum was the YouGov poll ten days out. That is what led to the sustained fear-mongering campaign of the last few days, and above all to the 'vow' that presented the safer option which some people sympathetic to change were persuaded to take. To the words 'if only' can be added 'it only'. It only required the 'vow' to sway 1 in 20 voters to be decisive, and it did.

If the poll had come later then it would have been too late to organise the response. Momentum could have swept YES to victory. For the YES campaign it was a poll too soon.

*

So what has happened since the referendum and, more importantly, where does all this take us?

In my resignation speech last September, I suggested that Westminster must have its feet held 'to the fire' in order to deliver its promises to Scotland. The promises made were for 'near federalism', 'devo to the max' or 'home rule'.

The Smith Commission offer has come and gone. My old friend Robert Smith could move his cross-party commission only at the pace of the slowest boat in the convoy. That boat, according to all accounts, was the Labour Party. The commission duly reported on 27 November. Its lowest common denominator position left 70 per cent of taxation and 85 per cent of welfare powers still to be controlled by Westminster. That may be many things, but it is not 'home rule' or 'close to federalism' or 'devo to the max'.

By 22 January, the Smith Commission had been translated into a UK government Command Paper which was extraordinary in both its lack of ambition and inherent contradictions.

Two examples will suffice. Smith had adopted a principle of 'no detriment'* in order to protect the Scottish Parliament from the usual process whereby the Treasury acts as judge and jury in any dispute over funding. This is the way all UK government departments are treated, and in every key respect

---

* The principle of 'no detriment' is outlined in the Smith Commission's report. The first part of the principle, that there should be 'No detriment as a result of the decision to devolve further power', seems clear enough. The second part is not: that there should be 'No detriment as a result of UK Government or Scottish Government policy decisions post-devolution.' Smith explains: 'Where either the UK or the Scottish Governments makes policy decisions that affect the tax receipts or expenditure of the other, the decision-making government will either reimburse the other if there is an additional cost, or receive a transfer from the other if there is a saving.'

This gives ample ground for argument and confusion because services and benefits overlap, as long as many policy areas are only partly devolved. There are precedents for being sceptical about leaving such vagueness in the lap of Treasury adjudication. For example, in 2001 the administration of First Minister Henry McLeish introduced payments for free personal care in Scotland. This resulted in a reduction of housing-benefit entitlements paid by Westminster. Despite McLeish's pleas to have access to this saving to help fund his policy, his own colleagues in London refused point-blank. It is not clear if there can be a satisfactory resolution when responsibilities are split. Hence one of the arguments for having a clear division of responsibilities as proposed by the Scottish Government.

Scotland (and Wales) are regarded by the Treasury mandarins as if they were mere extensions of Whitehall.

However, in the Command Paper the principle of 'no detriment' is taken to mean that any devolution of any policy area will be caught in a financial straitjacket that is so tight as to make it redundant. This is neatly illustrated in the following paragraph:

> 2.2.7 An outcome which requires the citizens of one part of the UK to make a greater contribution to fiscal consolidation as a result of the actions of devolved government would be contrary to the 'no detriment' principles set out in the Smith Commission Agreement. Therefore the fiscal framework must require Scotland to contribute proportionally to fiscal consolidation at the pace set out by the UK Government across devolved and reserved areas.

Further, the paper contains the following section, written apparently in all sobriety but certainly with no appreciation of its comic impact:

> As a result of the Smith Commission Agreement, the Scottish Parliament will control around 60 per cent of spending in Scotland and retain around 40 per cent of Scottish tax. This will therefore make the Scottish Government one of the most powerful sub-central governments in the OECD, just behind the Canadian provinces and Swiss cantons.

It will come as a great relief to the active citizenry of the ancient European nation of Scotland that their recent clarion call expressed in a national referendum has been well and truly heeded by Westminster – we are to be granted almost as much financial power as a Swiss canton!

The word 'retain' is used by the civil service drafters where taxation is concerned because VAT revenues are to be 'assigned' with no control by the Scottish Parliament, while the tax base of income tax in terms of tax reliefs and allowances is still held in London. Clearly it would be wrong to use the word 'control' over taxation where the Scottish government had no influence over the rates in the case of VAT, or the tax base in the case of income tax. Hence the classic Sir Humphrey deployment of the word 'retain'.

The Better Together parties claimed that the 'vow' had been redeemed. In reality, the Smith Commission watered down the 'vow' and the Command Paper diluted the Smith Commission.

Both the third sector and STUC poured buckets of cold water over the Smith Commission report and Command Paper, while Labour, after first claiming that the promise had been delivered in full, went into a sharp reverse within days. Gordon Brown made yet another political comeback, this time after his formal retirement, to launch the rather unoriginally entitled 'vow plus'. All this was rather too much for Labour's Better Together colleagues in the Tory and Liberal parties who pointed out that Labour had been actually advocating the 'vow minus' in the Smith Commission.

Labour's sudden about-turn on the 'vow' came about as part of the frenetic campaign of their new leader, Jim Murphy. The Blairite MP and Iraq war cheerleader was elected in December

2014 after the position fell vacant with the spectacular resignation of my old adversary Johann Lamont.

In one of the more memorable departures from office, Johann finally blew her top at 'London Labour' for their treatment of the Party in Scotland as a 'branch office'. With Labour trailing 10, 20 or even – in two MORI polls – almost 30 points behind the SNP, Murphy has tried activity as a substitute for strategy. There has been no cause too populist, no policy reversal too brazen, not to be given a test run by him as he tries desperately to reinvent himself as a crypto-nationalist. However, the revelation in February that he had claimed £1.30 for Irn-Bru from his Commons expenses made him look ridiculous, as did his blatantly populist call for the reintroduction of alcohol at football grounds. A YouGov poll of the same month showed him a full 50 per cent behind Nicola Sturgeon in popularity ratings.

The new First Minister has laid out a clear parliamentary strategy for the SNP, first turning to the real possibility of a balanced parliament. If Cameron could not win an election with an overall majority against a beleaguered Gordon Brown in 2010, it seems unlikely that he can succeed five years later. It might therefore have been assumed that this coalition government, which has systematically ensured the poorest sections of the community have sacrificed most during the recession, while looking after the richest, would have been deservedly swept out of office. But Ed Miliband instils neither the personal nor the policy confidence to sweep to power. The Labour opposition has failed time and time again to bring forward a programme to present a viable alternative to the coalition's austerity measures. Indeed, in all major aspects, Labour has merely mimicked them.

A balanced parliament is seen as a problem by the political establishment. It will create difficulties for the Westminster elite. But Westminster's difficulty is Scotland's opportunity.

A large block of SNP members at Westminster is entirely possible – indeed likely. Nicola has ruled out any deal – formal or informal – with the Conservatives. The reasons for this are clear and deeply rooted in Scottish society. The Tories have been in decline since the 1950s because they have been increasingly perceived to operate against the Scottish interest. It follows that any party that joins forces with them, as the Liberals have done in government and Labour did in the referendum campaign, is likely to pay a high political price.

Even if that were not so, then Cameron's appalling breach of faith on the morning after the referendum would have ruled out the Tories as people who could be relied upon to deliver any promise or commitment, however solemn, to the people of Scotland.

However, nothing else has been ruled out by the First Minister, and that again is entirely sensible. It is unlikely that the SNP would enter a formal coalition with the Labour Party. It is more probable that, given our experience of running a minority government in a balanced parliament in Scotland between 2007 and 2011, we would prefer to negotiate on a vote-by-vote basis. But Nicola is right to keep these options open.

Labour's mantra is that an SNP vote will make a Cameron prime ministership more likely. It is a familiar refrain, but it is patently not true. The ability of the Tories to survive in office is determined by the number of Conservatives elected in England, not by the number of non-Tories elected in Scotland.

In order to stay as PM, Cameron will have to survive a vote in the House of Commons. He will be opposed by the SNP in that vote, and with only one Tory MP in Scotland, and a possible Lib Dem wipeout, he will receive little or no help from Scotland as a whole.

As well as the existing parliamentary rules, which – contrary to Labour claims – do NOT provide for the leader of the largest party to become Prime Minister, there is also the new Parliament Act to consider. This makes it much more difficult to hold another election before the end of a five-year term, and therefore much more likely that an agreement will be needed to sustain a minority government in office. Only a vote of the Commons can force an election before the five years are up, and for obvious reasons if one side wants an election the other side probably does not. The Parliament Act therefore enhances the likelihood of minority administrations and greatly increases the potential power of minority parties.

Parroting that it is a choice between 'us' or 'them Tories' has worked many times for Labour before in Scotland. But the Better Together proposition of shoulder-to-shoulder campaigning has poisoned that particular well. We are now in a Scotland where the old political tunes have lost their resonance. The electorate is no longer prepared just to sing along.

Real delivery on the 'vow' will be front and centre of the SNP's approach to the election but, as the First Minister has emphasised, our appeal will be economic and social as well as constitutional. The Scottish government's submission to the Smith Commission spelt out what 'home rule', 'near federalism' or 'devo to the max' should really mean.

In contrast to the confusion and incoherence of the three degrees of unionism, the Scottish government outlined a clear opportunity to devolve everything bar defence, foreign affairs and monetary policy. And then pay a contribution to Westminster for these common services and make a negotiated payment for debt interest on past borrowings.

The Smith Commission principle of 'no detriment' could then be used in its proper way, with the Barnett* block grant or alternatively the remittance to Westminster adjusted to take account of the initial impact. No one could reasonably

* The Barnett formula is named after the late Joel Barnett, former Chief Secretary to the Treasury, who introduced it as a solution to Cabinet disputes in the run-up to the planned political devolution of 1979. It was modelled on the 1888 Goschen formula, which was devised by the then Chancellor George Goschen as a preparation for Irish Home Rule. Under Barnett much of 'identifiable' public spending is adjusted by population ratios. Thus increases in expenditure, say on health, in England are adjusted by the population ratio of Scotland (or Wales or Northern Ireland) to England and then by the percentage to which that service is devolved. That gives the Barnett 'consequential' for that spending department in each spending round, and the total from each subject determines the overall allocation. Often attacked as a means by which the three other nations of the UK can entrench their public spending advantage over England, in fact Barnett is a convergence formula when public spending is increasing. This is because over time the population shares of increases will dominate the overall total. The arguments for Barnett are that it offers a robust way of allocating spending, it provides compensation for the fact that parts of non-geographically identified spending, such as defence, are heavily weighted to parts of England, and in the case of Scotland it provides some (relatively small) return for the oil revenues accumulated by the Treasury over the period since Barnett was devised. The formula has been much criticised over the years, often mistakenly, and not least by Barnett himself, leading to the comparison with Palmerston's description of the Schleswig-Holstein question: only three people understood it – one's mad, one's dead and Joe Barnett has forgotten!

complain about further devolution which left the Scottish Parliament no better or worse off financially in year one. That is what any contribution should reflect. After the initial period the Parliament would prosper on the success of its own policies or rise to the challenge when problems occur. Clearly the Parliament has to be able to benefit from its own policies. It is just as important that it is not penalised for success as it is that it is not compensated for failure. That is what 'home rule', 'devo to the max' or 'close to federalism' actually means.

This approach will achieve in economic and financial terms what the late Donald Dewar achieved in political terms by devising the Scotland Act of 1998 to devolve everything which was not specifically reserved. For example, legislation on climate change, one of the great issues facing the planet, is devolved to the Scottish Parliament. This was because no one in 1998 thought it important enough to be listed in the Scotland Bill as reserved, and therefore it was by definition devolved. And so instead of a line-by-line, clause-by-clause struggle for each devolved competence there was a much shorter, more coherent Bill that listed the reserved functions and presumed everything else devolved.

At a stroke, Dewar's act of near-genius cut straight through the intractable problems which had becalmed devolution proposals for the previous generation. Instead of a succession of parliamentary skirmishes fought on each and every subject to be devolved, which had taken five years to no avail in the 1970s, the legislation sped through its main parliamentary processes in five months in 1998.

We are in a similar position now with finance. If we follow the Command Paper then the Scottish Parliament will be left trussed up in Westminster's financial straitjacket for years, even if the proposals are successfully delivered. There will be endless battles of attrition with the Treasury over the real financial impact of each and every Scottish government measure.

After due, proper and the most careful consideration, Sir Nicholas Macpherson will no doubt adjudicate in favour of his own department. Year by year, policy by policy, the Scottish position will be eroded as Westminster achieves by stealth what it cannot achieve politically at present – the erosion of the Barnett spending guarantees. Westminster will then over time both cut Scotland's spending advantage and also grant no control over Scotland's resource wealth or the real policy discretion to grow the economy.

However, if we cut the Gordian knot on finance just as Dewar cut it on legislation then a different and better prospectus opens up. There would be but one negotiation: to cover the remittance to Westminster. That would be on the Smith principle of 'no detriment'. After that, these payments would be indexed to an appropriate measure – perhaps spending in the remaining departments that were UK in their scope, such as defence and foreign affairs. From then on Scotland will have the ability to benefit from our successes and also take responsibility for our mistakes. The Treasury's iron grip of Scotland's finances would be ended once and for all. It will truly be 'devo to the max'.

Three examples show why this position opens up real home rule.

Air passenger duty (APD) has long been a target of the Scottish government for devolution, and indeed it is included in the Command Paper. A sizeable reduction in the duty would open up the prospect of a substantial boost to connectivity for business and additional tourism through direct flights.

A number of key studies have suggested a 'Laffer Curve' effect whereby a reduction in this specific tax could result in a boost to general tax revenues – one of the holy grails of public finance. The likely impact would undoubtedly be strong in Scotland. However, the boost to general taxation is dependent on control of the taxation base. Anything else would, at best, be fraught with difficulty in Treasury negotiations or, at worst, result in the Scottish government taking the hit of a decline in specific revenues and the UK Treasury taking the advantage of a lift in general taxation. One interpretation of the Command Paper would also leave the Scots stuck with the bill of any assumed decline in English flights, and therefore APD, as a result of increased competition from Scottish airports.

The second example is the affordability of the revolution in childcare, inspired by the work of the late Professor Ailsa McKay and pledged to be taken forward by the new First Minister. Little or none of the success in securing the expansion of women in work has been reflected in a boost to Scottish government revenues, even though the percentage of female employment is now nearly 5 per cent higher than the UK average. However, all of the cost of the expansion of nursery and childcare has been borne by the Scottish government.

To complete this revolution and seize the opportunity, with all the benefits that it offers to the future of Scottish society and to the balance and resilience of the economy, then the Scottish government should control the entire taxation base – not just the assignation of 40 per cent of it. Any other proposition will at very best slow down the affordability of the policy.

The third example concerns the health service. The realisation that the future of public funding of the Scottish health service was dependent on policy in England was one of the triggers in the referendum campaign which provoked the movement to YES. The more privatisation in England, the greater the pressure on spending in Scotland. Under the Barnett formula the funding available for Scottish spending on health is a direct proportion of that spent in England. If there is less public spending in England as a result of a shift to private finance then there is a knock-on impact in Scotland. The more off-the-books in England, the less on the Barnett books in Scotland.

In response, the Better Together parties contest that this is not the case because we can spend what we like in Scotland. However, the issue is not the right to spend, but the available income. The alternative claim by Alistair Darling during the referendum that the English health service was not really being privatised after all is even weaker, given that this same proposition is one of Labour's major 'weapons' in the general election campaign in England. The threat to Scottish health spending will not be countered by the Smith Commission proposals, but would be settled by 'devo to the max', 'home rule' or 'near federalism'.

In addition, the First Minister has already confirmed that, as long as there is an umbilical link between spending on health in England and available spending in Scotland, then SNP votes in the House of Commons to defend the integrity of the public health service in England are well justified.

The connection between the constitutional issue and the economic and social imperatives was one of the factors which powered the YES campaign forward in the final stages of the referendum. That connection can now do something similar for the SNP in the general election campaign in Scotland.

In an important speech in London on 10 February 2015 Nicola laid out the economic basis on which the SNP will fight the coming general election. Both Tory and Labour are committed to bringing the budget into balance by means of some further savage retrenchment in public spending. Nicola staked out some different and firmer ground, pointing out that, by extending the period allowed for full recovery of the finances, then an anti-austerity position is entirely credible and plausible. Indeed, given the deflationary risks present in the international economy, it is very necessary.

The current refusal of the Labour Party to countenance anything other than Treasury orthodoxy is a familiar weakness. My old boss at the Royal Bank in the 1980s, Grant Baird, himself a former Bank of England economist, used to recount a remark he attributed to former Chancellor James Callaghan, who had wrestled unsuccessfully with defending a fixed sterling exchange rate. When Anthony Barber, as Tory Chancellor, floated sterling in 1972, Callaghan mused: 'They never told me I could do that!'

Motivating the YES campaign right through the referendum was the hope that society could be ordered differently, that a fairer and more successful country could be worked for by securing the key levers of power. The Westminster elite have held them for too long for any good that they have been doing. By making that straightforward challenge to the continuing austerity plans of Labour and Tories, the First Minister has pitched her tent on that field, not of dreams, but of hope.

In addition, further credibility could be added to this alternative economic agenda by refusing to waste a full £100 billion in the lifetime costs of renewing the Trident nuclear system. The crucial 'gateway' decision is due next year which will commit the full expenditure on the Trident renewal. If that vote goes in favour then Trident goes ahead. If it goes against then Trident is at best cancelled or at worst postponed. In addition the recent revelation that Trident renewal is set to swallow up to one-third of the entire defence budget means that its affordability has become as big a question as its morality.

The First Minister's plan will have substantial appeal beyond the borders of Scotland, and, in anticipation of that, Nicola's approach to Leanne Wood of Plaid Cymru and Natalie Bennett of the Green Party in England represents sound strategy. It is of interest that this progressive agenda is being led by women. That kind of forward-looking politics is likely to make more hearts beat more quickly than another ever so weary procession of Labour's parliamentary army of invisible men from Scottish constituencies.

The framework for the SNP approach to the election is therefore clear:

- A strong group of SNP members working in conjunction with allies – and hopefully in a balanced Parliament – who will ensure the delivery of the 'vow', not in its anaemic version of the spring of 2015, but in its full-blooded promise of 2014;
- The presentation of an alternative to the economics of endless austerity which has gripped the

Westminster parties, combined with the cancellation of the replacement nuclear system that the UK clearly cannot afford;

- Opposition to the waste of time and effort of a Euro referendum or de minimis demanding a guarantee that any such vote will be subject to a triple lock of majorities in all of the component nations of the United Kingdom.

There will also be ample scope for more immediate economic and social demands.

The 'living wage' in the public sector is one of the key achievements of the administration which I led. Introduced in 2011 in the teeth of financial retrenchment, it pointed the way to a better and fairer society.

The Scottish government has made substantial strides in introducing it in government contracts; for example in the new ScotRail franchise. However, its general application is restricted by European competition policy, despite the fatuous claims of Labour to the contrary. This should be a major and early target for discussion in the Commission, with every likelihood of success. There is a general realisation across many European countries that there is a need to seize back the aspiration of a social Europe which was such a powerful vision in the 1980s and 1990s.

The protection of jobs in the oil industry will be another likely target.

On 1 January 2007, the price of Brent crude was $57.40. Eighteen months later it touched $140. Eighteen months after that it was down to $45. Last year it was back to $115. As I write it is just over $60, having recovered from below $50 at the start of the year.

No one really knows what the price of oil is going to be in the short term. It is a much safer assumption, however, that over the next thirty years the price will trend stronger, not weaker, and that oil shocks downwards, which will certainly happen, will be followed, as night follows day, by oil shocks upwards. The price which governs in the long term is the replacement cost of each new barrel.

Much more importantly, we know that the available resource offshore Scotland is up to 24 billion barrels. It could be more than this depending on the outcome of the range of discoveries west of Shetland, the timescale of West Coast exploration, which has, for military reasons, long been an underexplored area, and what happens with hard-to-reach resources in the North Sea. What is certain is that it will be a major resource for the next half-century.

We need immediate action to save jobs and protect that future. The track record of Westminster is to move like lightning to toughen tax when times are good and prices high but to move as if through treacle when prices are low and times are tough. No doubt the imminent arrival of a large squad of SNP MPs will concentrate the mind wonderfully. What is not achieved in the budget can be secured post-election.

A third possibility for immediate action will pay dividends for the North of England as well as Scotland. The prospect of tying up vast amounts of capital in slowly building a fast rail line which might reach the north of England in a generation or so has not commanded universal support. However, there is no reason at all why the real benefits of high-speed rail, which does not mean connectivity with London, but building connectivity between northern cities and producing thriving economic growth hubs, could not be secured. A Glasgow–Edinburgh–Newcastle line would be built much faster and carry more economic impact than merely waiting for Godot and 'high-speed rail'.

Similarly, improvements in the West Coast Line, the East Coast Line to Aberdeen and between Aberdeen and Inverness are the rail investments which make sense. Osborne claims to be addressing this, but the figures tell a very different story.

A report last year by the Institute for Public Policy Research showed that London's Crossrail alone was set to receive nine times more funding than all of the rail projects from the North of England's three regions combined. In terms of all infrastructure the spend per head in London amounted to £5,426 compared with £223 in the North East of England. A real restructuring of the transport budget to counter this inequity is long overdue and should be an SNP priority in the next Parliament.

*

The scene is now set for round two of a titanic struggle. The political stars have once again aligned to allow Scottish progress to be made.

When I entered the House of Commons in 1987 the place was still inhabited by political giants – Foot, Thatcher, Benn, Biffen, Heath. I didn't agree with most of them and some were well past their best, but Ted Heath in his dotage would be more than a match for Cameron in his prime. Neil Kinnock's worst day at the office would be regarded as a success for Ed Miliband.

In contrast to a discredited and weakened establishment at Westminster, the people who elect them are mobilised and strong. I turned the Scottish National Party into an avowed social democratic force, but the force that is with us now is as much to do with social media democracy as with social democracy. In this environment, the social media masses have a fair chance of humbling the tax-evading classes. I hope to see that front of battle lour at Westminster.

For all of my political life I have believed in Scottish independence. Since 1997 and the vote to establish a Scottish Parliament I have believed it to be likely. Since the referendum campaign of this year I have believed it to be a matter of when, not if.

There are a number of situations which could provide the circumstances. There are a number of events which could precipitate the next opportunity. There are a number of variables which will dictate the timing, a timing which ultimately lies in the hands of the people.

And that is the point. The YES side lost the vote but the referendum changed the nation. The people who emerged from the 100 days' campaign are different from those who embarked upon that journey. That changed nation will both create and secure the future opportunities for progress.

The means and procedure are now set. The Scottish people can, if they so wish at any Scottish election, vote for a party or parties who wish to put the issue to the touch once again.

After all, everyone deserves a second chance.

Every person and every nation.

Acknowledgements

This could be one of life's lessons.

I had thought that, having written countless articles, speeches and presentations, then producing a book might be something of the same, just more words. It isn't. It requires much more effort, both individual and collective.

This is despite the fact that I followed one of my granda's adages in writing this volume. In the introduction I describe how much I owe to my grandfather as indeed I owe to my grannie Salmond. That other Alex Salmond once told me that he adopted a two pan-drop strategy as a senior elder in St Ninian's Craigmailen parish kirk. When listening to the sermons of candidate ministers, Granda tested them against the time it took him to suck a pan drop. A one pan-drop minister he judged to be light and insubstantial. A three pan-drop man was long-winded and would bore the congregation to tears. However, a two pan-drop minister was worthy of great consideration, just the right balance between content and length. I have therefore tried to write a two pan-drop book!

Writing is therapeutic and certainly makes you think. Particularly about what you owe to the support of others.

My first thanks therefore are to my family. Foremost to my wife, Moira, who has been endlessly patient about the process, and decidedly firm in her opinions about the content. Keynes once said that 'it is astonishing the foolish things one can temporarily believe when one thinks too long alone'. With Moira's help I may have avoided at least some of that danger.

In a wider sense, writing something which is, in part at least, autobiographical gives me pause for thought about my wider family and how much I owe to their support. To Faither, to whom I dedicate the book along with my late mother. To my siblings Margaret, Gail and Bob, and their families: Neil and Ian (in the case of Margaret and Andrew) and Karen, Christina and Mark (in the case of Gail and David).

Maggie is herself a granny of two boys, Archie and Harris, thanks to Ian and Kay. Since her retirement, my big sister has blossomed into a considerable handicap golfer. Indeed she would in all likelihood now thrash me on a golf course. Such are the sacrifices of high office.

The real sacrifices are made by a politician's family. Those who are themselves involved in politics, like Gail and her two lovely daughters, Karen and Tina, but also those who aren't. All were called upon to defend the cause privately, and occasionally publicly, when their son, brother or uncle was leading a referendum campaign, and all unfailingly did. Luckily they have been grounded in the same secure earth as me.

I would like to record thanks to the Scottish civil service throughout my time in office. It is common in Westminster these days to blame the service for the failings of government.

This has not been my experience. Under first John Elvidge and more recently Peter Housden I always enjoyed huge support and effort from officials throughout government. They have attempted to carry forward the democratically chosen policy in the best traditions of the service.

A number are mentioned individually in the book and rightly so. Many, many more inevitably are not, and so I would like to place on record my thanks in particular to all of my private office present and past, press and events teams, my GCS drivers, protection officers and the Bute House staff. Somewhere in the bootleg section of social media is a 'last interview' at Bute between myself as First Minister and Jackie Bird of the BBC. If you can secure a copy, pay decent money for it. Alexander Anderson plays me, Geoff Aberdein plays Jackie, and my press and communications team, led by Aileen Easton and Tim Christie, play themselves. If you can forgive Geoff's legs and make-up then it does indicate a degree of mutual affection as well as the highest regard.

This brings me to the SPADs in government. If civil servants are traduced by Tory ministers then special advisers get traduced by everybody. In fact, led by Geoff Aberdein, they were committed, loyal and insightful. Like my private office team they did not always see the sunniest side of my nature. But unfailingly they responded above and beyond the call of duty.

I love the SNP parliamentary group. It had the great advantage of having a solidarity forged in the fire of minority government. With a tiny handful of exceptions, that spirit and positivity has translated into the period of majority government. Gill Paterson MSP, as group convener, is not someone I have always agreed with politically. He is, however, someone I could always rely on, without fail. Nicola Sturgeon has made a hugely successful start to her term as First Minister. She will be well supported by this highly talented group of parliamentarians. Our groups in Westminster led by Angus Robertson and in Europe by Ian Hudghton make up a formidable SNP parliamentary array.

My ministerial team, including the law officers, throughout my term as First Minister are due many thanks. As some may know, I am an admirer of Labour Prime Minister Harold Wilson. It is said that the one political gift that he lacked was the ability to sack people. In my case there were reasons I found this difficult. I can honestly say that I did not have a single failure in my ministerial team, and when changes were made it was because of the inevitable requirement to let other people show what they could do. This is one problem I now gladly bequeath to Nicola.

I led the SNP for the bulk of the last quarter of the century. Harold Macmillan once said that his problems with the Conservative Party lessened considerably once he became leader. By and large that was my experience with the SNP. What I do know is that I will never have the pleasure of leading a more committed and generous-hearted group of people. Few things make tears well up, but one that does is thinking of those generations of Scottish nationalists who put their hearts and souls into the cause with no hope whatsoever of political preferment, or even modest success. The SNP has now expanded by more than ten times within ten years. The task is to ensure that a mass-membership party retains the commitment and spirit of the women and men of principle who established and built the movement.

My local constituency party in the North East of Scotland has been unfailingly loyal. Everything I have in politics has been down to these people and the communities from which they spring. There was some press clatter late last year of me moving elsewhere in Scotland to contest a Westminster seat. Why on earth, when you have the honour of representing such people, would you ever even consider moving elsewhere? These fine folk are well served by a group of no fewer than twenty-eight local councillors on Aberdeenshire Council. Their excellent effort at community level makes the work of a constituency MSP much more productive. The councillors include my election agent, Stuart Pratt, who has guided me successfully through no fewer than eight parliamentary contests. He has agreed to try for an ninth in May.

My own constituency office, under a succession of staff, has long held down the job of running a local parliamentary office which was used by the entire country. That they have done it so well is entirely down to the calibre of these young women and men. Currently led by Fergus Mutch, the group is made up of Ann Marie Parry, Andrew Henderson, Stuart Donaldson and Gavin Mowat, who work for me as well as for North East MSP Christian Allard. They all rose to the challenge of the referendum with customary spirit and determination. I have also been greatly assisted by my two campaign drivers, James Tulloch and Jimmy Johnston, who must have listened to more speeches in more halls than the Official Report staff of the Scots Parliament!

In the production of this volume itself I would like to thank first the staff at Peters Fraser & Dunlop and particularly Caroline Michel, who first saw the potential for this book. Then HarperCollins for their unfailing courtesy in confronting seemingly impossible deadlines. This applies particularly to my editor, Martin Redfern, who responded gallantly to the challenge of learning whole new vocabularies in keeping this volume on the straight and narrow. In which regard I should also add my thanks to Angus Brendan MacNeil MP for his help with the Gaelic and Cllr Cryle Shand for his advice on Doric.

My lawyer and fellow parliamentary candidate Tasmina Ahmed-Sheikh contributed massively to the editing process as did my associate editor Alan Muir. These two, working with Martin, formed a powerful trio who kept me working almost as hard as they did. In this they were helped by my own staff Lorraine Kay and Lisa Gordon and my accountant, John Cairns.

Michael Russell MSP provided useful advice as did Joan McAlpine MSP in reading through the early drafts. The staff at The Marcliffe in Aberdeen, Continis, Jolly's and The George in Edinburgh are also due thanks for providing the setting for key drafting meetings

I should add that, just as with the referendum campaign itself, any omissions and mistakes are mine and mine alone.

In the tenth century, the monks at Deer Abbey in Aberdeenshire, a few miles from Strichen, rounded off their treasured biblical folio in Latin with the following colophon in common Gaelic (i.e. common to Scotland and Ireland). It demonstrates that Buchan wit, as biting as the wind, is rather more than a millennium old.

It reads: 'Be it on the conscience of anyone who reads this little book to say a prayer for the soul of the poor wretch who laboured so long in writing it.'

Alex Salmond MSP
Strichen, March 2015

PART II

Election Day

Thursday 7 May 2015

At breakfast, Moira asks me to predict the result, as she always does. I write '51' on a piece of paper, fold it and hand it to her.

I start the knock-up of voters late afternoon in Aberdeen. Unlike my previous constituencies in Aberdeenshire, the Gordon Westminster parliamentary seat reaches right into the city.

Few people are in and all who are have voted, save one guy who arrives on his motorcycle visiting his mum. This is a good sign. Not only does he want a selfie but it transpires that he has come back early from a bike rally in France to put his 'crossie in the richt place' – sounds to me that we are in for a high poll.

I steal a few moments having a kickabout with some of the local lads and notice that when the ball ends up near the wall onto the busy airport road, cars start hooting. As an experiment I stand on the wall, and just about all the commuting cars start hooting and waving. I wave back and ponder if I should just have stood there all day waving and dispensed entirely with the knock-up!

I head back to Inverurie in my 'snappy bus' via Bridge of Don and Dyce, where we are hoping for big and favourable turnouts. We believe that this traditionally SNP/Labour part of Aberdeen is going to give us pretty overwhelming support.

When I return to the campaign office I get the latest instalment of our exit poll, which we conduct over four diverse polling stations across the constituency. The only recent contest in which we have not conducted an exit poll was the referendum, and I have regretted it ever since. It is just about the one type of poll which is reliable.

The poll makes great reading. Indeed great is an understatement. Our vote is up nearly 30 per cent, and even allowing for the fact that the exit poll measures votes on the day, which will slightly exaggerate our support, it points to an overwhelming victory. If repeated around Scotland it will exceed even the wildest expectations and confirm the most optimistic polls.

I still go out in Inverurie and continue to knock up. The rain comes around 7 p.m. – annoying but late enough not to make a huge difference to turnout. Traditionally in the North East between 5 and 8 p.m. is our best time, as the workers with young families come back home, have their tea and then go out and vote SNP.

For fun and perhaps just a little superstition I decide to do a last 'jump and shout' in Uryside Drive, Inverurie, in a huge new development on the north-east of the town which is notable for having an SNP poster up on just about every house. I meet a bunch of young women having a 'make-up day' and hanging out of a top-floor window. This is my second campaign 'pamper party' in two days and the selfies are somewhat adventurous. I decide this might be a wise time to halt the formal campaign.

On my way back to Strichen I call in at the Ellon polling station where I had started the day some 12 hours earlier. One of our activists has been on polling-gate duty all day long. As I thank her it suddenly occurs to me that I had yet to see any other party activists at any polling station with the exception of a nice Liberal lady in Oldmeldrum. In contrast, every single polling station had a team of SNP folk busy on their knock-ups.

I meet a couple just back from holiday. This time they had not returned early like the guy on the motorbike, but their transatlantic flight had been late into London and so they had come straight to the polls in an airport taxi some 20 hours after leaving the United States. I thank them profusely. 'How do you know we voted for you?' they ask. 'A lucky guess,' I reply. They tell me they probably won't be staying up for the results programme.

On the way to Strichen, Nicola phones. She had been at a polling station in Govan and was concerned that someone had not met her eye. It is not unusual for this normally ice cool lady to have a campaign wobble. Indeed the only campaign I can remember her not having one was the referendum which we then lost. Mind you with the YES results in Glasgow there was probably no reason for her to worry.

I tell her we have an exit poll. 'What does it show?' she asks. 'Prepare for a landslide,' I reply.

I also take the opportunity to mention that I had placed a bet on her to win the first televised leadership debate. I haven't been quite sure if she would approve of me betting on her, but after all 11–2 is 11–2!

Just before Moira and I leave Strichen for the Aberdeen Conference and Exhibition Centre in Aberdeen the national exit poll, devised by John Curtice, comes over on Sky TV. For most people this must have been an extraordinary moment. For me the Scottish results confirm our own exit poll. And the results from England, showing the Tories doing better than forecast, are not a huge surprise to me either. A former Labour voter had made the point to me at one of our public meetings that if Miliband looks weak to us he would look weak in England as well. On the way to the count I watch Paddy Ashdown on my iPad saying that he would eat his hat if the Lib Dems are wiped out. That sight on its own would justify what is about to happen to the Liberal Democrats – the party that has put the moan into sanctimony and the Tories into power.

Despite the canvassing and the exit polls there is a difference between believing we are going to be successful and the first result confirming that belief. I am on the broadcasting gantry at the conference centre at around 2.15 a.m. when the first Scottish result comes through. It is from Kilmarnock. On a good night our candidate, Alan Brown, would have won it with just over 20,000 votes. The returning officer starts the SNP total with the word 'thirty'.

Over the next few hours two things become clear. First, the SNP landslide has arrived incarnate, and second the Tories are coming uncomfortably close to an overall majority.

At 4.30 a.m. I make an acceptance speech proclaiming that the 'Scottish lion has roared'.

Introduction

If the election result in England turned out to be a psephologist's nightmare then the results in Scotland were a pollster's dream.

In every major respect the porridge of polling set shortly after the referendum and it continued through to election day. The evidence was clear enough, with the first election poll conducted by MORI for STV in late October 2014 showing the SNP at over 50 per cent. Therefore the reason that the 56-seat landslide was unexpected is that everyone (including myself with my '51' forecast) in the run-up to the poll expected some degree of slippage. It was after all a Westminster election.

That there was no such loss in support was largely due to the exceptional performance of Nicola Sturgeon, in the first leadership debate certainly, but even more importantly in raising the standard against austerity throughout the campaign. In this book's original epilogue I identified as really important the speech Nicola made in London on 10 February. That set out the SNP's anti-austerity stall and gave the SNP campaign what Labour lacked – a strong theme and one consistently and vigorously pursued.

However, the fact that the SNP breakthrough was forecast in the polls does not make it any less dramatic. The Tories won an unexpected overall majority, but with just 37 per cent of the vote across Britain. The SNP won 50 per cent in Scotland.

The swings to the SNP were on a scale which would have been extraordinary in a by-election. It had been joked during the campaign that the sole Labour MP left in Scotland would be the less than memorable Willie Bain in Glasgow North East. Willie was sitting on nearly 70 per cent of the vote. In fact he lost to Anne McLaughlin by more than 9,000 votes on a record swing of nearly 40 per cent!

No party in recent democratic political history has achieved anything close to a mandate on that epic scale. That mandate was to oppose austerity economics as practised by the coalition and now amplified by a majority Tory government. That mandate was to secure, not the watered-down version of the 'vow' represented by the Smith Commission but the 'home rule', 'devo to the max' or 'close to federalism' that was promised before the referendum. It was in response to these matters that the Scottish lion roared and the government will ignore them at their peril.

This new addition to the book provides a blow-by-blow account of the last few days of a remarkable election campaign. Then we have a look at the election aftermath and take in some of the daily highlights as an extraordinarily able SNP group take the Westminster parliament by storm.

This was a very different type of election for me, given that it is one that I fought as a constituency candidate as opposed to as a political leader. My long-serving, long-suffering and highly successful election agent Cllr Stuart Pratt used to point out that every election I fought as leader of the SNP, and then as First Minister, resulted in an increased majority. His conclusion was that the less time I was able to spend campaigning locally as a candidate the more people voted for me! This election was an opportunity to put the Pratt dictum to the test in reverse. Prepare therefore for the delights of Newmachar, Rhynie, Insch and Ellon, and an insight into how a constituency election campaign is best fought. I have concentrated on the last two weeks of the campaign when the pace hots up and tempers occasionally get frayed.

For the final portion of the diary we switch back to the high politics of the Palace of Westminster in the aftermath of the election. As I write this new chapter in early August it is not yet three months since the election. It seems a great deal longer, given that the days have been packed with political drama and the beginning of the contesting of the major issues – austerity, Scotland and Europe – that will dictate the politics of the next few years and therefore the outcome of the Scottish constitutional question.

The book finishes with a look at where Scottish politics are likely to go now. The first edition of the book managed to predict pretty successfully the result of the election in Scotland but did rather less well in predicting the outcome in England, where I was hoping for a balanced parliament rather than a Tory majority.

However, as has already been amply demonstrated, in parliamentary terms, the new Tory government is far from invulnerable. In constitutional terms, the future is Scotland's to determine.

Pre-Election Diary

Saturday 18 April

A touch of role reversal this Saturday as the constituency awaits the visit of Party leader Nicola Sturgeon accompanied by the national press pack. For simplicity's sake we decide on a walkabout in Inverurie, which has a smashing town square for campaigning. It is where we had the homecoming reception for the town's Commonwealth medallists Hannah Miley and wrestler Viorel Etko last August.

As we make our preparations we see the Liberal candidate, Christine Jardine, has left her car in the car park in an attempt to get her stickers into our photos. This is pretty desperate stuff but highly amusing.

The main woman arrives to a heroine's reception. For someone who has been going non-stop since the referendum campaign Nicola looks and sounds remarkably fresh. We make some impromptu speeches, take plenty of selfies and go shopping in Mitchells dairy where I pour the First Minister a cup of tea. We then get photographed beside Hannah Miley's golden coo. The pictures will look good.

There is not much time for political talk but Nicola tells me that the Party's private polling is 'too good to release', placing us at near 50 per cent, and she seems confident that the manifesto launch on Monday will keep up the campaign momentum.

I dash back to Strichen and then back to Inverurie for David and Chenyere Pack's wedding blessing at Thainstone House Hotel. David's father Brian is my seconder in the campaign and a long-term friend. The happy couple get a rousing start helped greatly by the superb food. I suppose that when a reception includes just about every top fairmer in Aberdeenshire it is as well that the joint is perfectly roasted. It is.

The reception is also enlivened by the bride's lovely Nigerian relatives. If only I had time to (or indeed could) boogie.

Sunday 19 April

We have our campaign meetings on Sundays and this one is very positive. Our premises are above the Fly Cup in Inverurie, a community café staffed by young adults with disabilities. There is plenty of space and these are ideal campaign rooms.

The campaign is proceeding at a pitch-perfect pace. Our canvassing is on track and showing 52 per cent support and gradually rising. We have registered lots of people to vote but are still concerned that a number of people seem to have dropped off the electoral roll since the referendum, despite assurances to the contrary from the registration officers. I have written an article for tomorrow's *National* on that very point.

We decide on the layout of our last major publication – the campaign newspaper – which we deploy from next weekend, and decide to use some of the cracking pictures of Nicola and me from yesterday's walkabout.

Coming back to Strichen with Stuart Pratt I ask him for a forecast result. 'Forty-seven per cent,' he says without any hesitation whatsoever. What about the others? I ask. 'Nae idea, dinnae care,' replies the less than Delphic oracle of Pitsligo.

Monday 20 April

The manifesto launch outside Edinburgh doesn't disappoint. It is an event on an epic scale and makes the efforts of the other parties look puny in comparison.

All parties need a bit of luck with timing and Nicola gets hers, first with the release of two further and unexpected Ashcroft polls showing us ahead in two Edinburgh constituencies where we came fourth in 2010, and second with Boris Johnson comparing Nicola and the SNP to King Herod, thieves, foxes, weevils and scorpions all in a single article. With typically less originality his *Telegraph* colleague Iain Martin sends a tweet in which he compares the manifesto launch to a Nazi rally.

This pair, writing from the platform of a propaganda sheet already discredited by the 'Frenchgate' episode,* actually help

* 'Frenchgate' is the rather unoriginal name given to the murky episode in which the *Daily Telegraph* attempted to destabilise the SNP election campaign. On 4 April the paper published what it claimed to be a contemporaneous account of a meeting between the French Ambassador and the Scottish First Minister, during which the First Minister supposedly 'backed' David Cameron. This was immediately and vigorously denied by the First Minister and the French Ambassador and by the French Consul General in Edinburgh, who it turned out was the unwitting indirect source of the account. It quickly emerged that the memo was not in fact a record of the meeting but a note prepared by a Scotland Office civil servant about one week later

us substantially. I ponder if that ever occurs to them. They do however symbolise what it is to be *Better Together*. Boris is English, Martin Scottish. They are perfectly at one – unified in buffoonery.

Tuesday 21 April

I'm off to a book signing in Edinburgh, where I will take in a meeting for SNP candidate Tommy Sheppard and receive an honorary doctorate from Glasgow University.

The book signing is stowed out while the meeting with Tommy is at the Spoon Bar in Nicolson Street, Edinburgh, and is in the form of a pie and a pint session. Tommy is brimming

---

after a conversation with the Consul General. Even the author of the memo had his doubts and added to the note that something could have been 'lost in translation'. The First Minister demanded a leak inquiry from the Cabinet Secretary and complained to the new press standards organisation, IPSO. She achieved an unprecedented 'double first', with the leak inquiry finding the culprit and IPSO requiring the *Telegraph* to publish a full correction. The inquiry reported on 22 May and revealed that the leak came from Euan Roddin, the special adviser to former Secretary of State Alistair Carmichael, on the instruction of his boss. Carmichael had claimed in the election campaign that he had only heard about the memo from a journalist! He apologised, gave up his redundancy payment and said he would have resigned if he had still been in office! However a number of his constituents are pursuing him through the electoral courts, arguing that his deception affected the narrow result in Orkney and Shetland. The humiliation for the *Telegraph* was just as great, with IPSO ruling comprehensively against the paper on 10 June for clear breaches of the editorial code and requiring the front-page correction. However these welcome developments came only after the election, the result of which the leak and its reporting was designed to influence. At the time of writing Alistair Carmichael remains a Member of Parliament and the *Daily Telegraph* remains in publication.

with confidence about his prospects in Edinburgh East and as a former Assistant General Secretary of the Scottish Labour Party should not be subject to candidatitis. This well-known condition afflicts first-time candidates (particularly SNP ones) who through inexperience think they are winning their seat regardless of political circumstances.

It is a fun meeting and greatly enlivened by today's news that Jim Murphy's claim of 'no cuts from Labour' under Ed Balls's spending plans has unravelled in response to journalistic inquiry. Murphy looks and sounds like an ever more desperate figure. He has adapted his referendum 'Irn-Bru lone man of the streets' campaign to take along a crowd of around 20 placard-waving T-shirt-adorned party activists. It seems no one has ever explained to him that the idea of street campaigning is to connect with crowds, not to take them with you. As a campaign tactic it is simply bonkers. In an unconscious irony the Tories have wheeled out 'soapbox' John Major to make dire warnings of overweening SNP influence in the next parliament.

This gives me a political theme for my lecture at Glasgow University, where they are making me a doctor of the university. I make the point that you cannot seriously call on Scotland to stay and 'lead' the United Kingdom in a referendum campaign and then get upset six months later when you realise that role might become a speaking part as opposed to the usual bit part!

I have put a fair amount of effort into my honorary degree speech. The ceremony is very formal, in the impressive surroundings of Bute Hall, and I deliver a lecture on the University's most famous son, Adam Smith. The thesis is on how his two great works, *The Theory of Moral Sentiments* and the better known *Wealth of Nations*, must be read together to understand the moral philosophy that underpins Smith's economics.

'No society can be truly happy of which the far greater part of the members are poor and miserable' is not a quote from Smith that most Tories would recognise, but then that is what tends to happen when you believe the Adam Smith Institute rather than the man himself.

At a splendid dinner afterwards with Principal Muscatelli and his senior staff I take the temperature of the campaign from those academically observing rather than politically participating. Everything I am hearing now tells me that the polls are real enough. There is a coalition backing the party far broader than the YES supporters in the referendum. Around this dinner table, there are people who almost certainly voted NO but who are about to vote for the SNP. Among the students I am told the SNP movement is a tidal wave.

One of the academics tells me quietly that Gordon Brown is getting a doctorate next week as a diplomatic move, after some blowback from my appointment. I presume that Dr Brown appreciates all that I have done for him!

Wednesday 22 April

I start off with a breakfast meeting in Aberdeen.

Due to a diary mix-up I didn't know I was expected at the early morning oil and gas hustings until last night, when the *Scottish Daily Mail* journalist Alan Roden tweeted that I was snubbing the industry and only interested in the personal glory of honorary degrees, not the jobs of oil workers. I phoned his editor Andy Harries to thank the paper personally for alerting me to the mix-up – that should put Alan in really solid with his boss! I then enjoy the looks of real disappointment on the faces of my political opponents when I turn up bright and early and bright and breezy.

Danny Alexander is the Lib Dem representative on the panel. He has that grey fixed look of a man attempting to deny to himself what must be blindingly obvious from his own canvassing. I was in Inverness last week and would put a substantial bet on his political demise – indeed if the odds weren't so ridiculously cramped I would have done exactly that. In contrast Anne Begg, the Labour MP for Aberdeen South, looks rather more genuinely relaxed, and the challenge of winning her seat should not be underestimated. The Tory from Aberdeenshire West and Kincardine is absurdly upbeat. Unless something unique is happening in my part of Aberdeenshire then I would be confident that the young member of my office staff and SNP candidate Stuart Donaldson, an endearingly likeable and impressive 23-year-old, would be a fair bit ahead. However I make a mental note to do some more canvassing in both these seats before the election is over.

The day is enlivened by the release of a film recorded on a Tory mobile-phone account of a public meeting at the Gaelic College, Sabhal Mòr Ostaig, which took place a couple of weeks back. In it I had I joked that I would be writing Miliband's Budget. I really should demand better-quality filming of my campaign speeches. The attempt to present it as a video nasty brings the Tory 'anti-Scottish' campaign to a new humourless low.*

Thursday 23 April

Today there is a BBC radio hustings in Inverurie. I have had a substantial bust-up with the BBC about the ticket allocation. Earlier in the campaign Nicola had by far her most difficult debate in front of an Aberdeen audience. I really know the North East of Scotland and it was not a typical Aberdonian group. Indeed I recognised a disturbing number of political activists in the BBC audience, including Hugh Pennington – a delightful retired academic expert on germs, but a Labour supporter who thinks the SNP are something akin to the things he used to look at under his microscope. Public audiences are meant to be exactly that: members of the public, not activists with an axe to grind.

I discovered that the BBC were at it again and this 'constituency audience' in the Inverurie mart turns out to be stacked with activists, many not even from the Gordon constituency. I am far from pleased, particularly because I had turned down

---

* It is the case that there were more campaign posters of me in London than of David Cameron and Ed Miliband combined. I can have no complaints about the style in which I was portrayed. The first, with Ed Miliband in my top pocket, had a touch of the US version of *House of Cards* about it, while the second version, with me portrayed as a pickpocket, had a passing resemblance to that dashing chap in the old Milk Tray adverts! It was Gordon Brown who described the Tory campaign as 'anti-Scottish'. Interestingly, London, where these Tory posters were mostly deployed, produced the Tories' worst result of the election in England.

Question Time in order to stay faithful to my local station, and even tinker with the idea of boycotting the event. However, we are winning and winning well, and so wiser counsel prevails. I determine to go along and smile my way through whatever provocation comes.

The meeting passes and without any serious mishap. There is a claque of Tory/Liberal/Labour supporters – a Better Together reunion. But in truth they sound sad and mad rather than bad or dangerous to know.

Friday 24 April

The National has a great front page today on Gordon Brown's latest campaign reincarnation. 'Deja Vow' is their headline. However, his latest promise – £1 million to stock up food banks – doesn't really cut it in terms of transformational announcements. Gordon is beginning to resemble an old volcano – each eruption less significant than the last.

We start the day at a meeting with the Health Board Chief Executive Malcolm Wright about Brimmond medical practice in Dyce. The closure of this practice could have emerged as a major problem for us during the campaign. However a vigorous approach turns it into something of an advantage: a chance to show what full-on SNP representation can achieve. At this meeting the local MSP Mark McDonald and I get the key assurance we seek that under all circumstances the Health Board will ensure continuity of primary medical care, and from the existing premises.

On my way to Gadies, a restaurant-cum-craft centre near Oyne, to a constituency book signing, I listen to the broadcast of yesterday's radio debate, which comes over pretty well. The signing is packed out and the following concert with the extraordinary Robyn Stapleton is an absolute joy. During the interval I perform a duet with celebrated local journalist and folk musician Frieda Morrison, singing the haunting traditional song from my home town Linlithgow, 'The Four Marys'. This is very much against Moira's advice but to the considerable delight of an enthusiastic crowd.*

This campaign is going well.

Saturday 25 April

This Saturday we have hundreds of SNP activists delivering our new newspaper and canvassing around the constituency.

I decide to concentrate on the coastal villages of Balmedie, Newburgh and Collieston. Support is high and the already huge campaign team is added to by a number of new SNP activists who have come up for the weekend from around Scotland.

This is almost entirely the result of the Lib Dems' extensive briefing that they are poised to give me a bloody nose. The *Mail*, *Telegraph* and *Scotsman* find such a prospect too difficult to resist, and so print this nonsense. Second only to the struggling UKIP for electoral fantasy, the result of this Liberal briefing is to galvanise SNP supporters from around the country to volunteer their services and spend an entertaining weekend in (more or less) sunny Aberdeenshire.

* For those with a strong disposition this can be seen at www.youtube.com/watch?v=pJBuNNd0jFU

When we get to picturesque Collieston, where there are 200 or so inhabitants and no mobile-phone reception except at the very end of the pier, we find we have arrived in the middle of a regatta. This is a lovely village where the locals are diverse and interesting people. They are delighted to find out that we have arranged a public meeting for the hall on Monday. This is a first for Collieston. Meanwhile the campaign team are delighted to find both a barbecue and the tiny ice-cream shop.

Sunday 26 April

'Team Alex' are in high form at the Sunday meeting. Our social media campaign is dominating, and that is reflected in the YouGov online constituency analysis. However, tonight we turn our attention to the more traditional activity of polling-day organisation. This is going to be particularly important given that most of our activists are new people who have never fought an election.

There are varying views on the effectiveness of polling-day organisation. It is probably correct that it matters much more when the poll is low, as in a local election or even more so a local by-election. However, even in a high-poll contest like this one I still maintain that an efficient polling-day effort contributes up to 2 per cent to the vote, perhaps more when combined with electronic techniques. At street level our polling-day effort is particularly effective when, as in this election, our opponents are very, very short of people.

On the way home I ask the oracle Pratty what the percentage support will be. 'Forty-seven per cent,' comes the immediate answer. 'Surely our big campaign momentum is moving that up?' I say. 'Allowed for that,' says the sage of Pitsligo.

Monday 27 April

Mike and Cameron, Moira's part-time gardeners, ask me to inspect my advertising hoarding at Strichen, of which they are particularly proud. *Still Game** I call them – they are handy guys and both solid SNP men.

I'm off to Deveron dental practice in Huntly, which I opened when I was First Minister and is now having its fifth birthday party.

NHS dentistry is one of the success stories of the SNP administration and the Deveron dental practice is a prime example. A few years back there were queues down the streets of North East towns as people tried desperately to sign up for an NHS dentist. Now the dentists advertise for their NHS patients, who include virtually every child in the country. The number of dentists is up by 60 per cent, thanks largely to the new dental school in Aberdeen.

Deveron dental practice is a case in point. It now employs 21 staff and has a patient list of over 6,000. I meet one of its original patients. Hugh Thomson is not too well but is campaigning hard from his mobility scooter. There are some great pictures and a good time is had by all. The *Daily Record* is particularly excited that I agree to get my teeth cleaned sporting a pair of futuristic protective glasses!

---

* The popular BBC Scotland comedy series featuring two lively pensioners.

From Huntly we go back down to the coast to take in public meetings in Collieston and Newburgh. Gavin Esler of the BBC has been looking for a venue to fill one of our community meetings, and so tiny Collieston, with around one-third of the population packed into the compact village hall, makes it onto the network 10 o'clock News. Gavin is a first-rate journalist with a real understanding of Scotland. 'Is the landslide going to happen?' he asks over a pint afterwards. 'Yes,' I reply.

I rush back to Strichen via Tesco's in Ellon as I suddenly remember my message line from Moira. The staff find it highly amusing when I squeeze in with what I think is seconds to spare before ten o'clock. The store shuts at midnight!

Tuesday 28 April

I have been combining my election tours with book-signing events and today I am off to my home town of Linlithgow and then to a full public meeting in Alloa.

But first to Edinburgh, where I have promised Edinburgh South West candidate Joanna Cherry a campaign visit. We spend a productive time at Clovenstone boxing club in Wester Hailes, where the very useful professional boxer Craig McEwan, an ex-Commonwealth medallist, has spent lots of time coaching the local youngsters in his dad's training centre.

I heartily approve of amateur boxing, although I have the gravest doubts about the professional game. There are few other sports which reach youngsters in deprived areas in the way that boxing can. This is a great gym and I am impressed by the way that the distinguished QC Joanna is natural with these young people from one of Edinburgh's toughest schemes.

The reaction is great. This is Wester Hailes, this is a general election. If this is typical she is going in by a barrowload.

Off tae Lithgae, where I had been so moved by the reception during the referendum campaign. If that was a tremor then today is off the campaign Richter scale. It is with great difficulty that I extract myself away from local candidate Martyn Day and his engaged campaign team.

I have a book signing and public meeting in Alloa with Elaine C. Smith and the candidate Tasmina Ahmed-Sheikh. This is a highlight of the campaign, with a full town hall and a funny, engaging, inspirational meeting.

Elaine is a marvellous force of nature and a really important figure in Scottish public life. She reprises the 'back of the bus' routine which had been so influential in the referendum campaign debates – the idea that Labour's attitude to Scotland is to tell us to go to the back of the bus and shut up. Indeed it is one of the moments that people mention as being influential in their personal conversion to the YES cause. In front of this supportive audience she is in high form.

This diverse and beautiful constituency of Ochil and South Perthshire could have been designed for Tasmina. Her ability and enthusiasm have already inspired a large and highly motivated campaign team and this packed town hall audience just adore her style.

The question-and-answer session and the book signing go on for so long that we have to totally abandon plans for a post-match meal. I have a bag of crisps and a cup of tea instead, and it is near midnight when I return to Edinburgh.

On the road I reflect that it would be difficult not to conclude that Edinburgh, the Lothians and the 'wee county' of

Clackmannanshire are now firmly in the SNP camp. Tomorrow I set off for a brief tour of the west of Scotland and the Borders.

Wednesday 29 April

First thing to East Kilbride for a book signing in Waterstones. All of these events have been hugely well attended, but this one is totally fu' to the gunnels. I have made it a rule to sign every book before leaving. As a result I end up hours late by the time I get to Hamilton for an endorsement photo with local candidates Angela Crawley and Margaret Ferrier, plus Marion Fellows from the next-door constituency of Motherwell.

The huge campaign team had waited patiently for my arrival with spirits undimmed, as had Radio 5 Live, with whom I conduct one of the easier interviews of my career. I had just received news of the STV MORI poll showing the SNP on an extraordinary 54 per cent and social media is alive with reports of Jim Murphy being interviewed about the poll while doing the hokey-cokey with a group of pensioners!

In that context, being asked provocative questions about what Nigel Farage says about the SNP is neither here nor there. John Pienaar is seriously impressed about what he is finding in Scotland and is beginning to believe that an SNP clean sweep is possible. It isn't, of course, but we could get close to it if we can take the three Borders seats. Much earlier this year I had held meetings in Dumfries and Kelso in front of huge audiences and believe that anything is possible. The Labour seat of Dumfries is well within our current compass. However, the seats of lone Tory David Mundell and the Liberal Michael Moore will be tough nuts to crack.

We had decided to have a major fundraiser in the North East to help secure victory in Moore's Berwickshire seat, where John Lamont for the Tories was also a dangerous challenger. My sister Gail is the SNP election agent and the local and vigorous candidate Calum Kerr is a 'braw lad' for the Borders.

Thus we invited Berwickshire to join a hugely successful fund-raising auction we had held jointly with North East Fife, Livingston and Ochil and South Perthshire. The injection of substantial funds to a constituency that had seldom before had any serious money at all is proving important in competing with the headquarters-funded operations of the Liberals and Tories.

I head off for a street meeting in Gala and a town hall meeting in Hawick which goes with a bang. Calum Kerr has developed enormously since his adoption meeting in Kelso in February and turns in a totally assured and confident performance. After careful reflection I add Berwickshire to my list of flutters in this campaign. It is about the last seat in Scotland where you can get decent odds against an SNP victory.

I demand of Calum that when elected he conducts an immediate campaign to secure better internet connectivity in the Borders. 'Why are you asking?' he says. 'So that next time I am travelling in the Borders I can watch Jim Murphy doing the hokey-cokey on my iPad,' I reply.

Thursday 30 April

The *Scottish Sun* has declared for the SNP in a spectacular front page showing Nicola as Princess Leia from *Star Wars*. Overcoming my disappointment at being cast as Yoda and not

Luke Skywalker, I offer the *Sun* the opportunity to film me delivering a message in a Yoda voice: 'You must feel the force around you, Princess Leia. I am pleased with the *Scottish Sun*. I am.'

Back to Gordon for the last local hustings of the campaign – the NFU meeting in Oldmeldrum. This is the last of eight hustings with the local candidates. The young Labour candidate, Braden Davy, who I think has done really well at the public meetings, doesn't turn up – perhaps a sign that his boss Anne Begg is in a spot of bother in Aberdeen. Instead we get Barney Crockett, the former leader of the Council in Aberdeen. Braden would have done better.

The Tory candidate, Colin Clark, cuts an impressive figure but his politics are far too dry for this area. If the constituency were composed entirely of michty fairmers then he might be the ideal candidate. But it isn't and he is not.

However, both the Labour and Tory candidates are certainly above average. It would be difficult to say the same about the Liberal Christine Jardine. I understand, of course, that she has her heart set on becoming an MP, and things must have been going swimmingly until I came along and upset her applecart. However, none of this explains her demeanour, which carries the air of being permanently miffed, usually about me. She is not just catty but far too obviously so – rather like the claque of Better Together activists at this meeting. One said that I wasn't a real nationalist because I wanted to dilute the racial purity of the constituency through immigration, while another asked how I could be trusted with the constituency as a self-confessed punter. I replied to the former that his cut-glass accent must be concealing his own

Garioch background and to the latter I said that I'd been known to back a few horses and even have an occasional drink on a Sunday. Their behaviour is bad enough to provoke the NFU Committee to apologise, pointing out that they had no idea who these people were!

As I explain over a drink afterwards to the *Herald*'s Vicky Allan, they are really a godsend to any candidate. There is nothing like basking in the glow of being unjustly and personally attacked. The bar in Methlick is solidly behind the SNP. I don't mention to Vicky that Methlick is just outside the Gordon constituency boundary!

Friday 1 May

We have identified that the Aberdeen City part of the seat is the key to this election. The Labour vote in Bridge of Don and Dyce is melting to the SNP and we should concentrate a great deal of effort on these areas.

So today after some campaigning at the mart in Inverurie, I head off to Bridge of Don before dipping into Aberdeen South to give Callum McCaig a helping hand. Of all the seats in the North East it is the one which causes me most concern. Banff and Buchan is safe as houses, as is Gordon. I believe that the shire tends to move together and therefore Aberdeenshire West will be going the same way. In Aberdeen North we have a great organisation, and the Labour candidate Richard Baker is completely unelectable in just about any circumstances.

That leaves Aberdeen South, where Dame Anne Begg is a gritty, determined MP and deservedly well dug in to the seat. Earlier in the year I had tried in vain to get the popular local hotelier Stewart Spence to run. Stewart would have been on first-name terms with the denizens of all the plusher areas of Aberdeen South and therefore eminently electable. He declined, but luckily the young personable councillor Callum McCaig put his hat in the ring at the very last moment.

If I had doubts before the canvass then they were immediately dispelled afterwards in a quick run though Kincorth, the massive council estate on the south of the city. Support is flowing to the SNP like a river, and after a productive couple of hours we end up being coaxed into the Abbot Bar, where the locals are vociferously supportive to a man and woman.

I finish the day with a public meeting in Dyce at the Menzies hotel. We had decided in our blitz of public meetings to leave no stone unturned and therefore we were using up both Friday nights and Sundays. Every meeting has attracted a decent audience and this is no exception. In addition every meeting throws up an idea or piece of wisdom.

Attending the meeting is Libby Brooks of the *Guardian*. Libby warmed to me much earlier in the election when we were canvassing some big detached houses in Inverurie. We came across a young lad dressed like the Michelin man about to jump out of a bedroom window about 25 ft off the ground onto a tiny mattress in the garden. He was on a dare with his wee brother and a couple of pals. My mind went racing back to anxiously peering over the top diving board at Falkirk baths when I was a nipper.

At any rate the task is to talk him down without him losing face, albeit that losing face can be better than losing a leg. I do this by the expedient of asking him for a selfie in his get-up. He agrees to this and the journalist is suitably amazed.

'All in a day's canvassing,' I tell Libby later. 'Mind you, it cost me a tenner to stage that incident just to impress you!'

Saturday 2 May

This is shock-and-awe Saturday, where by force of numbers we intend to demonstrate in every area of the constituency that we are overpowering the other campaigns.

In succession therefore we shock Ellon, Newmachar and Kintore and awe Inverurie, Daviot and Old Meldrum. I have got it into my head that Kintore might be a weak spot in our campaign. This was based on nothing more than a less than enthusiastic response (i.e. a very rude gesture) to our snappy bus on one of last week's visits. Even the most experienced candidates like myself tend to magnify personal experiences and accord them undue significance.

My solution is to have a public meeting in the town, which has been duly set for tomorrow, given that Monday is a public holiday with no hall available. A Sunday meeting is a first in our area, but my office manager, Fergus Mutch, reassures me that we will be fine. The reception today is noticeably warm in Kintore, which indicates that my fears were based on nothing at all.

This is like a mini-referendum with the local meetings reverberating through social media.

Sunday 3 May

Vicky Allan's constituency report in the *Sunday Herald* is very positive and sports an excellent picture of my snappy bus. It may not be the most elegant, innovative or modern of campaign techniques but it is still really effective for street campaigning. Rather like the old swingometer, it has been overtaken in an electronic age, but when it comes to the last few days of a campaign there is nothing like an old-fashioned battlebus for profile and creating momentum.

The Kintore meeting goes well, with no drop-off in the big crowds despite being a Sunday night. I take a mental note for future campaigns.

The campaign meeting is in jovial mood, with all our plans laid for the next few days, and a very large group is gathering for the polling-day instruction. However I decide to slip away to have dinner with SNP council group leader Hamish Vernal and his wife Mo. Hamish wants to fill me in on developments in the Council. He believes that, assuming things go well in the election, then the shaky Tory-led administration of the Council will collapse as momentum swings to the SNP.*

Before I leave the meeting I ask Stuart for his estimate of our vote. 'Forty-seven per cent,' replies the ancient canvasser without hesitation.

Monday 4 May

I have my final article of the campaign in *The National* today in which I predict that Jim Murphy will be lucky to see midsummer's day as Labour leader. I watch a recording of the final leaders' debate in Scotland, which is a bad-tempered affair, poorly controlled by the BBC's Glen Campbell. However,

---

* The Tory administration duly fell on Monday 8 June, to be replaced by an SNP-led administration.

the key to the proceedings is the demeanour of Murphy. His look is that of a politically dead man walking.

We travel around the western towns and villages in the constituency, starting at the Huntly Marketmuir (May Day celebrations) then through to Rhynie, Lumsden, Kennethmont, Insch and Oyne. I meet a Tory supporter on the gate at the Marketmuir. He is a jovial chap who believes we are going to win and win well. We are doing really well in Huntly, largely thanks to the efforts of my proposer and greatly respected local councillor Joanna Strathdee.

Before we set off for Rhynie I call in to see an old friend and prospective constituent, Bill McKay, better known as Sir William McKay, author of the McKay report on responses to the West Lothian Question and former senior clerk of the House of Commons. I am looking for advice on parliamentary procedure in the event of a hung parliament.

On to Rhynie, which is the highest village in the constituency. I have a journalist and photographer from Bloomberg in tow. In the square where the locals have prepared a great reception for us I introduce the photographer to one of the village worthies. Much impressed that Bloomberg have come to Rhynie, the wag remarks that he will in future change his newspaper order from the *FT* and rely on Bloomberg exclusively for his financial advice! We have a cup of tea with Lottie Coutts and her cat Simone. This lovely lady is one of the village's oldest inhabitants and very pleased to serve up shortbread to both my campaign team and Bloomberg.

On the way back to Insch we stop off at the Dreams Daycare playgroup where I demonstrate that I am a dab hand at air hockey and conduct some interviews with Bloomberg and the

Irish Times. There is little resistance now to the idea that the SNP are set for a sensational result and much attention is now focused on our role in a hung parliament.

We finish off at Insch golf club. There is a particularly warm welcome in a place where I once managed to win a trophy way back in 2007. Indeed, as far as I know I am the only First Minister to actually win a golf tournament while in office. I dropped a note at the time to the Honorary President of the club – Prime Minister Gordon Brown, whose father was once the local Minister.

Tuesday 5 May

An early start with my former staff member Lynsey-Anne, who has returned to help me in the election. We visit Gray and Adams in Fraserburgh with my successor in Banff and Buchan, Eilidh Whiteford, and then head to a coffee morning in Dyce.

I keep a promise by going off to campaign for Stuart Donaldson in Kemnay. A nicer young lad it would be difficult to meet and I think he is set to make a big stir in West Aberdeenshire. It is a rainy day and so I introduce Stuart to a campaign technique I learned from that legendary street campaigner Winnie Ewing. We visit every shop and take care to buy something in each (with the exception of the veterinary surgeons). It is a way of creating a buzz on a rainy day.

By the afternoon we are back in Bridge of Don, where I can feel our majority increasing every time we campaign there. We keep up the 'jump and shout' through the afternoon before going to Ellon for our last public meeting at the Station Hotel. It is hugely attended and boosts morale even further since, as this is the final meeting, 'Team Alex' is also there in great strength. All of these events are amplified many times over on social media. This campaign is coming to a great climax.

Wednesday 6 May

Eve of poll depends on a tight schedule of campaigning around the constituency from Ellon to Inverurie, to Huntly and then back to Bucksburn.

At Huntly we meet a pensioners' bus party from Peterhead. This allows some very efficient campaigning – two constituencies in one go. At Bucksburn in the evening I come across a 'pamper party'. This is my first-ever such event and something I feel I have missed out on in my life thus far.

There is little doubt from the reaction on the doors that this election is now done and dusted.

On the way back to Strichen we have an impromptu rally with the team who had been gathered at the Ellon campaign rooms for more polling-day training. The crowd must have swelled to some 200 or so and I give them a rousing speech. The address to the campaign team in the car park of Ellon may not rate in historical significance with Robert Bruce's address to the troops on the field of Bannockburn – but it wasn't at all bad.

Post-Election Diary

Friday 8 May

When we get back to Strichen from Aberdeen Conference Centre in the early hours of the morning the magnitude of the SNP victory is clear. In Gordon, the Pitsligo seer is but 1 per cent out. Our percentage is 48. 'You're slipping,' I tell my election agent with some relish.

My sister Gail texts me to say that Berwickshire has gone to a recount but omits to tell me who had asked for it. This is particularly dramatic, since the very last thing I had said to her last week was that 'anything under 500, insist on a bundle check' and of course it's only the side who are behind that ever ask for a recount. I phone and eventually get through to her. She tells me, '*They* asked.' I knew we'd won.

By the time I get to bed for a few hours' sleep we have 56 seats and SNP candidate Drew Hendry's defeat of Danny Alexander has provided Scotland's 'Portillo moment'. The downside is the Tory majority of 12. However, I have been here before. In the 1992 election John Major won an unexpected majority of 21, which vanished like snow off a dyke in the face of the European rebellion. History could repeat itself and on that very issue. The difference is that the SNP had but 'three in '93' and near twenty times that number of MPs in 2015.

This determines my view on what role I should play in the new parliament. I had never thought leading the group to be a serious option. Even with two people who had worked together as umbilically as Nicola and me over so many years, it is simply not sensible for an immediate past leader to lead an opposition parliamentary group – especially one which is as large as the governing one in the Scottish parliament. The result would inevitably be the emergence of rival power centres, and that would benefit no one. Of course political parties should have a collective leadership but there should never be a doubt about who leads.

In any case Angus Robertson has proved a highly successful leader of the SNP as an opposition party in the Westminster parliament since 2007. If there had been the prospect of going into office in a balance-of-power situation then there would have been different priorities to consider. In those circumstances the most crucial point would have been governmental experience to avoid the fate of the truly hapless Liberal Democrats. However, coalition with Labour has not been likely for some time.

With the tight Commons position and Europe a touchstone issue, the International brief has many opportunities to both forward Scotland's cause and contribute to serious issues. In addition it should be possible to assemble a really talented parliamentary team given the calibre of people available.

Saturday 9 May

We are gathered at the Forth Bridge for a memorable photo-call. All are present and correct with the exceptions of Angus Brendan MacNeil and Ian Blackford, understandable given the distances to their far-flung constituencies.

The old blood-red crossing is soon set for world heritage status. Of all the famous photos that have been taken here, this one in particular, as an illustration of the tsunami which has swept over Scottish politics, takes some beating.

Monday 11 May

We repeat the photocall outside St Stephen's entrance of the House of Commons. One thing is pretty evident and pretty quickly. There is a collective fascination with the SNP group from the metropolitan media and a very large hostility. You get the impression from the Commons hacks that they would like to hide the silver from unwanted interlopers. The contrast with the House of Commons staff could not be greater. Superbly marshalled by the down-to-earth Serjeant at Arms, Lawrence Ward, they are determined to make the newcomers feel at home.

Amid all the high politics it is crucial to get the new members installed into offices and staffed up as soon as possible. Luckily, Pete Wishart, our accommodation whip, is as wily and forceful as they come, and very quickly good office possibilities emerge. I now realise why I spent seven and a half years as First Minister and Privy Councillor. It is the best way to get a cracking office in the Commons!

David Cameron's normal reaction to a political crisis is to do nothing and hope that something will turn up. This will likely be his initial reaction to Scotland. There will be mouthings of respect but the attempt will be made to run the government of Scotland as business as usual.

An early indication is the reappointment of lone Tory David Mundell as Secretary of State. A wiser move would have been to amalgamate the territorial ministries and deal with the devolved administrations directly. It will make Scottish Questions pretty interesting with one sole Tory Daniel facing 56 Scottish lions.

Tasmina makes an immediate mark by persuading the House of Commons library to stock *The National*. Interestingly, today's paper has a report on a Dublin auction in which €1,500 has been paid for James Connolly's Scottish Labour Party membership card of 1892. Two points are of interest. First, Connolly joined the Scottish Labour Party, not the Labour Party, which had yet to be formed. Second, the images of the two leaders on the card are James Keir Hardie, later founder of the Independent Labour Party, and Robert Cunninghame Graham, later founder of the SNP!

Wednesday 13 May

Group leader Angus Robertson is making good progress in getting the appointments together. I assemble a talented overseas team including Angus MacNeil as my deputy, Stephen Gethins, the new North East Fife MP, on Europe, Tasmina Ahmed-Sheikh on International Trade and Investment, Patrick Grady, who has wide experience of developing-world charities, on International Development and Lisa Cameron, the East Kilbride MP, on Climate Justice. We will be assisted by Peter Grant, the former Fife Council leader, and Stuart Donaldson MP. This is a really able group of people and we intend to pursue the government as a pack.

However, the first government problem looks likely on the repeal of the Human Rights Act. Today I am sounded out separately by no fewer than three Tory backbenchers, all determined to frustrate Theresa May's plans. I put them in touch with Joanna Cherry, our new Justice and Home Affairs Spokesperson. Unless Cameron knows something I don't I cannot see how he has a majority on this, given that the Irish parties will be reluctant to further rock the peace agreement boat. It will be an early test of the government's resolve.

Saturday 16 May

Today's papers are full of the meeting at Bute House between David Cameron and Nicola Sturgeon. Nicola had told me on Thursday that she expected Cameron to take a minimalist approach – to concede as little as he can get away with. This sounds very like the Prime Minister, whose obsession with the tactics of the moment and lack of interest in the long term are the reasons why he has subcontracted his political strategy to the Chancellor of the Exchequer, just as he contracted out the election campaign to Lynton Crosby. However, Westminster political history is littered with leaders who concede too little and too late to restless nations.

The breaking story, however, is the demise of James Murphy, the 'saviour of the union' (as a brilliant parody film terms him),* a full month before my pre-election forecast of midsummer's day. Despite surviving a vote of no confidence by means of voting for himself and drafting in ex-spook Baroness Ramsay (as a representative of the Scottish Labour parliamentary group!), the bold Jim then resigns without telling his colleagues what he was about to do. He then says he is staying on for a month to rewrite the party rulebook!

Murphy's resignation is as meaningless as his predecessor's was effective. Johann Lamont correctly identified the 'branch office' syndrome as killing Labour in Scotland. Murphy bizarrely allocates responsibility to Len McCluskey. Apart from being one of the most absurd press conferences I have ever watched, I find it interesting that he was trying so hard to stay. Perhaps it is connected with the UK leadership election and is a sign that the Labour right wing are expecting big trouble at mill.

Friday 22 May

The publicity surrounding the new group continues apace – some of it is welcome but some less so. The perfectly legitimate necessity of securing a proper position on the opposition benches is interpreted as an attempt to dislodge the octogenarian Labour legend Dennis Skinner. That may have been down to some over-enthusiasm in the ranks, as in reality Dennis is much more of a potential ally than a rival. A truce is arranged.

---

* This vignette is available for viewing on YouTube as 'Jim Murphy – Saviour of the Union' by Bonnie Prince Bob: www.youtube.com/watch?v=afRE3RwLwaE

More productively, one of our new members, Brendan O'Hara, the new Defence spokesperson, finds a subject to get his teeth into. The newspaper revelations from Able Seaman William McNeilly about the weaknesses in safety procedures at the Faslane nuclear submarine base on the Clyde open up an issue which is going to be central to this parliament.

I take Brendan through the full gamut of parliamentary procedures that he could use to raise the issue in the Commons, including securing one of the first debates in the new parliament. This sets off an interesting discussion with the Commons clerks as to whether a member can make his maiden speech on a motion for the adjournment. The eventual answer is yes, but that it would set a precedent for the future. On a hunch I apply for the adjournment, as do a large number of our colleagues. By an amazing coincidence it is my application that comes out of the ballot, and so the debate is secured but no precedent created. Ballots in the House of Commons, rather like the Lord God Almighty, often move in mysterious ways.

I am asked by a couple of characters from the *Daily Mail* whether Mhairi Black and Joanna Cherry are gay and if it is true that the SNP group has the highest incidence of gay members of any parliamentary group. On the second point I say that of course the SNP excels in all things and on the first that I have no earthly idea. However, I phone the office to alert my colleagues to these inquiries, particularly to the one about Mhairi, in case friends and family need to be told. The response comes back that the young lady is perfectly relaxed. She grows higher in my estimation on a daily basis.

Someone lower in my estimation is Alistair Carmichael, who is the subject of the first leak inquiry in the history of the civil service to actually find the leaker! This is 'Frenchgate' again. It turns out that it was Carmichael and his special adviser, despite the explicit claim during the election that he had heard it first from a journalist. Whether he would have been exposed if he had still been in office is a hypothetical but interesting question. Carmichael adopts the unusual defence that he would have resigned if he had still been Secretary of State but since he isn't he doesn't have to. His constituents seem to have other ideas.

Monday 25 May

We have a Group meeting in the Grand Committee room in the upper committee corridor. We fill the entire room to overflowing, which brings home the scale of the SNP triumph. I have been in Westminster when we had to run around to look like a crowd. Now we really are a crowd.

And it's not just the quantity. There is real quality in this group. With an age range spanning almost half a century and a hugely diverse set of backgrounds, this could develop into a truly formidable parliamentary group.

Wednesday 27 May

If the War of Jenkins' Ear was a pretty pointless exercise then the War of Skinner's Bottom was even more futile. Luckily the truce holds. Dennis remains in his place flanked on all sides by 'The 56', all sporting the white rose of Scotland.*

I added my own bit of colour to the Queen's speech proceedings by breenging through the doors to the Members' Lobby with but seconds to spare. I had been doing a TV piece in Central Lobby and managed to squeeze in just before Black Rod put in an appearance. The resulting photo goes viral and the guys on the door ask for copies for their mantelpieces.

The Queen's Speech is full of Tory red meat – anti-immigrant, pro-censorship, anti-poor – and George Osborne's soundbites. Her Majesty the Queen actually has to recite phrases such as 'the northern powerhouse' and kids must 'earn or learn'. Ah how she must yearn for the days when prime ministers were phrase-makers like Churchill or Macmillan and the Queen's Speech didn't sound like the product of a Lynton Crosby focus group.

Perhaps it is the corgi that didn't bark that is of most significance. There is no mention of the Human Rights Act, just the tentative proposal for a British Bill of Rights. As I suspected the arithmetic doesn't favour the government's prejudices.

The Group's clapping of Angus Robertson's speech draws a stern rebuke from the Speaker. I think this is all good. It illustrates one of the patent nonsenses of Westminster. However, there will be bigger battles to come. In the late Eighties Dafydd, now Lord, Wigley and I were disciplined by the then Deputy Speaker at around the same time, me for intervening in the

* I am asked in the Chamber why we are sporting a 'Yorkist rose', which allows me to recite the McDiarmid lines: 'The Rose of all the world is not for me, I want for my part, Only the little white rose of Scotland, That smells sharp and sweet – and breaks the heart.'

Budget, Wigley for inadvertently detaching the arm of the Speaker's chair when making a good point to him rather too forcibly.

I pointed out to Wigley at the time that breaking the rules by design was better than breaking the furniture by mistake!

Thursday 28 May

Tommy Sheppard's impressively crafted maiden speech beautifully makes the point about clapping and draws praise from the Speaker about the solidarity of the SNP Group.

Michael Gove's discomfort at being challenged on all sides on the Human Rights Act means he decides to wind up early. This results in us getting extra time for the adjournment debate on Trident and also a little bit of parliamentary history for Brendan O'Hara. Denied the chance to make his maiden speech in an adjournment debate, Brendan had spoken yesterday in the first day of the debate of the loyal address. However, I also gave him some of my speaking time in the adjournment debate, given that he is the local MP for Faslane naval base as well as the Defence spokesperson of the SNP Group.

This means that Brendan ends up making substantive speeches in the first two days of parliament. I quickly check the record and no one, but no one, has ever managed that before. As we hold court with the press corps after the debate I point this out. 'Not even Pitt the Younger managed that,' I joke. 'Just call me O'Hara the Elder,' responds the bold Brendan.

Elsewhere lone Tory Mundell is having difficulty explaining why the constant repetition in the Scotland Bill of the phrase 'must have obtained the agreement of the Secretary of State' doesn't constitute a veto. Most people will conclude that if it reads like a veto and sounds like a veto and looks like a veto then it probably is a veto.

Sunday 31 May

I have a great time at the Hay Festival.

Immediately after breakfast my generous hosts Rob and Revel allow me the opportunity to hit a golf ball past Bill Clinton's best attempt and into the River Wye. This I do, although it takes me several goes. Mind you, if I hadn't managed, I still might be there hitting ball after ball from Wales into England!

The festival itself is huge fun and Dame Helena Kennedy is an engaging inquisitor. I am a big admirer of Helena's and indeed asked her to become Scotland's Solicitor General a few years back. Unfortunately she had just accepted an appointment as principal of an Oxford college, and after much soul searching gave up her chance of ministerial office.

This audience on the Welsh border are really friendly and the book signing afterwards goes on for hours. We drive to London after the show with historian Simon Schama, who is a charming and interesting man but one who makes me appear taciturn.

After a stop for a pint in Cheltenham we continue our journey and Simon continues his everlasting fund of stories and observations. As I nod off to sleep in the back seat Simon without breaking sentence says 'Just take a nap' and then continues unabated.

Tuesday 2 June

A sad day begins with the newsflash about the death of Charles Kennedy. I liked Charles a very great deal. Most people did. Indeed his greatest attribute as a politician was his likeability. He combined that with a generosity of spirit and a sound political instinct which stood his party in good stead, particularly over Iraq.

In the middle of a number of tributes I do an interview for BBC News 24. I am asked by Norman Smith about Charles's role in the Better Together campaign. That role was non-existent and so I reply that his heart wasn't really in Better Together but that he would have been a major figure in the coming European referendum campaign.

It's meant to be nothing other than a diplomatic and kind way of avoiding saying that he wasn't well enough to play a prominent role. It certainly wasn't to suggest that he was some sort of secret nationalist, which would have been a ridiculous thing to say. However, that is exactly what is claimed in the social media and repeated by the usual suspects in the dead-wood press. They don't really believe it, of course, just want a stick with which to beat the SNP. I am sorely tempted to say a great deal more but in the immediate aftermath of someone's death it seems an inappropriate time to engage in a silly political debate. I content myself with a mild statement correcting the misleading impression and repeating my condolences.*

---

* However, there has been some passage of time since then. The reason I knew Charles's heart wasn't in Better Together is that he attacked it publicly in separate interviews with the *Sunday Post* and the BBC. He was particularly scathing about George Osborne's embargo

Wednesday 10 June

I have decided to apply for the *Guinness Book of Records*.

After voting in the morning some 27 times for Chairs of Select Committees in Westminster I rush to Scotland for the Community Empowerment Bill third stage, where I vote a further 44 times. Seventy-one votes in two parliaments on the same day must be some sort of record. Indeed it will be impossible to emulate. Someone may well sit in two parliaments and vote on the same day, but the coincidence between Select Committee chair votes, which are some of the very few Westminster votes not determined at great length through the lobbies, and multiple votes in the Scottish parliament will in all likelihood never happen again.

Our key conversations with Tory backbenchers on the European Bill are proceeding very well. Indeed I am now confident that the government is facing at least two defeats – the first on the timing of the referendum, specifically the Prime Minister's attempt to hold it on the same day as the Scottish elections. The government is also in trouble in their attempt to restrict the purdah period before the referendum.

I have taken as many of our new members as possible through the process of procedure on how to gain the best positions with amendments and how to secure the help of the Commons clerks, who are there to support the House, not the

---

on sterling, and critical of it being backed by Danny Alexander and Ed Balls. He said it was no way to conduct a campaign with an eye to the future. Those who knew Charles rather better than I did, like former Liberal Democrat MP Lembit Opik, made the same points online.

government. Many are keen learners and will emerge as significant parliamentarians.

As we proceed through the extraordinary range and depth of maiden speeches this Group is looking ever more impressive. With Labour in a catatonic state, as witnessed by their failure to oppose the European referendum Bill at second reading yesterday, then the claim that the SNP is emerging as the real opposition is gaining ground and indeed substance.

Friday 12 June

At the Borders book festival and playing to another packed house in Melrose. This time my interrogator is BBC journalist Shelley Jofre, who has just completed a splendid film for *Panorama* on Nicola entitled 'Is this the most dangerous woman in Britain?' She tells me that this was her last work for the BBC, as her young family must come first. Moira and I go for tea before the event with Shelley's family, my sister Gail's family and their new MP Calum Kerr, who is full of the joys of attending that day's Common Riding.

I am told by the stewards to expect a bit of snash from the 500-strong audience. In the event the Tories among us are like lambs. The conversation is vital and entertaining and another indication that the mobilisation seen in the referendum and the election is continuing apace.

My failed nemesis Alan Cochrane of the *Telegraph* is also here with his book and is due up tomorrow. Gail goes on a scouting mission round the tiny tent C in which he is to perform and counts around 50 chairs laid out. Seems a lot to me!

Tuesday 16 June

There is more proof positive that Labour have taken leave of their senses and abdicated as an opposition. Yesterday late on, and only when staring defeat in the face, the government caved in and tabled a drafting amendment to rule out the Euro poll taking place on the same day as the Scottish elections next May.

It was a sign of real disorganisation and surprise on the part of the government whips as they realised that the Tory rebels were not bluffing. Nor were they bluffing in calling time on the blatant government attempt to avoid a proper purdah period. The debate allows me the opportunity to recall the conduct of government ministers and particularly civil servants, including Treasury Permanent Secretary Nicholas Macpherson, during the Scottish referendum. The government whips circulate a panicky letter around their backbenches pleading for no rebellion, but despite that 27 Tories rebel, more than enough to defeat the government. The amendment is still defeated, though, by 288 to 97, because the official Labour line was to sit on their hands.

In parliamentary terms, it was as close to a penalty kick as you can get. Rumours abound of a split between Labour's acting leader Harriet Harman, who wanted to vote, and Hilary Benn, who was set on abstention. I comment that 'faced with an open goal Labour contrived to miss the ball'.

In contrast to the Referendum Bill, which is causing the government all kinds of grief, the Scotland Bill is moving through with a total refusal to accept any amendments. In parliamentary terms it is tidier but in political terms it is even more problematic.

Thursday 18 June

On BBC *Question Time* with David Davies, Caroline Flint, *Financial Times* Editor Lionel Barber and *Times* columnist Melanie Phillips. It is a good panel and a very fair programme, dominated by the subjects of Europe and terrorism.

What interests me more than anything is the open-mindedness of the High Wycombe audience. Before the programme during the warm-up, when they are doing the sound checks, it is pointed out that they cannot hear me. 'Good thing too,' says a rather pukka voice to pretty widespread applause. However, by the end of the programme the audience has warmed up to me considerably. Another half-hour with them and High Wycombe could be another SNP target seat!

Davies is a substantial politician. It is interesting that back in the day when he was beaten by Cameron for the Tory leadership he would have been regarded as a right-winger. In fact his social liberalism is an attractive aspect of his politics, and even his euro-scepticism comes across as principled compared with the flimflam that passes for belief in Downing Street.

Wednesday 24 June

A curious Royal story breaks out among the usual press suspects. It is particularly curious since it seems to have some foundation, unlike most of the anti-Scottish bile that they publish. The source appears to be Sir Alan Reid, Keeper of the Privy Purse, who, in an 'off the record' briefing which seems to have developed chaotically into an 'on the record' one, has suggested that the palace finances would lose out from the coming devolution to Scotland of the Crown Estate.

This was enough to launch the *Telegraph*, *Times* and *Mail* into apoplexy, claiming that the nasty Scots were going to short-change the Queen, and that secret republican Nicola Sturgeon didn't share my fealty to the Windsor cause. It is bonkers, of course, and old-hat. The revenue from the Crown Estate is only a guide for the Royal Grant, which is paid direct by the Treasury. It is not the source of royal funding. By the end of the day the story has started to totally fall apart and Sir Alan Reid is eating humble pie.

However, it raises some interesting questions. The source of the story now forced into headlong retreat was either making a clumsy attempt to divert attention from the £150 million austerity-busting refurbishment of Buckingham Palace or alternatively didn't understand the nature of royal finances.

Speaking as one whose royal credentials have seldom been questioned – at least not recently – I'm not at all sure if this is the ace card that unionists think it is. A more difficult question for the Scottish government might have been: 'Why shouldn't the Royal finances be subject to the same austerity as the budgets of her Majesty's subjects?'

Monday 29 June

The Prime Minister makes a statement on the Tunisian atrocity but combines it with one on the European summit. The Speaker, who in fairness usually has good judgement, allows this tasteless nonsense. He should not have done so. The relatives of the dead and everyone else are entitled to hear a considered parliamentary response from their Prime Minister without it being contaminated by party political arguments about Europe.

It is early days, of course, but there is little in the official response which points to any new thinking about our foreign and security policy. On the contrary the response would seem to be to extend and intensify our participation in the bombing campaign across the Middle East.

One refreshing idea which is being promoted by the SNP's Tasmina Ahmed-Sheikh and a number of Conservative MPs gets to the heart of the battle for hearts and minds in which we are engaged and suggests changing the way we refer to ISIS or ISIL. Daesh, sometime spelled Daiish or Da'esh, is short for al-Dawla al-Islamiya f'il al-Iraq wa ash-Sham. Many Arabic-speaking media organisations refer to the group as such, and there is an argument that it is appropriately pejorative, deriving from a mixture of rough translations from the individual Arabic words.

However, the real point of using Daesh is that it separates the terrorists from the religion they claim to represent and from the false dream of a new caliphate that they claim to pursue. That argument is surely correct.

Thursday 2 July

Leader of the House Chris Grayling introduced the proposals for Evel – English Votes for English Laws – to general parliamentary contempt punctuated by hilarity. I rather like Grayling. He manages to maintain an air of exasperated good will even under strong fire. However, he has really drawn the short straw in presenting this total dog's breakfast. There was a reason why Tam Dalyell posed the West Lothian Question, and that is he believed there was no answer to it short of independence or a unitary state. There was a reason that Bill McKay's committee did not propose blocking powers for English MPs within the Westminster parliament, and that is they realised that you cannot set up a de facto English parliament within the House of Commons.

All of this hard logic seems to have bypassed the Tories, and Grayling has been left picking up the pieces.

Sunday 5 July

A packed weekend for politics, with Greece preparing to defy European instruction and austerity in a referendum and my parody site, AngrySalmond, starting a column for *The National*!

I am not entirely sure if everyone will realise that the hilarious column with its fruity language is indeed a spoof, given the picture of me above it admittedly wearing a pink beret. At any rate my emails should be revealing over the next few days.

The *Sunday Herald* has discovered that Liberal candidate the permanently miffed Christine Jardine spent twice as much as the SNP in failing to win the Gordon constituency. It will be the same in all the Lib Dem seats. They will have spent twice as much in losing as the SNP did in winning, and next to none of their money will have been raised locally.

It turns out that the historian Professor Jill Stephenson and one of the 'compelling voices in support of the union' has called Mhairi Black 'a slut' online. Apart from being a very silly person, Ms Stephenson, emeritus professor at the University of Edinburgh, is an example of the extraordinary brass neck of unionism. As I've already mentioned, the only piece of academic research on social media abuse from Strathclyde University academic Dr Mark Shephard indicated that independence supporters are more sinned against than online sinners. However, that will not stop the dead-wood press trying to paint online abuse as an indy supporter prerogative. Ironically the papers which claim this – the *Mail*, the *Scotsman* and the *Telegraph* – carry websites where the level of sheer abuse is off the scale.

In my column for the *Courier* and *Press and Journal* I describe the Evel proposals as creating a 'Keystone Cops parliament' with people rushing in and out depending on the subject.

Wednesday 8 July

The first Tory Budget for 19 years, and George Osborne does not disappoint his backbenches, who roar on his deeply regressive Budget. Osborne seeks to trap Labour by cloaking his assault on the poor in the language of the 'living wage'. However, it does not require extended analysis to see that his measures will result in millions of working families being substantially worse off.

No Tory tummy is left untickled as austerity becomes incarnate. The Budget will come unstuck on the number of the working poor who will lose out badly. The cheering Tory benches should beware of the words of Walpole: 'Today they are ringing the bells. Soon they will be wringing their hands.'

The extension of austerity and yesterday's pummelling on Evel (when they ran away from a vote to stave off defeat) are both areas where the Tories are taking big risks. Some of their arrogance will be curbed in the Commons. Rather more of it will require the electorate to instruct them further.

Sunday 12 July

Harriet Harman adds to Labour's woes by suggesting on the weekend TV programmes that Labour will not oppose the Tory proposals on welfare. It is difficult to understand her logic unless she is acting as an undercover agent for Jeremy Corbyn in the Labour leadership race. If she doesn't have a change of heart then this means real trouble for Labour.

Rickie Fowler wins the Aberdeen Asset Scottish Open. It is strange to be watching it at home rather than being up with the action, but the decision to host the tournament at Gullane is fully vindicated and Rickie's win is a box-office triumph for the NBC coverage.

Like many of my colleagues I spend the weekend thinking about how to react to the Tory proposal to sabotage the anti-fox hunting legislation in England. There are two things which persuade me we should vote. One is the massive lobby of people from England asking for our help to oppose something we don't approve of. Second is the clear necessity to oppose a government that is determined to ride roughshod over all opposition. Of course we would rather strengthen the Scotland Bill, stop the assault on the poor and vulnerable or force a climbdown on Evel. However, retreats and climbdowns become a habit if there are enough of them, and this is the one that is available.

Tuesday 14 July

The decision to vote on fox hunting is spectacularly vindicated as the government retreat on their proposals. This is the fourth time the Tories have been outfoxed – on Evel, on the referendum, on the Human Rights Act and now on hunting.

The Tory benches and the Prime Minister are furious, while the cry rings out 'Tally-No!' from the SNP benches.

It provides the perfect backcloth to a stunning maiden speech from Mhairi Black. I had lunch with Mhairi last week and she gave me her speech to read. I didn't suggest changing a single word. It is one of the rare parliamentary performances that reach out to real people. How foolish that silly Edinburgh professor must feel now.

Thursday 16 July

I appear on the BBC's late-night political programme *This Week* with a Greek comedian understandably upset at the behaviour of the European powers in forcing Greece to accept what is effectively the original austerity package.

It is a move that pro-Europeans may come to regret, and I say so on the programme. I also identify what could be the next governmental reverse: the totally disgusting proposal that one of the only ways a woman can continue to receive child benefit for a third child is to establish that the child was the result of being raped.

It is a particularly nasty aspect of the Budget which was first spotted by SNP MP Alison Thewliss and pointedly raised by Angus Robertson at Prime Minister's Questions yesterday.

I also explain why Jeremy Corbyn is doing so well in the Labour leadership contest. I say that whether people agree with him or not, at least they know where he stands. He, at least, is not one of nature's abstainers.

Monday 20 July

A hugely significant day in the Commons.

Michael Fallon runs into real parliamentary trouble trying to explain why British pilots embedded with US forces were busy bombing Syria against the explicit will of parliament, and struggles to offer any precedent. The truth is that both Fallon and Cameron have their itchy fingers on the trigger. Like the Bourbons they have forgotten nothing and learnt nothing.

Labour then splits on the key welfare votes, with 48 rebels joining the SNP in the lobbies against the Tories. With members of no fewer than eight political parties lining up to vote against the government, on crude Commons arithmetic the Tories could have been defeated if the Labour leadership had not abstained. At the very least it would have been a damned close-run thing. The political damage is all with Labour and the real damage all with our constituents. One consequence will be to give Jeremy Corbyn further momentum in the leadership contest.

Tuesday 21 July

Labour finishes the parliamentary session on the Budget by doing what they have been best at throughout the last few weeks – abstaining.

They seem to have totally lost the parliamentary plot in a more and more bizarre and convoluted procession of blunders. At its heart is a genuine confusion over how to recover from a catastrophic defeat. Is the right answer to tack right and rediscover the Blairite Third Way, or is it better, Sturgeon-style, to reject the assumptions behind austerity economics and provide an alternative, not a substitute?

The problem is that the first requires a charismatic leader who can take strong positions on a limited number of issues to emphasise the narrow differences between the opposition and a struggling government, while agreeing with the government on much else. Thus Blair talked about a fresh start, while Gordon Brown attempted to seduce the City.

The second requires a candidate with enough credibility to withstand the inevitable assault from the mainstream right-wing media. Much as I respect Jeremy Corbyn for his long-standing record of being largely right on international affairs, he is going to struggle to be seen as an alternative prime minister.

Thus, in a symbolic move, the SNP finish the session by occupying the Labour benches, this time with little or no resistance. After the events of the past few weeks, nobody seriously questioned our right to be there.

Scotland's Future In Scotland's Hands

There was just a moment, after the photocall of the new Group at St Stephen's entrance to the House of Commons, which brought home to me the full extent of the dramatic political change that has transformed the Scottish political landscape.

All 55 of my SNP colleagues were there, crowded into that famous place. I have never had more than five colleagues at any time since I was first elected as an MP. It was in exactly that same spot I was once interviewed, surrounded by the Westminster press pack, after halting the Budget speech in 1988. I was on my own that day. Now we are a parliamentary force to be reckoned with. It has been an extraordinary development and it was a proud moment.

Some of these new members I know well. Hannah Bardell was my first office manager in Inverurie, Stephen Gethins had worked for me in Westminster and been a Scottish government SPAD, Tasmina Ahmed-Sheikh a First Ministerial Adviser, Patrick Grady the SNP National Secretary. I wrote for Brendan O'Hara when he edited the Celtic fanzine *Not the View* more than 20 years ago, while Stuart Donaldson had campaigned for me as a tot in his carrycot in the 1992 election.

Most of the other MPs are experienced and hugely effective SNP campaigners. I have gone to bat for them in local and parliamentary by-elections over the years. For example Roger Mullin, the new MP for Gordon Brown's old seat of Kirkcaldy and Cowdenbeath, was the candidate in the Paisley North by-election just a few weeks after I became SNP leader for the first time in 1990.

Others in the SNP Group, however, are people who had newly emerged to political prominence in the YES campaign itself. Michelle Thomson, Tommy Sheppard, Philippa Whitford, Calum Kerr, Kirsten Oswald, Richard Arkless, Lisa Cameron and John Nicolson are just a few examples of these new people motivated to become involved in representative politics by the referendum experience.

Over the last three months since the election it has become clear that this is a richly talented group of MPs – person for person the most able I have ever seen. An initially sceptical Westminster press corps have come to grudgingly accept the calibre of the 56 sent to Westminster from Scotland.

The reason for this exceptional standard is twofold. First, virtually all of these MPs had to battle their way through very crowded selection meetings. Real quality was required to emerge successfully from that process. Second, the decision I made last autumn as SNP leader to allow the vast new intake of members to stand for election gave the SNP the biggest talent pool to choose from, not just of this election but in Scottish political history.

But the enthusiasm and the excitement of being part of such a large political group is tempered with the arithmetic reality of the return of a majority Conservative government.

Labour's catastrophic mistakes in their approach to the election had two implications – and for both Ed Miliband should carry the responsibility. First there was his strategic decision in January 2011 to appoint Ed Balls as his Shadow Chancellor after Alan Johnson fell by the political wayside. In that one fateful decision he both attached himself to the economic failures of the last Labour government and also limited his options in presenting a real economic alternative to the Tory-led coalition. Second, in the immediate run-up to the election there was a paralysis instead of a response to the Lynton Crosby-inspired anti-Scottish campaign that Labour would only return to office on the backs of the SNP. The very first time he was challenged at Prime Minister's Questions on this theme all Miliband had to say was that the Prime Minister had effectively conceded the election – that it was now accepted that he, the Labour leader, was going to be Prime Minister. He could have made a virtue of progressive parties potentially agreeing on how to shape the future.

Instead Miliband first tried to ignore the charge and then culminated this folly in the election campaign itself by the ridiculous declaration that he would rather not be Prime Minister than deal with the SNP. A more inept, pathetic and cowardly way to deal with a political attack would be difficult to envisage.

The campaign may not have been winnable for Labour, but the Tories could have been stopped with a better leader fashioning a better campaign. Even with a feeble opposition in England, the Tories won their majority with but 37 per cent of the overall vote. The campaign was there for the taking and the Tories were there for the stopping.

But Miliband wasn't that kind of leader.

However, a majority of twelve does not put the Tories beyond parliamentary reach. On the contrary, the majority hasn't proved to be particularly secure over the last five weeks, never mind the next five years. At the start of a parliament with an unexpected overall majority and the Labour Party in total turmoil the Tories can be forgiven for believing in their own invulnerability.

In reality there will be few glad confident mornings again as politics and the force of political gravity start raining on the Tory parade. The SNP have already established ourselves as a determined opposition and all opportunities for progressing that further will be pursued in the new parliament.

When I was a child I used to believe that if I shut my eyes then no one could see me. This toddler's-eye view of politics sums up the Tories' response to the challenge from Scotland. Their plan is to continue the pretence that the powers on offer in the Scotland Bill match the commitments made in the 'vow', to ignore the outright rejection of this approach at a general election (in which the SNP vote was greater than that of the three unionist parties in Scotland put together), and then to demand that the SNP government explain how they will reverse the billions of pounds of welfare cuts that are part of the Tory programme – without Scotland having the economic and social powers to pursue a different course.

Not all unionists are signed up to this 'head under the blanket' approach.

Edward Leigh, the Conservative MP for Gainsborough, is as convinced a unionist as they come. Indeed he was foremost in demanding that the three London leaders unite to offer the 'vow' in the desperate last days of the referendum campaign. But this is what he said in the Scotland Bill debate on 15 June:

> We are making the same mistakes that were made on the Irish Question in the 19th century: we are giving too little, too late ... I do not believe it is possible to dribble out complex tax powers such as thresholds, VAT and airport tax, while also maintaining support for the Union. The Smith Commission was a rapid scissors-and-tape job in response to a vow that was hastily put together by panicked Unionist politicians in the last days of the referendum campaign. Perhaps it was adequate for its time, but I have read it very carefully – it is not that long – and it has now been overtaken by events.

A wiser policy would have been to come to terms with the Scottish aspirations and to do so in a spirit of generosity. The Smith Commission proposed inadequate powers but its principles 5 and 6 (of no detriment and no financial advantage) offered the route map to move to 'devo to the max', 'home rule' or 'close to federalism' in an orderly and accepted way.

However, 'Downing Street statesmanship' is beginning to rival 'military intelligence' as one of life's great oxymorons.

In the Independence White Paper I postulated that it would take a political generation for there to be another independence referendum. My view was based on the history of a devolution referendum in 1979, followed 18 years later by one in 1997. I repeated that judgement often enough.

But circumstances change, and Downing Street is well on the way to providing that 'difference in material circumstances' which will dramatically shorten my forecast timescale: by the refusal to honour the 'vow', by the failure to recognise an electoral mandate from Scotland, by choosing 'austerity to the max' instead of 'devo to the max', and by running risks with Scotland's European future. Each of these issues could light the blue touchpaper for a further poll. Cameron's claim that he can prevent a ballot is no more than posturing. He has no more power to do that than King Canute had to stop the tide lapping up the beach at Westminster.

If the SNP and/or any other party achieve a mandate and then a majority in the Scottish parliament for a referendum, a referendum there shall be. And no amount of Tory huffing and puffing will stop one. Equally there can only be such a ballot if the Scottish people so will. It is a matter that will be determined by the people and determined on a timescale of their choice.

Since the coming of the parliament in 1999 I have thought that independence was a likelihood. Since the referendum and the transformation it provoked in Scottish political attitudes, I have thought independence inevitable. Since the election, and the reaction of the Tories to the SNP landslide, I have thought that 'indy ref 2' will arrive on a much sharper timescale.

The people – the real guardians of Scotland – spoke in the referendum. They spoke again by majority in the election. They will not be prevented from speaking again.

Scotland's future is in Scotland's hands.

Alex Salmond.

Alex Salmond MP and MSP

Strichen, August 2015